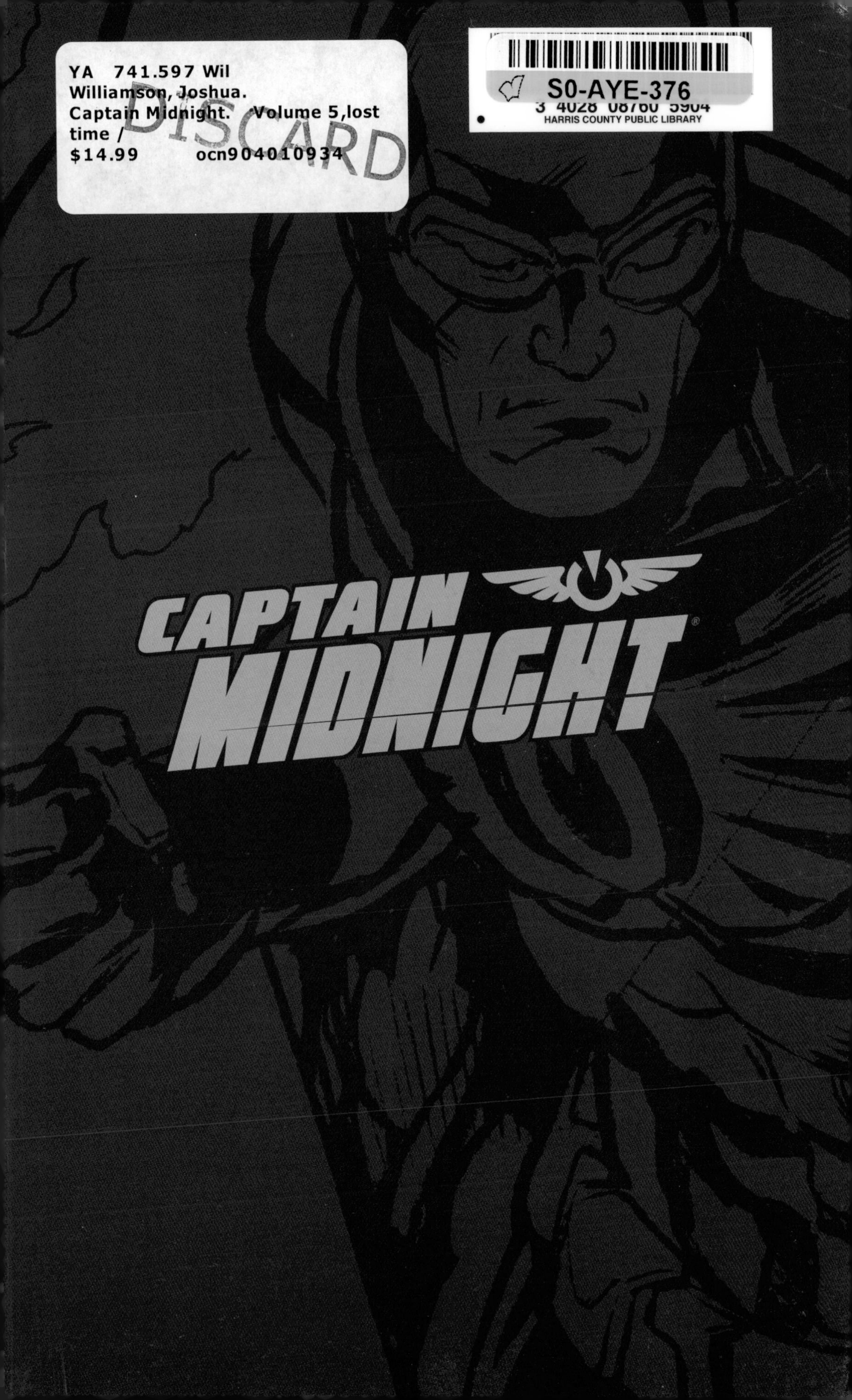
CAPTAIN
MIDNIGHT®

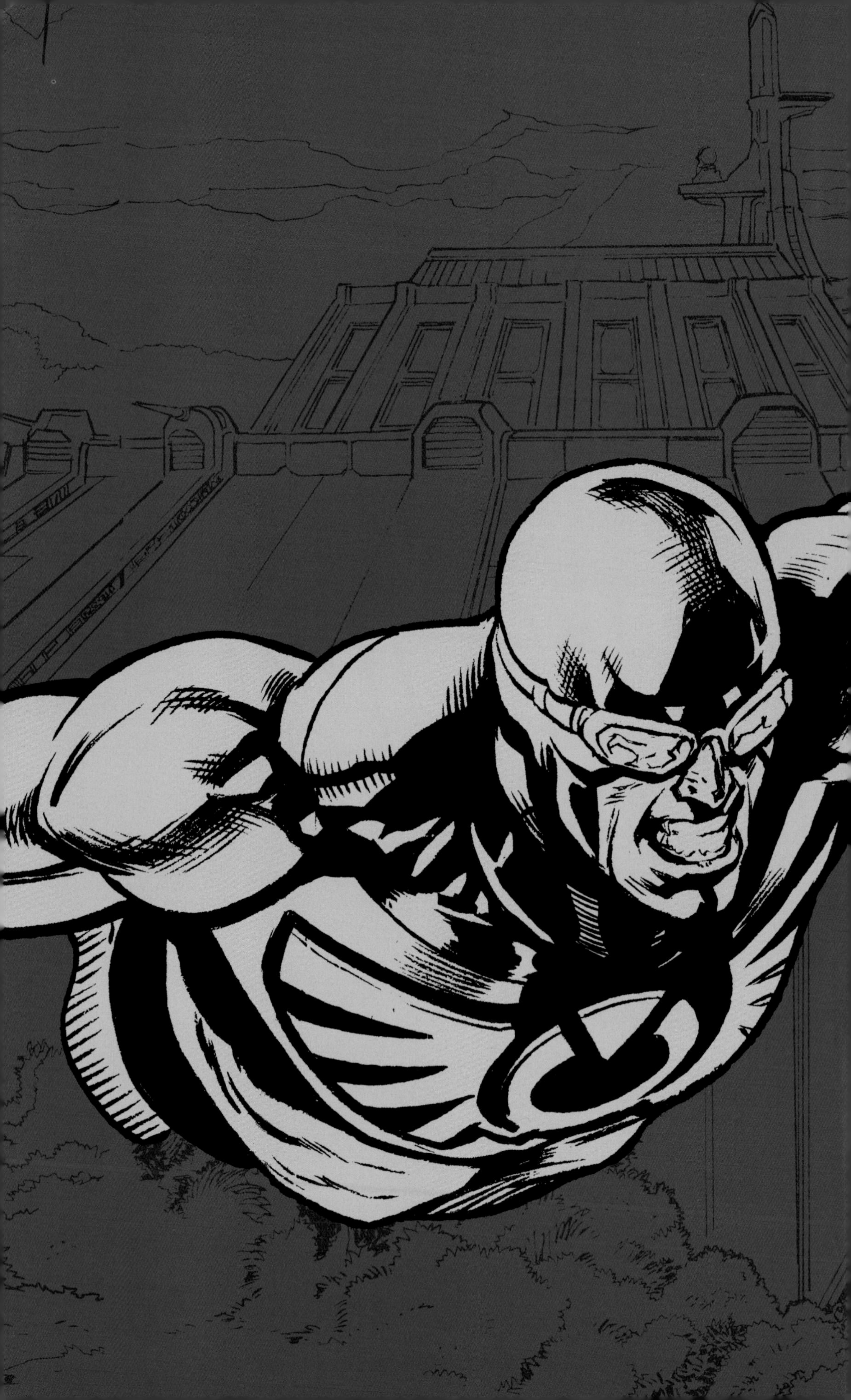

CAPTAIN MIDNIGHT

VOLUME 5 LOST TIME

STORY BY

JOSHUA WILLIAMSON

ART BY

FERNANDO DAGNINO

COLORS BY

JAVIER MENA

LETTERS BY

NATE PIEKOS OF **BLAMBOT**®

COVER BY

MICHAEL BROUSSARD

CHAPTER BREAK ART BY

DUSTIN NGUYEN
(CHAPTER 1)

MICHAEL BROUSSARD
(CHAPTERS 2–4)

DARK HORSE BOOKS

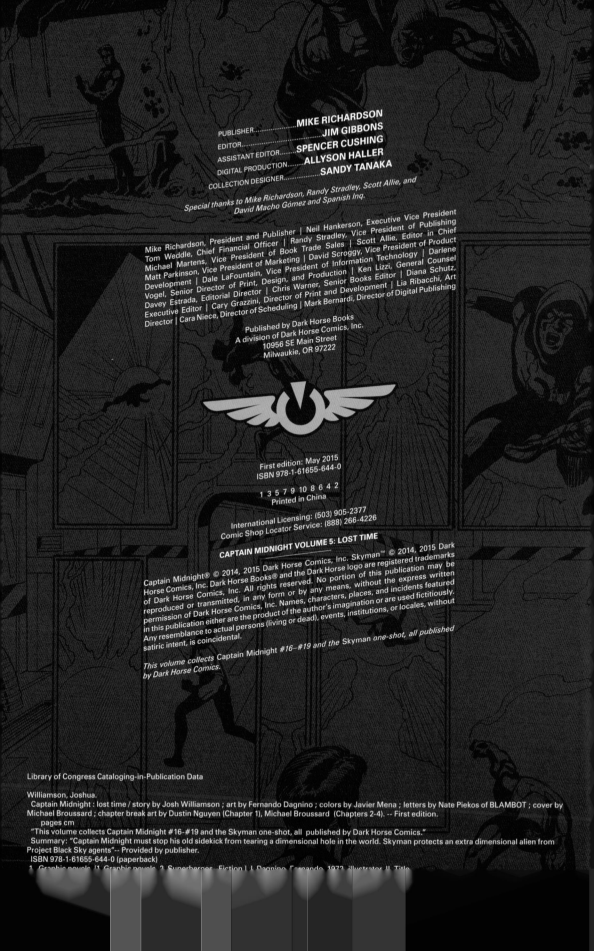

PUBLISHER....................**MIKE RICHARDSON**
EDITOR............................**JIM GIBBONS**
ASSISTANT EDITOR............**SPENCER CUSHING**
DIGITAL PRODUCTION........**ALLYSON HALLER**
COLLECTION DESIGNER.................**SANDY TANAKA**

*Special thanks to Mike Richardson, Randy Stradley, Scott Allie, and
David Macho Gómez and Spanish Inq.*

Mike Richardson, President and Publisher | Neil Hankerson, Executive Vice President
Tom Weddle, Chief Financial Officer | Randy Stradley, Vice President of Publishing
Michael Martens, Vice President of Book Trade Sales | Scott Allie, Editor in Chief
Matt Parkinson, Vice President of Marketing | David Scroggy, Vice President of Product
Development | Dale LaFountain, Vice President of Information Technology | Darlene
Vogel, Senior Director of Print, Design, and Production | Ken Lizzi, General Counsel
Davey Estrada, Editorial Director | Chris Warner, Senior Books Editor | Diana Schutz,
Executive Editor | Cary Grazzini, Director of Print and Development | Lia Ribacchi, Art
Director | Cara Niece, Director of Scheduling | Mark Bernardi, Director of Digital Publishing

Published by Dark Horse Books
A division of Dark Horse Comics, Inc.
10956 SE Main Street
Milwaukie, OR 97222

First edition: May 2015
ISBN 978-1-61655-644-0

1 3 5 7 9 10 8 6 4 2
Printed in China

International Licensing: (503) 905-2377
Comic Shop Locator Service: (888) 266-4226

CAPTAIN MIDNIGHT VOLUME 5: LOST TIME

Captain Midnight® © 2014, 2015 Dark Horse Comics, Inc. Skyman™ © 2014, 2015 Dark
Horse Comics, Inc. Dark Horse Books® and the Dark Horse logo are registered trademarks
of Dark Horse Comics, Inc. All rights reserved. No portion of this publication may be
reproduced or transmitted, in any form or by any means, without the express written
permission of Dark Horse Comics, Inc. Names, characters, places, and incidents featured
in this publication either are the product of the author's imagination or are used fictitiously.
Any resemblance to actual persons (living or dead), events, institutions, or locales, without
satiric intent, is coincidental.

This volume collects Captain Midnight #16–#19 and the Skyman one-shot, all published
by Dark Horse Comics.

Library of Congress Cataloging-in-Publication Data

Williamson, Joshua.
  Captain Midnight : lost time / story by Josh Williamson ; art by Fernando Dagnino ; colors by Javier Mena ; letters by Nate Piekos of BLAMBOT ; cover by
Michael Broussard ; chapter break art by Dustin Nguyen (Chapter 1), Michael Broussard (Chapters 2-4). -- First edition.
       pages cm
  "This volume collects Captain Midnight #16-#19 and the Skyman one-shot, all published by Dark Horse Comics."
  Summary: "Captain Midnight must stop his old sidekick from tearing a dimensional hole in the world. Skyman protects an extra dimensional alien from
Project Black Sky agents"-- Provided by publisher.
  ISBN 978-1-61655-644-0 (paperback)
  1. Graphic novels |1. Graphic novels 2. Superheroes- Fiction | I. Dagnino, Fernando, 1973- illustrator. II. Title.

CHAPTER 1

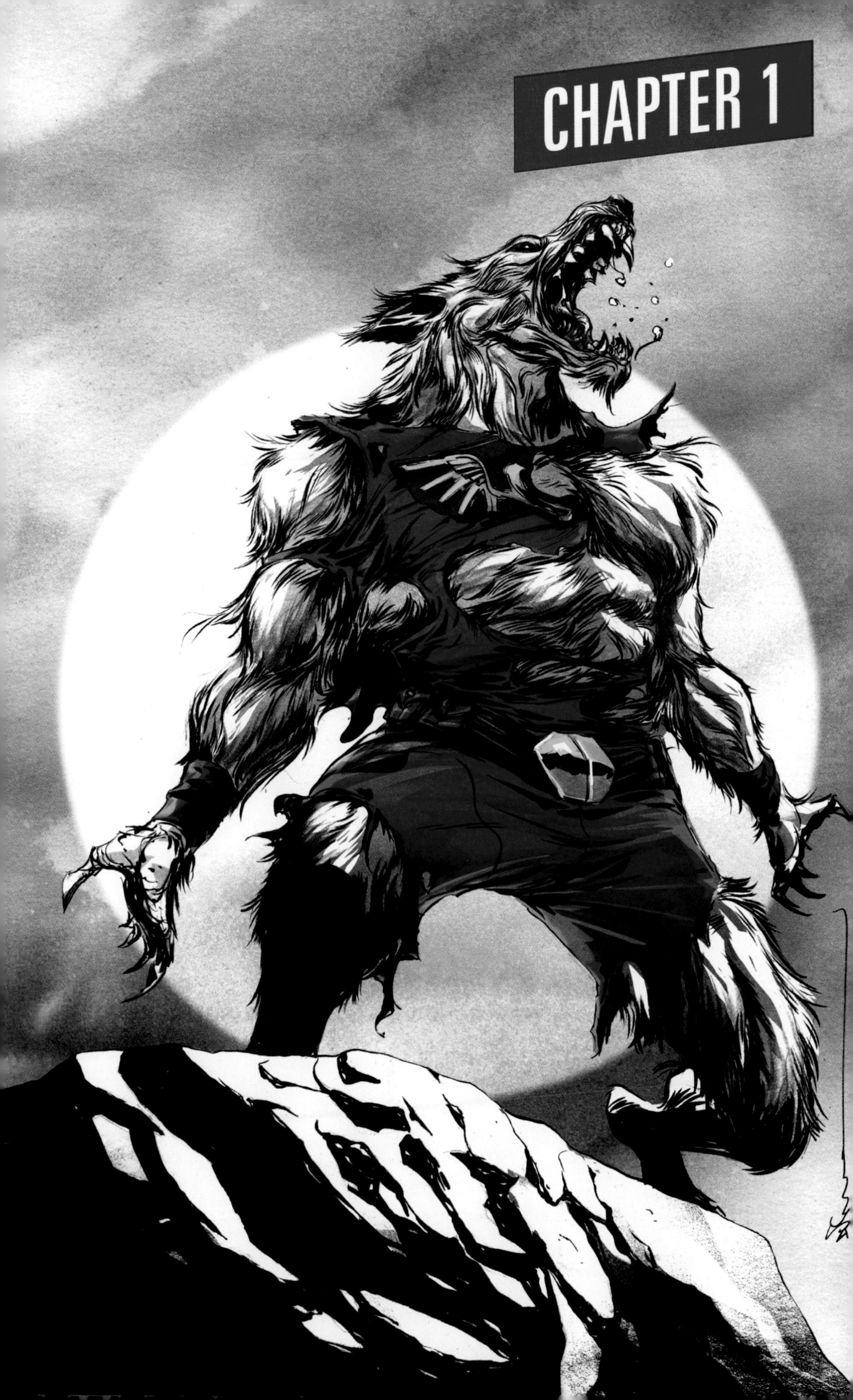

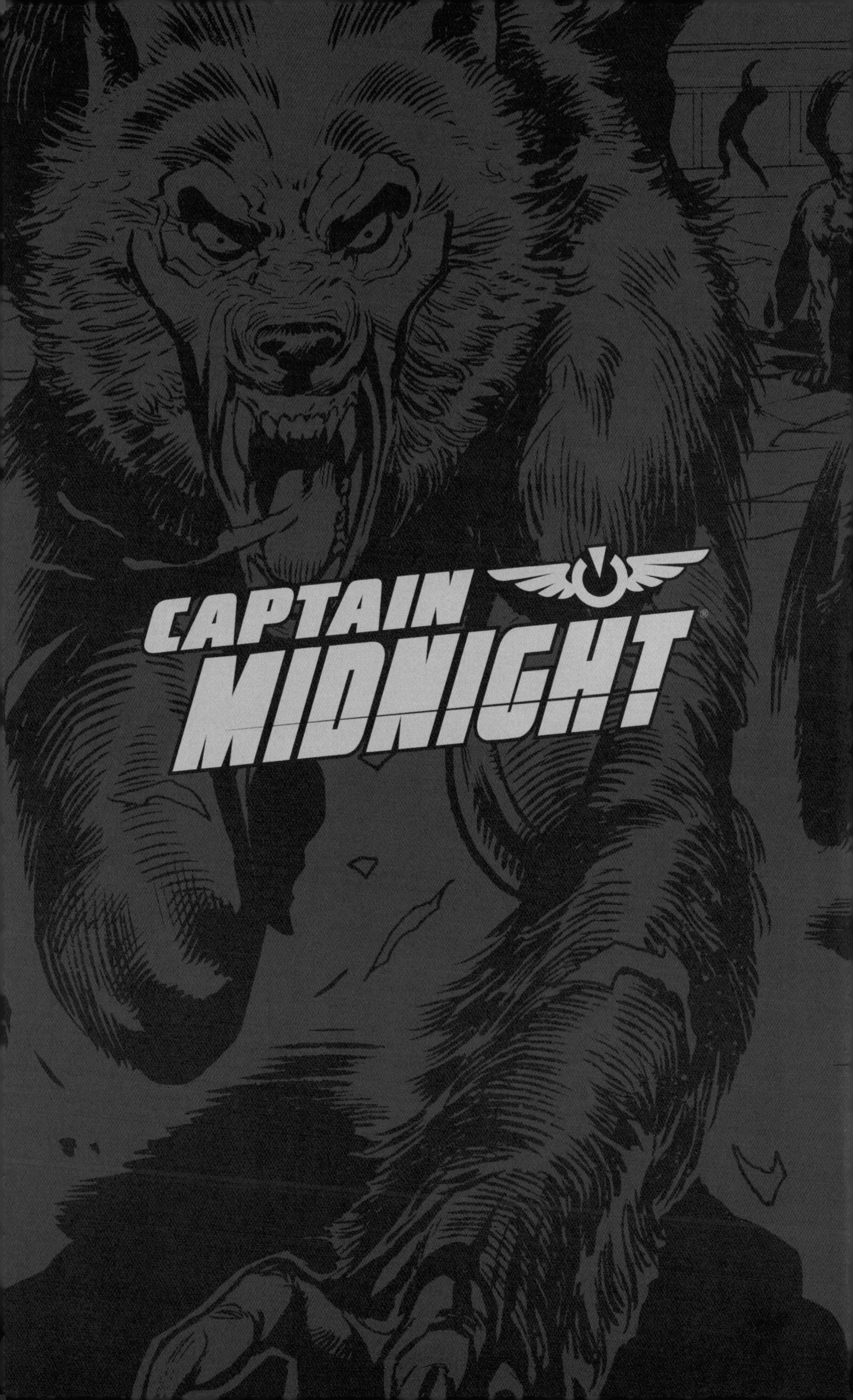
CAPTAIN MIDNIGHT

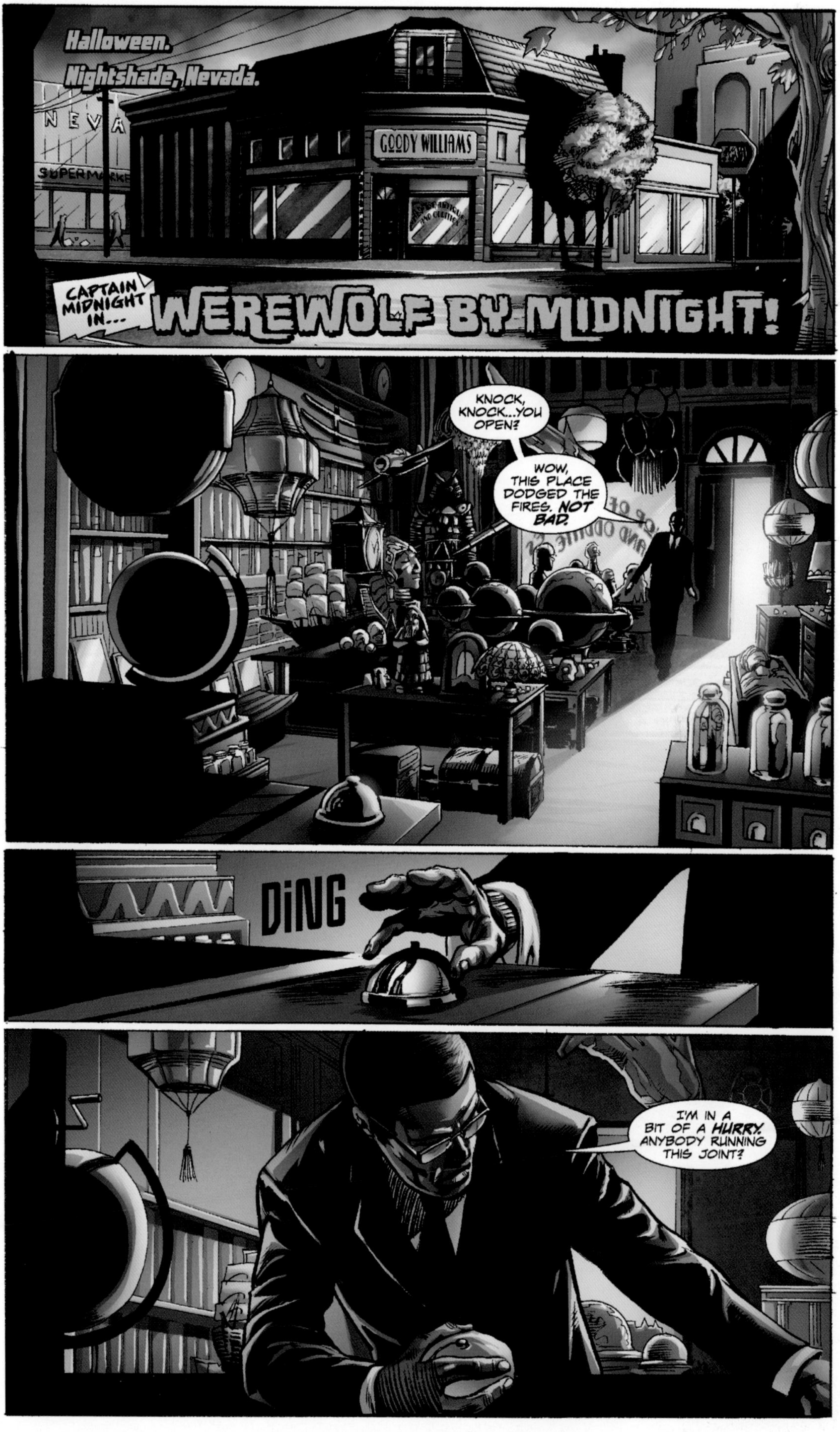

Halloween.
Nightshade, Nevada.
NEVA
SUPERMARKE
GOODY WILLIAMS
CAPTAIN MIDNIGHT IN...
WEREWOLF BY MIDNIGHT!
KNOCK, KNOCK...YOU OPEN?
WOW, THIS PLACE DODGED THE FIRES. NOT BAD.
DiNG
I'M IN A BIT OF A HURRY. ANYBODY RUNNING THIS JOINT?

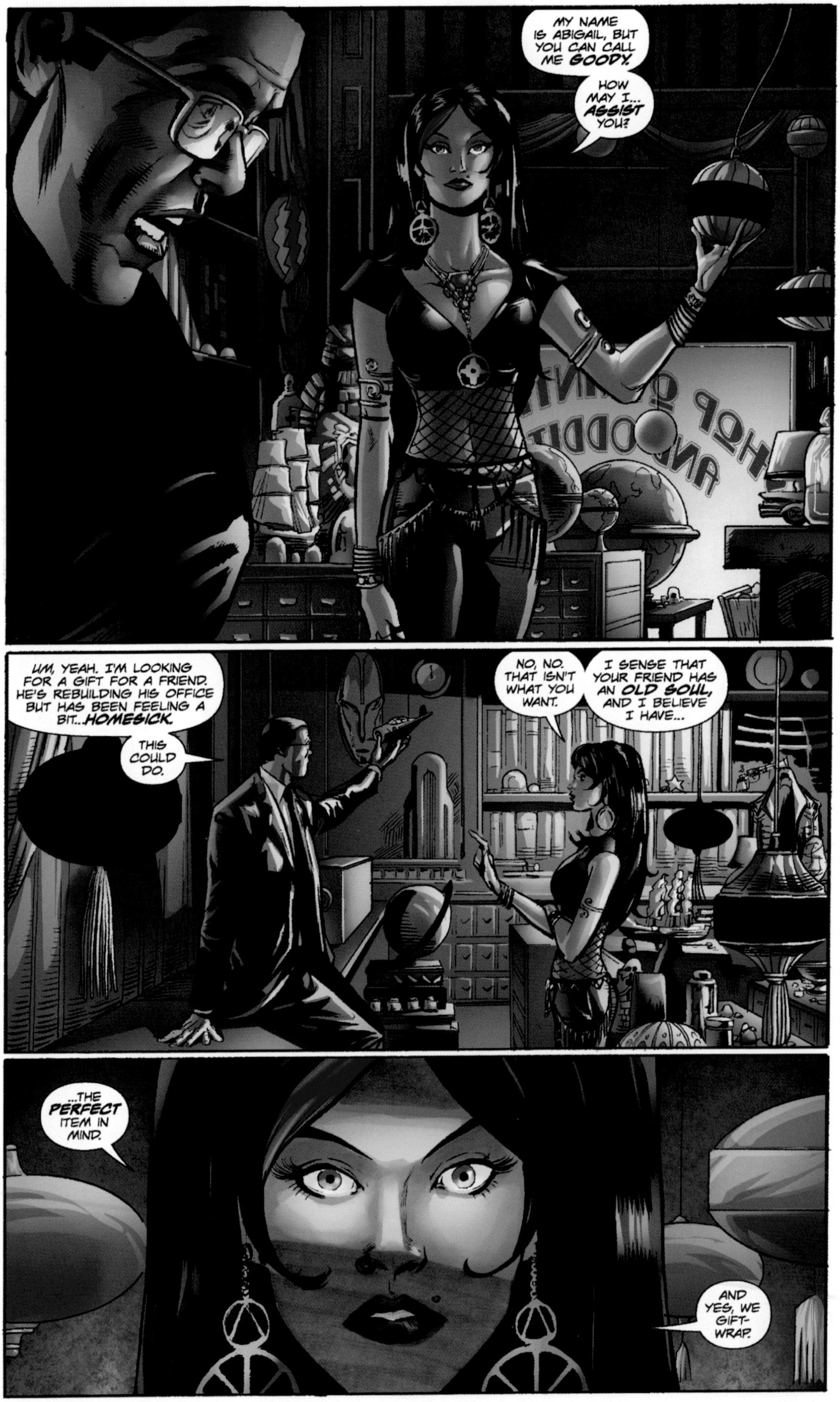
MY NAME IS ABIGAIL, BUT YOU CAN CALL ME GOODY.
HOW MAY I... ASSIST YOU?
HOP Q... AND ODDIT...
UM, YEAH. I'M LOOKING FOR A GIFT FOR A FRIEND. HE'S REBUILDING HIS OFFICE BUT HAS BEEN FEELING A BIT...HOMESICK.
THIS COULD DO.
NO, NO. THAT ISN'T WHAT YOU WANT.
I SENSE THAT YOUR FRIEND HAS AN OLD SOUL, AND I BELIEVE I HAVE...
...THE PERFECT ITEM IN MIND.
AND YES, WE GIFT-WRAP.

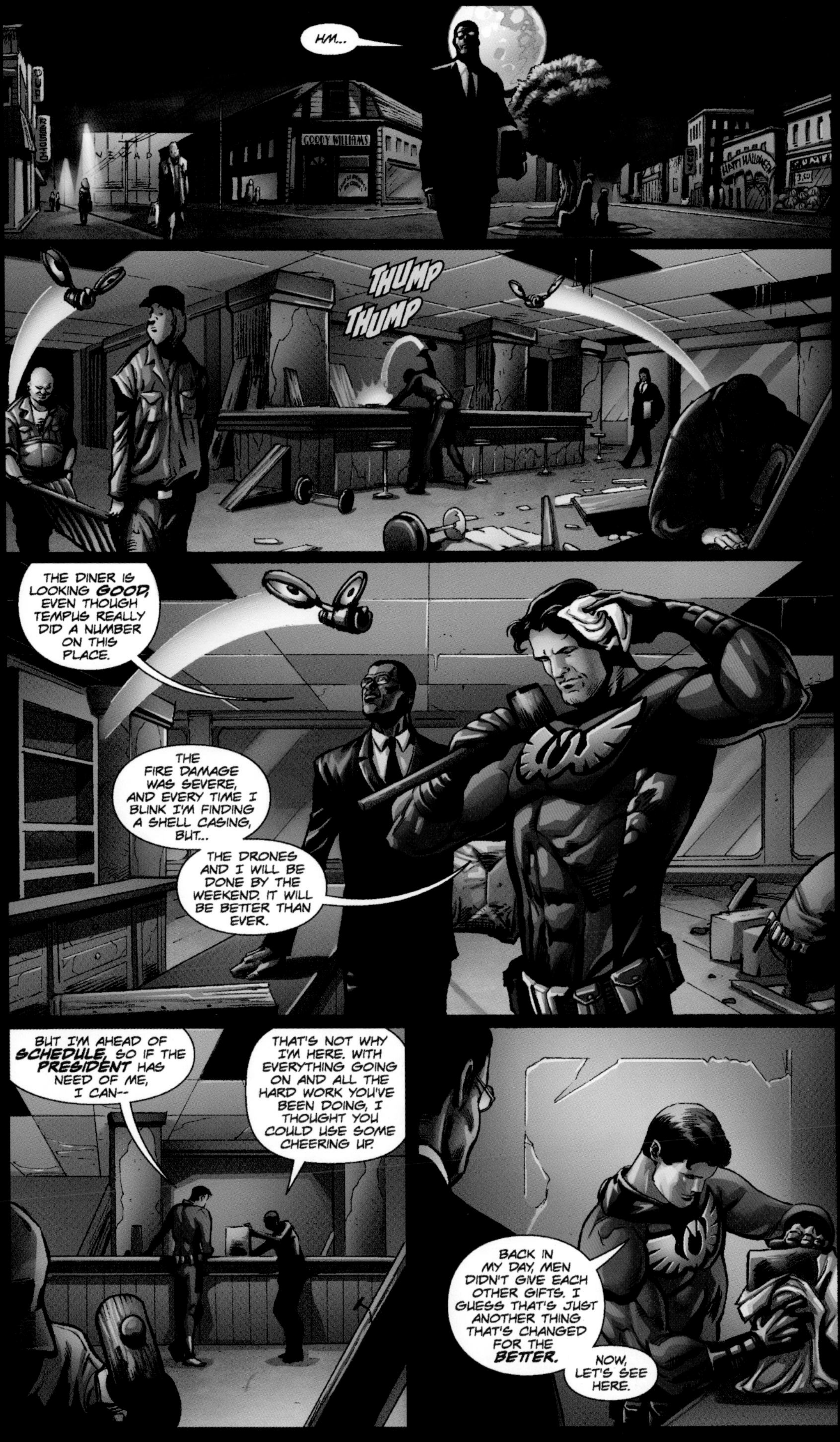
HM...
GOODY WILLIAMS
HAPPY HALLOWEEN
THUMP THUMP
THE DINER IS LOOKING GOOD, EVEN THOUGH TEMPUS REALLY DID A NUMBER ON THIS PLACE.
THE FIRE DAMAGE WAS SEVERE, AND EVERY TIME I BLINK I'M FINDING A SHELL CASING, BUT...
THE DRONES AND I WILL BE DONE BY THE WEEKEND. IT WILL BE BETTER THAN EVER.
BUT I'M AHEAD OF SCHEDULE, SO IF THE PRESIDENT HAS NEED OF ME, I CAN--
THAT'S NOT WHY I'M HERE. WITH EVERYTHING GOING ON AND ALL THE HARD WORK YOU'VE BEEN DOING, I THOUGHT YOU COULD USE SOME CHEERING UP.
BACK IN MY DAY, MEN DIDN'T GIVE EACH OTHER GIFTS. I GUESS THAT'S JUST ANOTHER THING THAT'S CHANGED FOR THE BETTER.
NOW, LET'S SEE HERE.

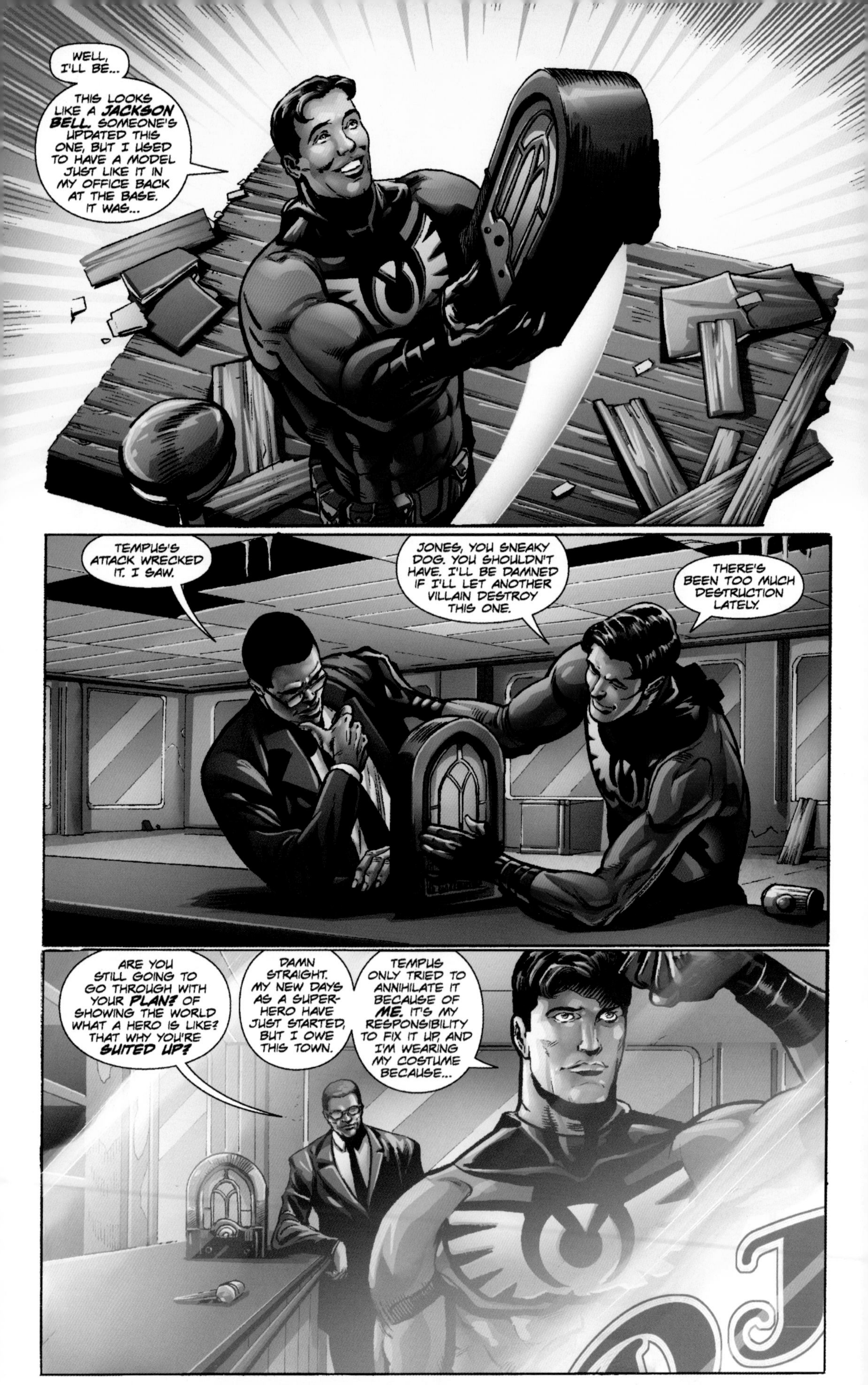
WELL, I'LL BE...
THIS LOOKS LIKE A **JACKSON BELL.** SOMEONE'S UPDATED THIS ONE, BUT I USED TO HAVE A MODEL JUST LIKE IT IN MY OFFICE BACK AT THE BASE. IT WAS...
TEMPUS'S ATTACK WRECKED IT. I SAW.
JONES, YOU SNEAKY DOG. YOU SHOULDN'T HAVE. I'LL BE DAMNED IF I'LL LET ANOTHER VILLAIN DESTROY THIS ONE.
THERE'S BEEN TOO MUCH DESTRUCTION LATELY.
ARE YOU STILL GOING TO GO THROUGH WITH YOUR **PLAN?** OF SHOWING THE WORLD WHAT A HERO IS LIKE? THAT WHY YOU'RE **SUITED UP?**
DAMN STRAIGHT. MY NEW DAYS AS A SUPER-HERO HAVE JUST STARTED, BUT I OWE THIS TOWN.
TEMPUS ONLY TRIED TO ANNIHILATE IT BECAUSE OF **ME.** IT'S MY RESPONSIBILITY TO FIX IT UP, AND I'M WEARING MY COSTUME BECAUSE...

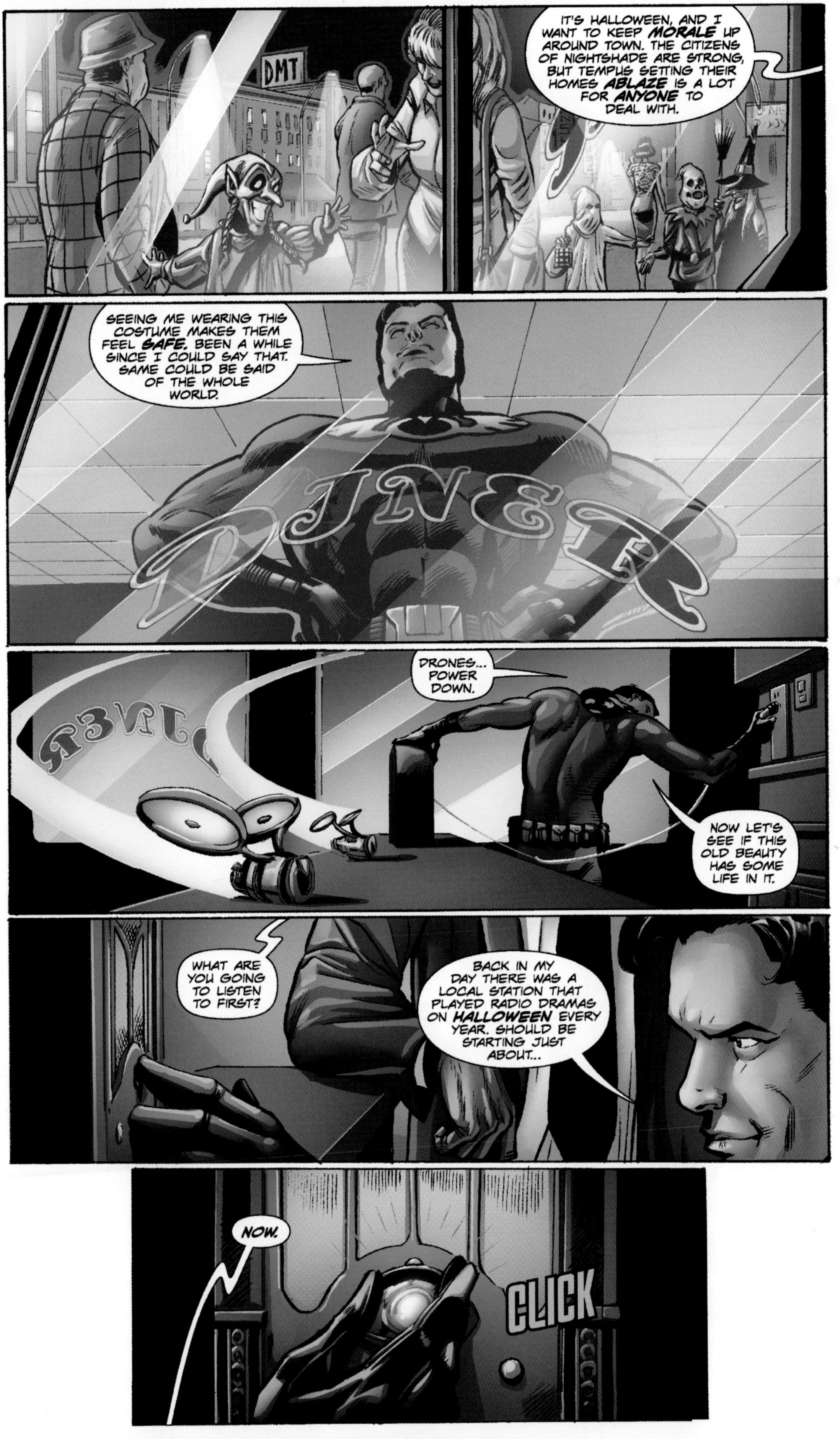
DMT
IT'S HALLOWEEN, AND I WANT TO KEEP MORALE UP AROUND TOWN. THE CITIZENS OF NIGHTSHADE ARE STRONG, BUT TEMPUS SETTING THEIR HOMES ABLAZE IS A LOT FOR ANYONE TO DEAL WITH.
SEEING ME WEARING THIS COSTUME MAKES THEM FEEL SAFE. BEEN A WHILE SINCE I COULD SAY THAT. SAME COULD BE SAID OF THE WHOLE WORLD.
DINER
DRONES... POWER DOWN.
NOW LET'S SEE IF THIS OLD BEAUTY HAS SOME LIFE IN IT.
WHAT ARE YOU GOING TO LISTEN TO FIRST?
BACK IN MY DAY THERE WAS A LOCAL STATION THAT PLAYED RADIO DRAMAS ON HALLOWEEN EVERY YEAR. SHOULD BE STARTING JUST ABOUT...
NOW.
CLICK

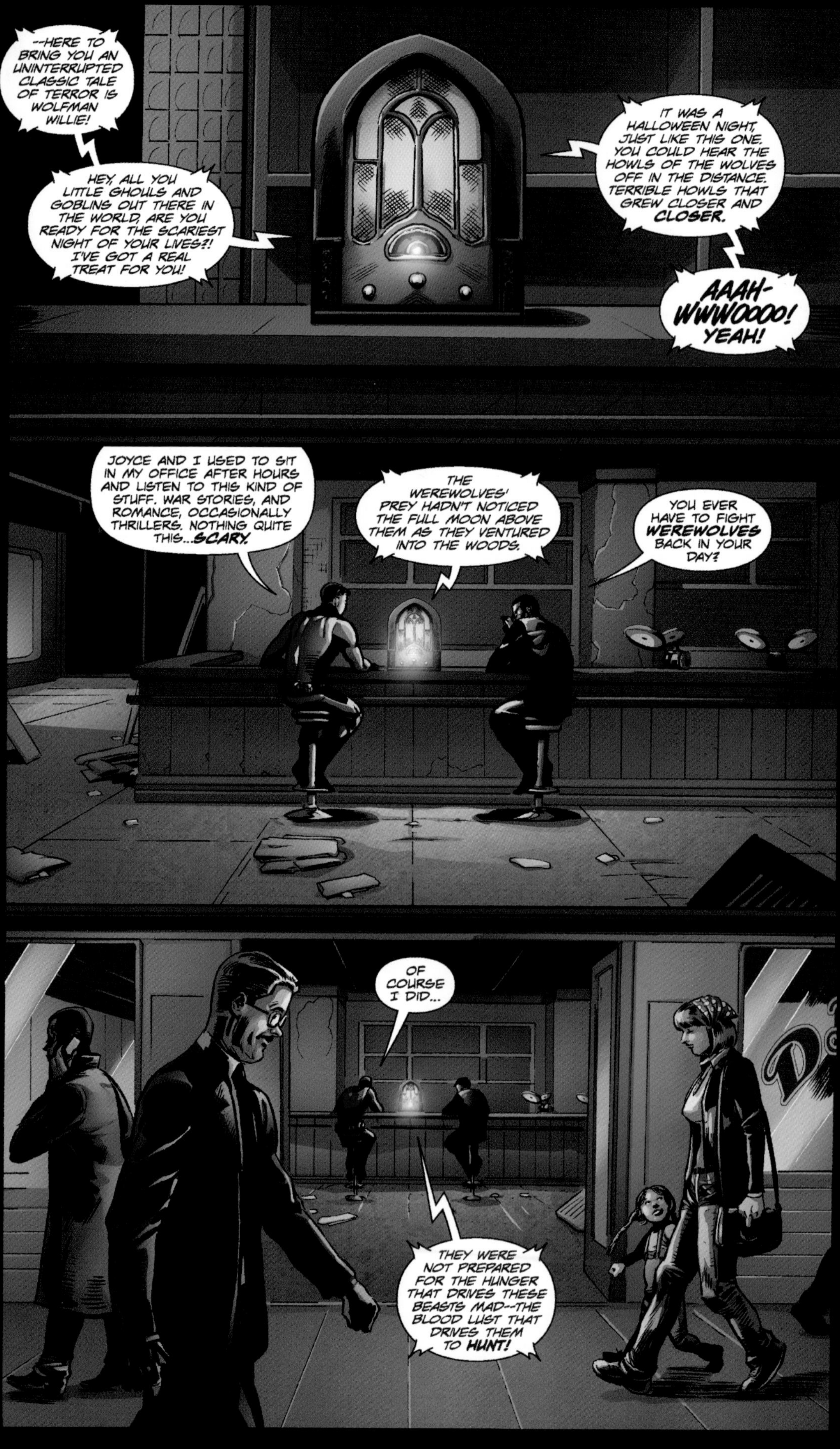
--HERE TO BRING YOU AN UNINTERRUPTED CLASSIC TALE OF TERROR IS WOLFMAN WILLIE!
HEY, ALL YOU LITTLE GHOULS AND GOBLINS OUT THERE IN THE WORLD, ARE YOU READY FOR THE SCARIEST NIGHT OF YOUR LIVES?! I'VE GOT A REAL TREAT FOR YOU!
IT WAS A HALLOWEEN NIGHT, JUST LIKE THIS ONE. YOU COULD HEAR THE HOWLS OF THE WOLVES OFF IN THE DISTANCE. TERRIBLE HOWLS THAT GREW CLOSER AND CLOSER.
AAAH-WWWOOOO! YEAH!
JOYCE AND I USED TO SIT IN MY OFFICE AFTER HOURS AND LISTEN TO THIS KIND OF STUFF. WAR STORIES, AND ROMANCE, OCCASIONALLY THRILLERS. NOTHING QUITE THIS...SCARY.
THE WEREWOLVES' PREY HADN'T NOTICED THE FULL MOON ABOVE THEM AS THEY VENTURED INTO THE WOODS.
YOU EVER HAVE TO FIGHT WEREWOLVES BACK IN YOUR DAY?
OF COURSE I DID...
THEY WERE NOT PREPARED FOR THE HUNGER THAT DRIVES THESE BEASTS MAD--THE BLOOD LUST THAT DRIVES THEM TO HUNT!

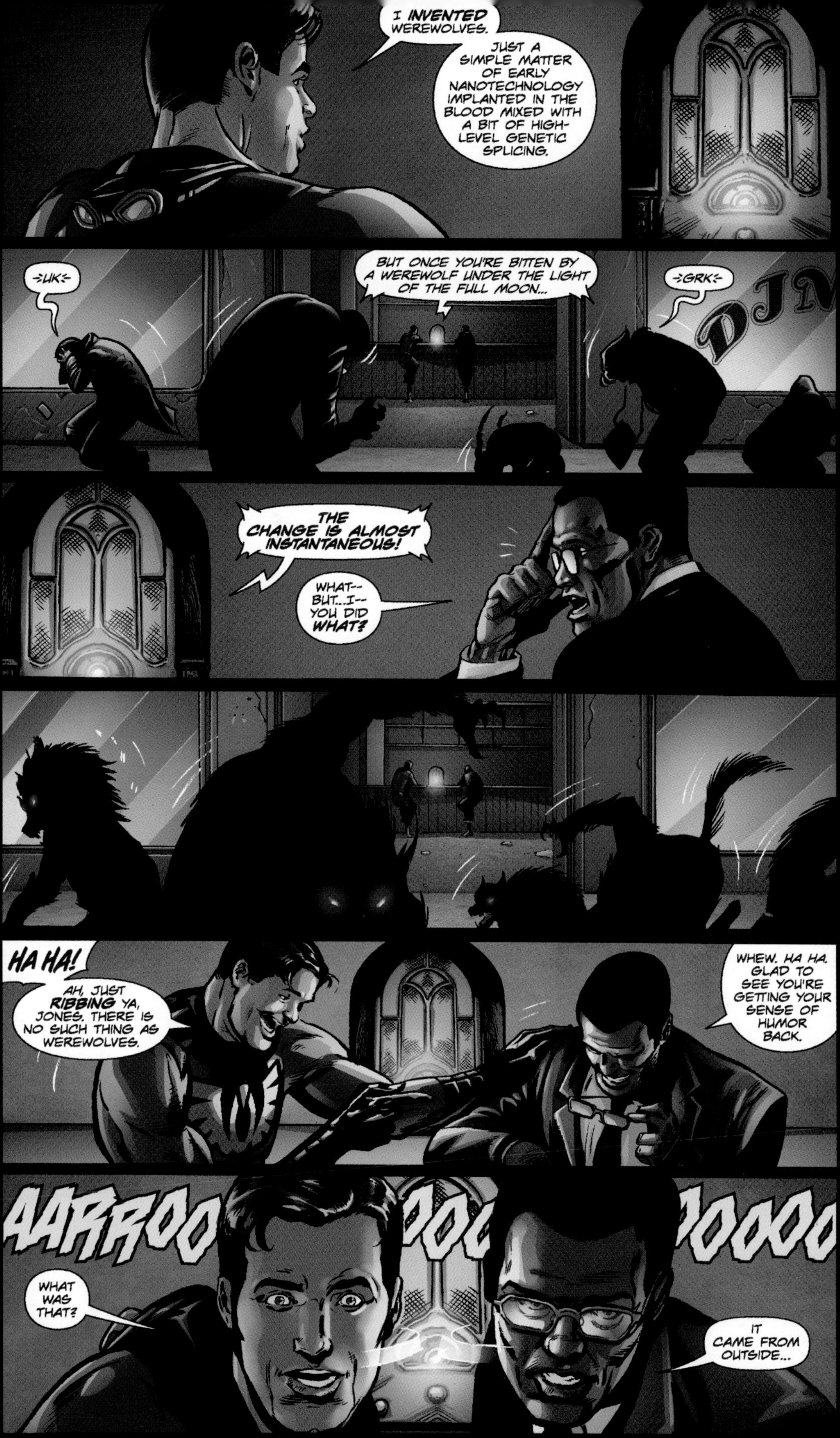
I INVENTED WEREWOLVES.
JUST A SIMPLE MATTER OF EARLY NANOTECHNOLOGY IMPLANTED IN THE BLOOD MIXED WITH A BIT OF HIGH-LEVEL GENETIC SPLICING.
UK
BUT ONCE YOU'RE BITTEN BY A WEREWOLF UNDER THE LIGHT OF THE FULL MOON...
GRK
THE CHANGE IS ALMOST INSTANTANEOUS!
WHAT-- BUT...I-- YOU DID WHAT?
HA HA!
AH, JUST RIBBING YA, JONES. THERE IS NO SUCH THING AS WEREWOLVES.
WHEW. HA HA. GLAD TO SEE YOU'RE GETTING YOUR SENSE OF HUMOR BACK.
AARROOOOOOOOOO
WHAT WAS THAT?
IT CAME FROM OUTSIDE...

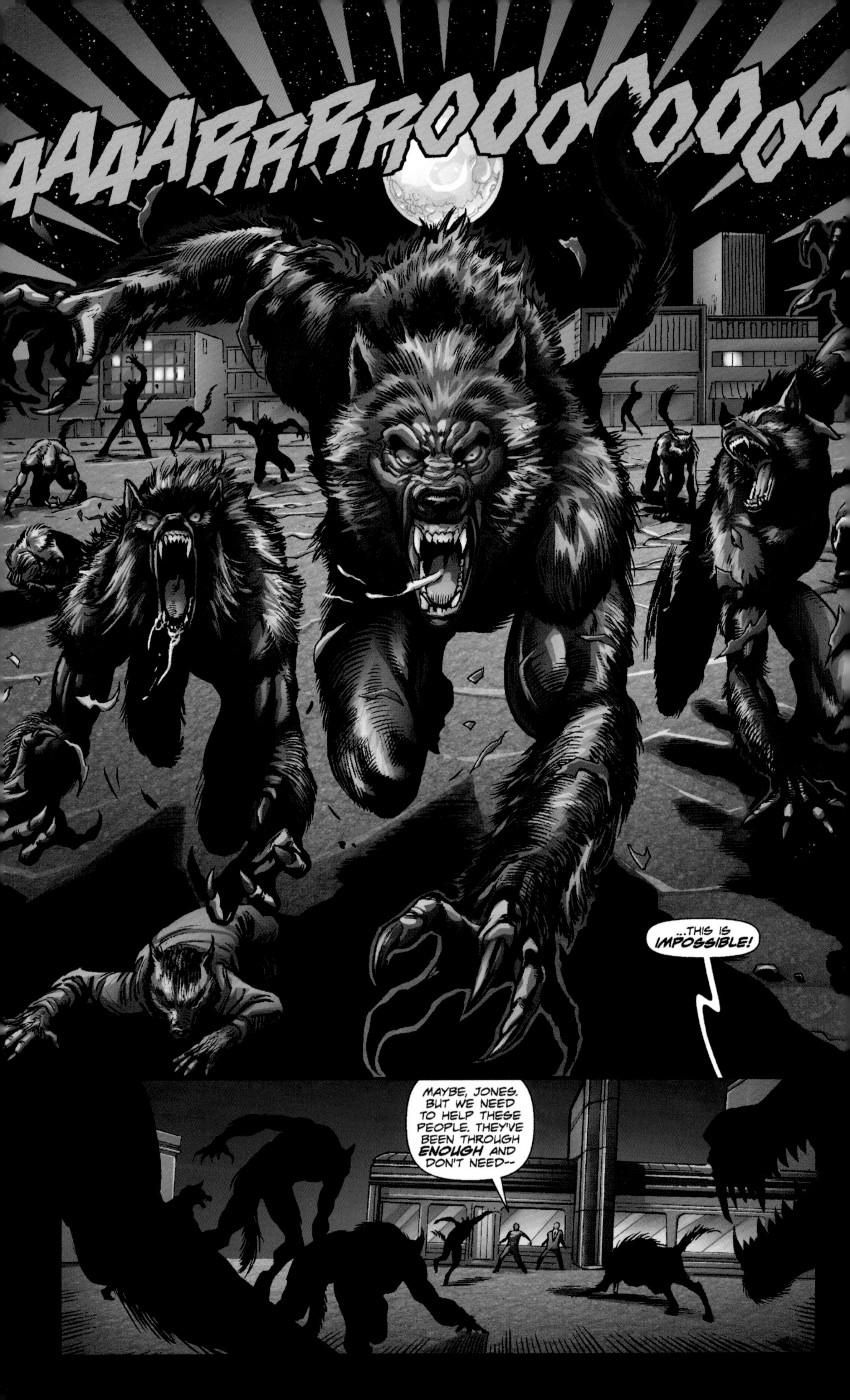
AAAARRRRROOOOOOOO
...THIS IS IMPOSSIBLE!
MAYBE, JONES. BUT WE NEED TO HELP THESE PEOPLE. THEY'VE BEEN THROUGH ENOUGH AND DON'T NEED--

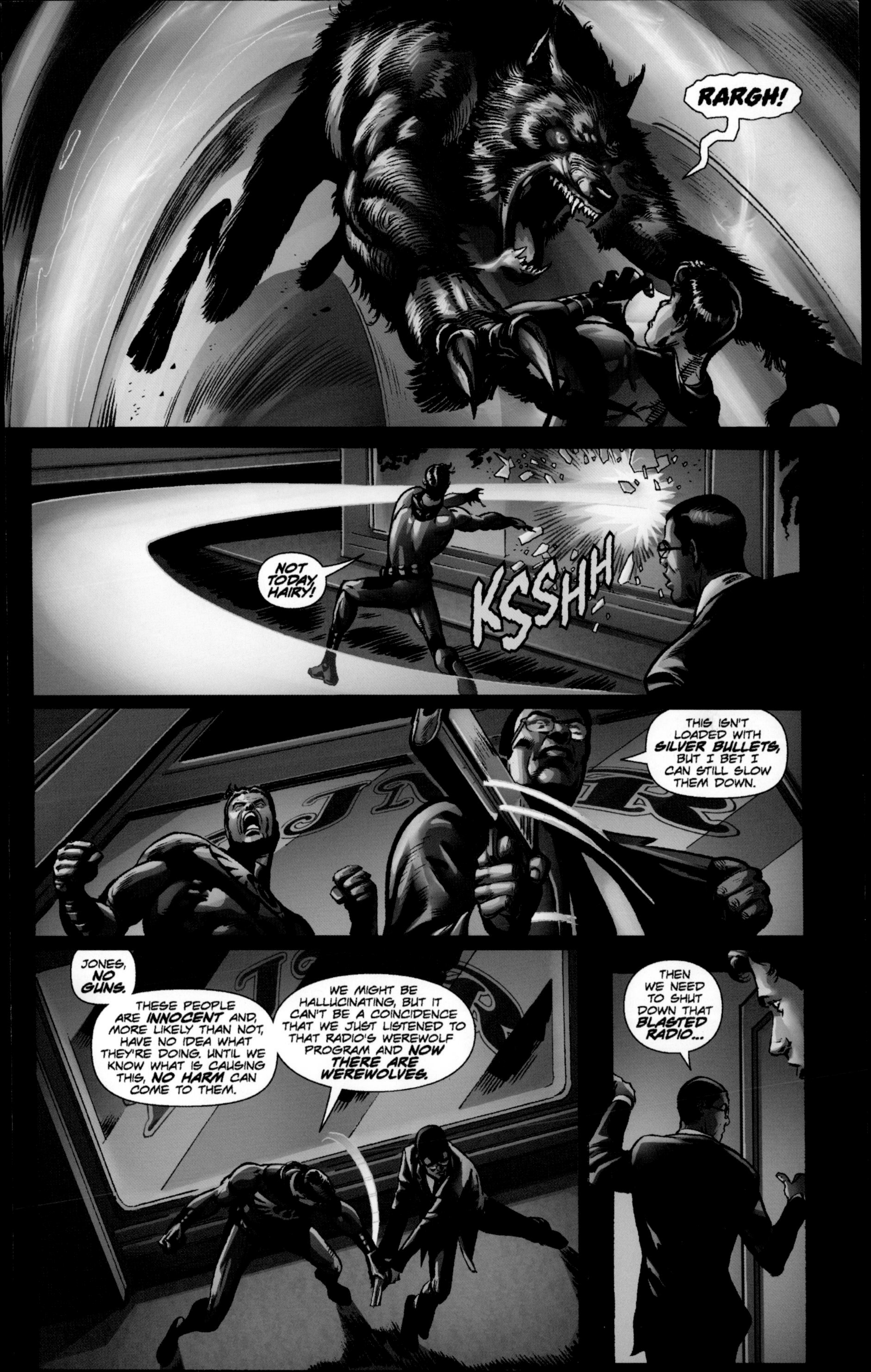
RARGH!
NOT TODAY, HAIRY!
KSSHH!
THIS ISN'T LOADED WITH SILVER BULLETS, BUT I BET I CAN STILL SLOW THEM DOWN.
JONES, NO GUNS.
THESE PEOPLE ARE INNOCENT AND, MORE LIKELY THAN NOT, HAVE NO IDEA WHAT THEY'RE DOING. UNTIL WE KNOW WHAT IS CAUSING THIS, NO HARM CAN COME TO THEM.
WE MIGHT BE HALLUCINATING, BUT IT CAN'T BE A COINCIDENCE THAT WE JUST LISTENED TO THAT RADIO'S WEREWOLF PROGRAM AND NOW THERE ARE WEREWOLVES.
THEN WE NEED TO SHUT DOWN THAT BLASTED RADIO...

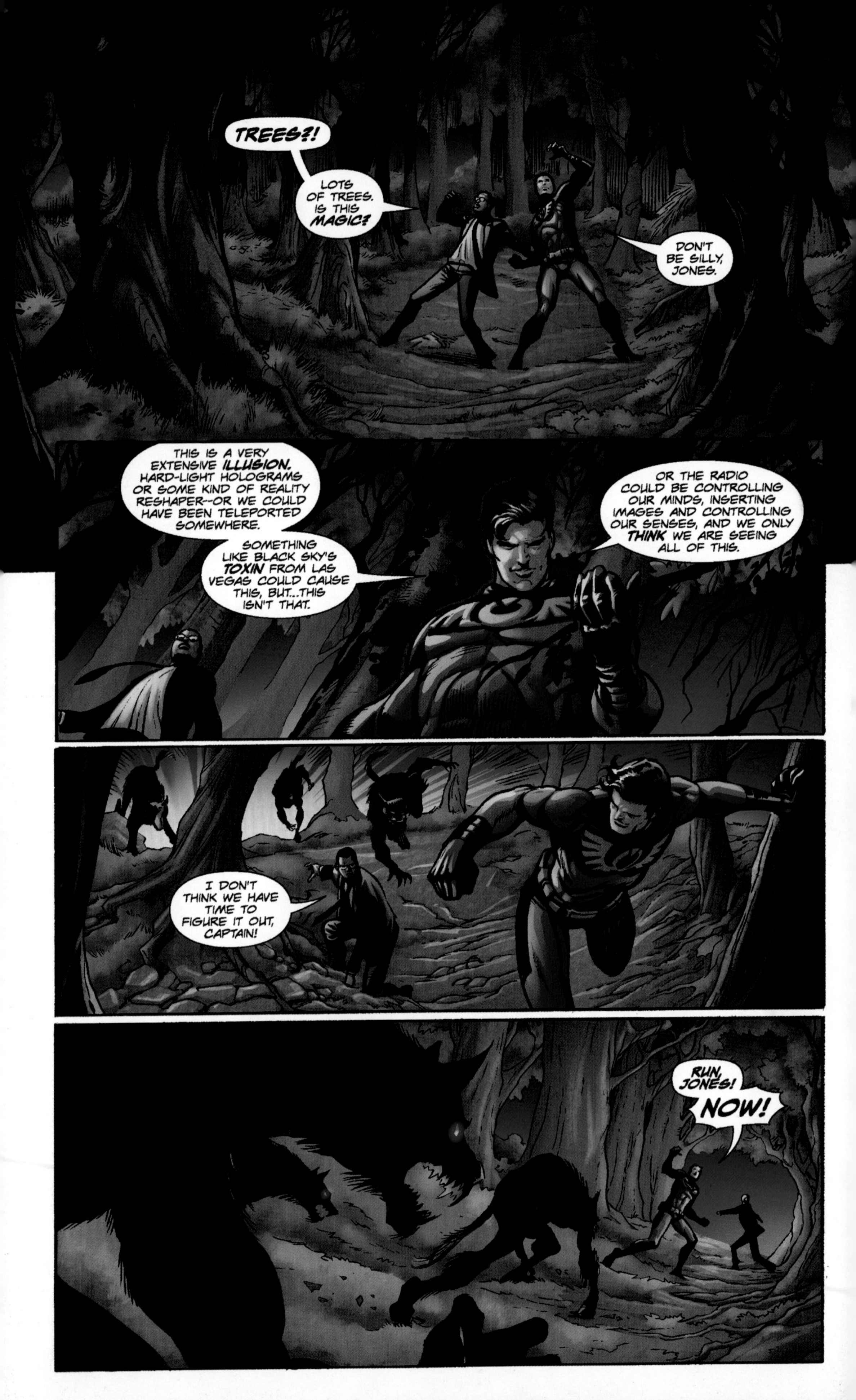
TREES?!
LOTS OF TREES. IS THIS MAGIC?
DON'T BE SILLY, JONES.
THIS IS A VERY EXTENSIVE ILLUSION. HARD-LIGHT HOLOGRAMS OR SOME KIND OF REALITY RESHAPER--OR WE COULD HAVE BEEN TELEPORTED SOMEWHERE.
SOMETHING LIKE BLACK SKY'S TOXIN FROM LAS VEGAS COULD CAUSE THIS, BUT...THIS ISN'T THAT.
OR THE RADIO COULD BE CONTROLLING OUR MINDS, INSERTING IMAGES AND CONTROLLING OUR SENSES, AND WE ONLY THINK WE ARE SEEING ALL OF THIS.
I DON'T THINK WE HAVE TIME TO FIGURE IT OUT, CAPTAIN!
RUN, JONES! NOW!

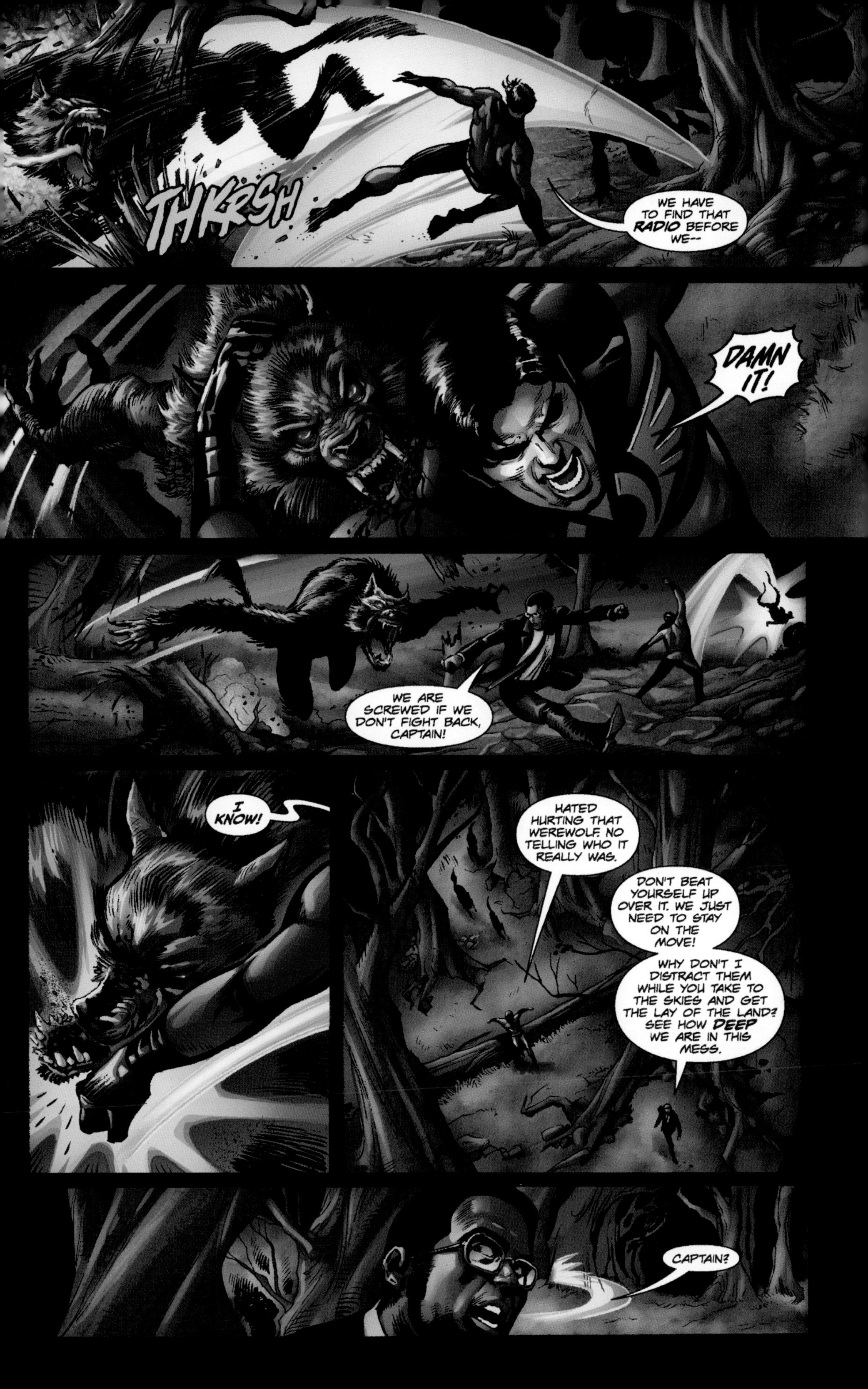
THKRSH
WE HAVE TO FIND THAT RADIO BEFORE WE--
DAMN IT!
WE ARE SCREWED IF WE DON'T FIGHT BACK, CAPTAIN!
I KNOW!
HATED HURTING THAT WEREWOLF. NO TELLING WHO IT REALLY WAS.
DON'T BEAT YOURSELF UP OVER IT. WE JUST NEED TO STAY ON THE MOVE!
WHY DON'T I DISTRACT THEM WHILE YOU TAKE TO THE SKIES AND GET THE LAY OF THE LAND? SEE HOW DEEP WE ARE IN THIS MESS.
CAPTAIN?

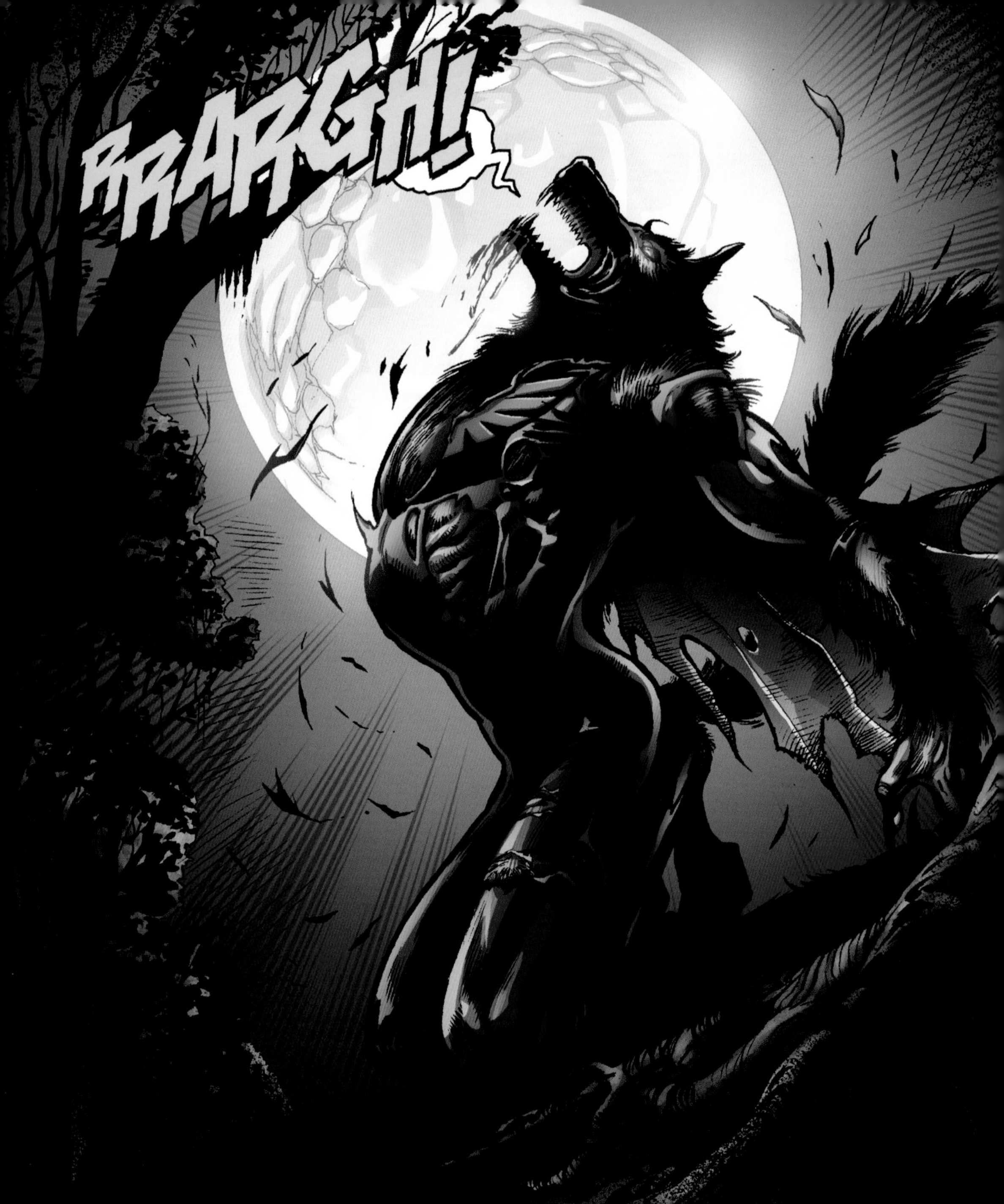
RRARGH!

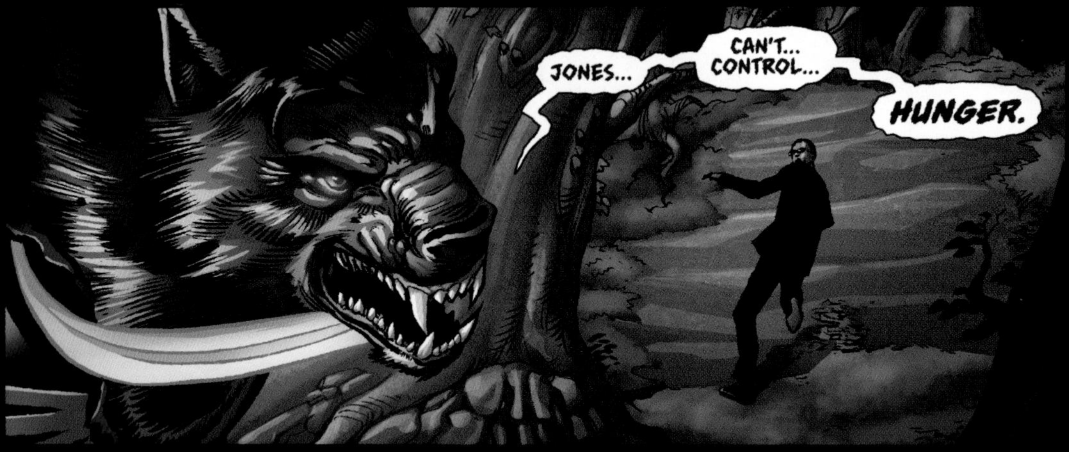
JONES...
CAN'T... CONTROL...
HUNGER.

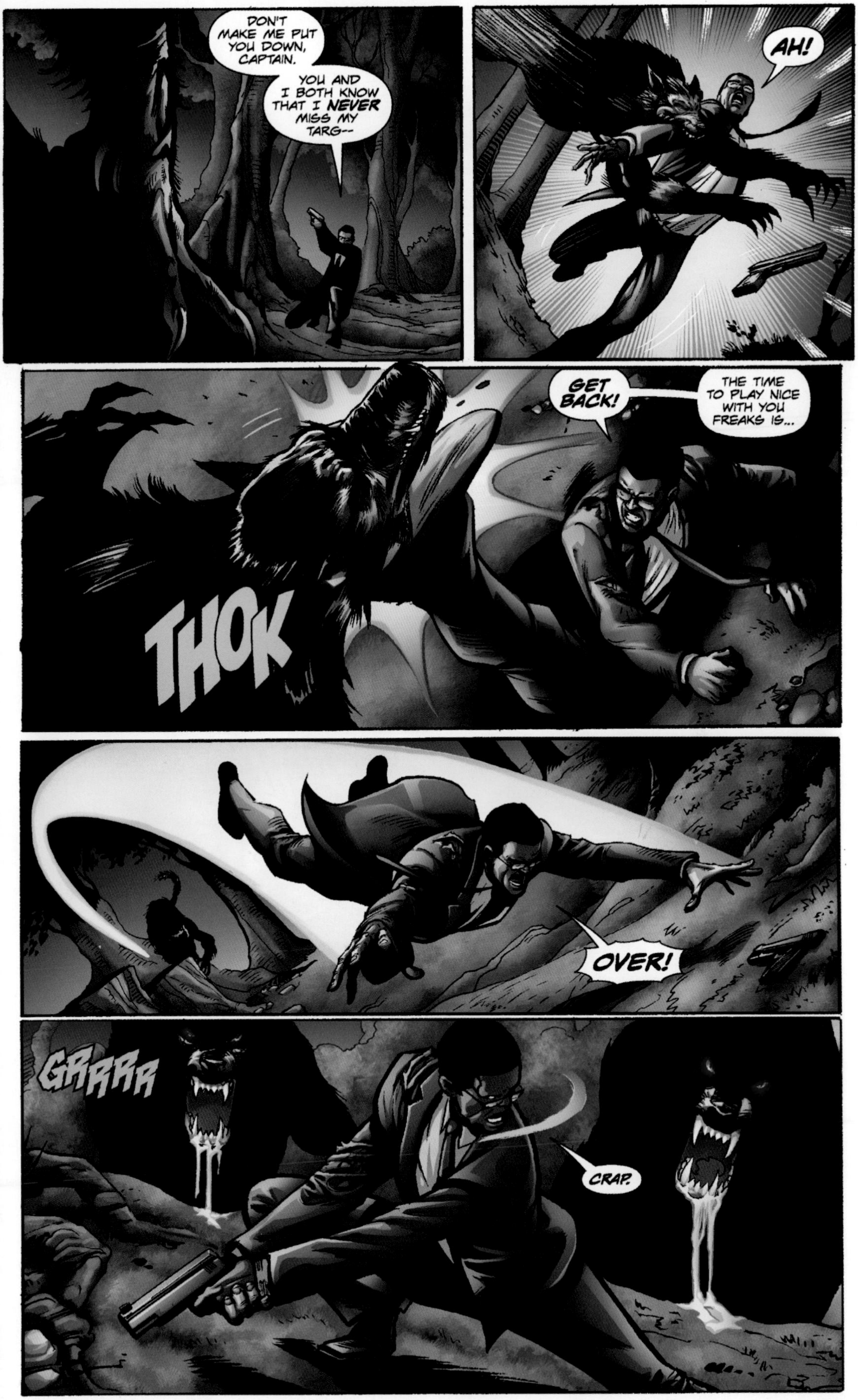
DON'T MAKE ME PUT YOU DOWN, CAPTAIN.
YOU AND I BOTH KNOW THAT I NEVER MISS MY TARG--
AH!
GET BACK!
THE TIME TO PLAY NICE WITH YOU FREAKS IS...
THOK
OVER!
GRRRR
CRAP.

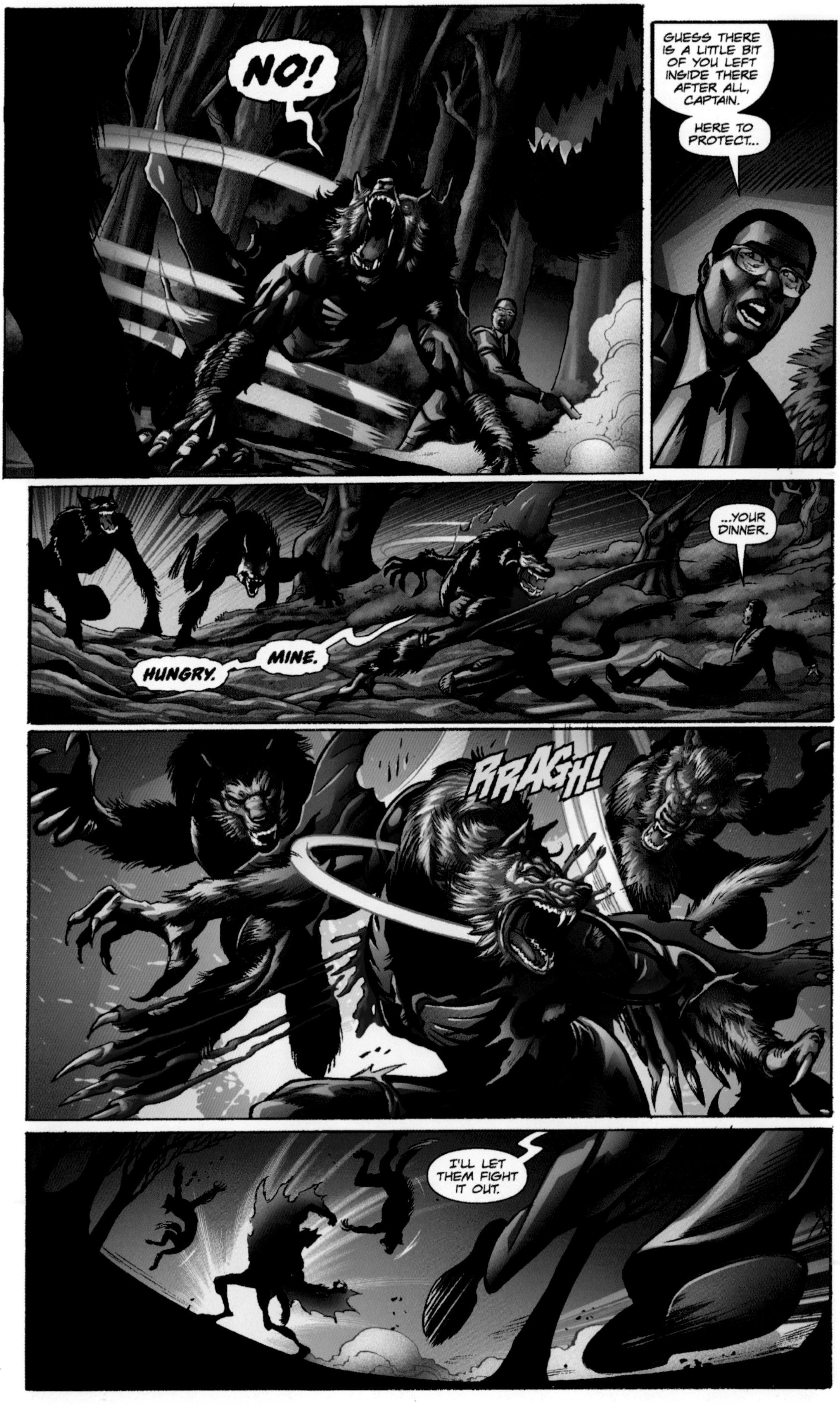
NO!
GUESS THERE IS A LITTLE BIT OF YOU LEFT INSIDE THERE AFTER ALL, CAPTAIN.
HERE TO PROTECT...
...YOUR DINNER.
HUNGRY.
MINE.
RRAGH!
I'LL LET THEM FIGHT IT OUT.

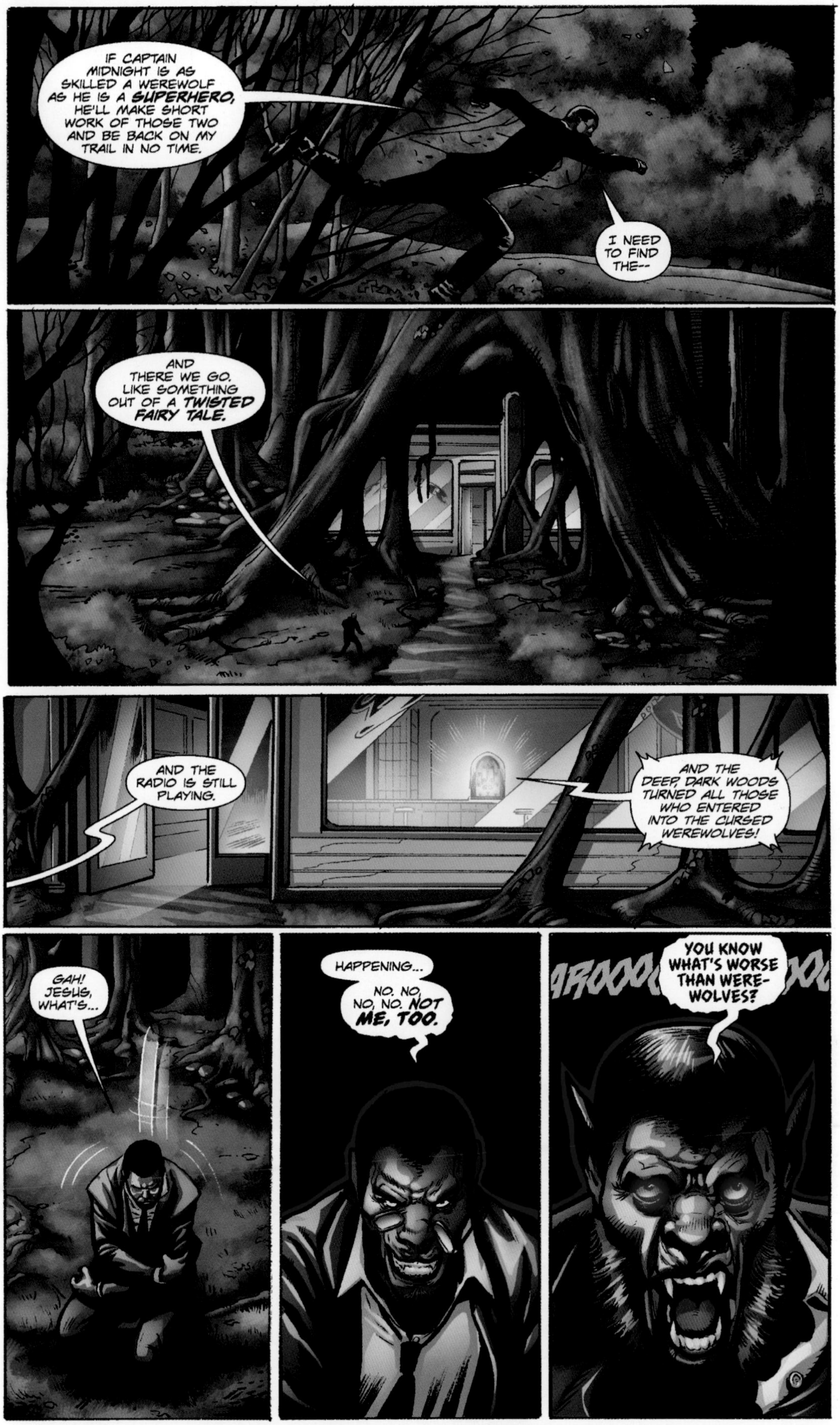
IF CAPTAIN MIDNIGHT IS AS SKILLED A WEREWOLF AS HE IS A **SUPERHERO,** HE'LL MAKE SHORT WORK OF THOSE TWO AND BE BACK ON MY TRAIL IN NO TIME.
I NEED TO FIND THE--
AND THERE WE GO. LIKE SOMETHING OUT OF A **TWISTED FAIRY TALE.**
AND THE RADIO IS STILL PLAYING.
AND THE DEEP, DARK WOODS TURNED ALL THOSE WHO ENTERED INTO THE CURSED WEREWOLVES!
GAH! JESUS, WHAT'S...
HAPPENING...
NO. NO, NO, NO. **NOT ME, TOO.**
YOU KNOW WHAT'S WORSE THAN WERE-WOLVES?

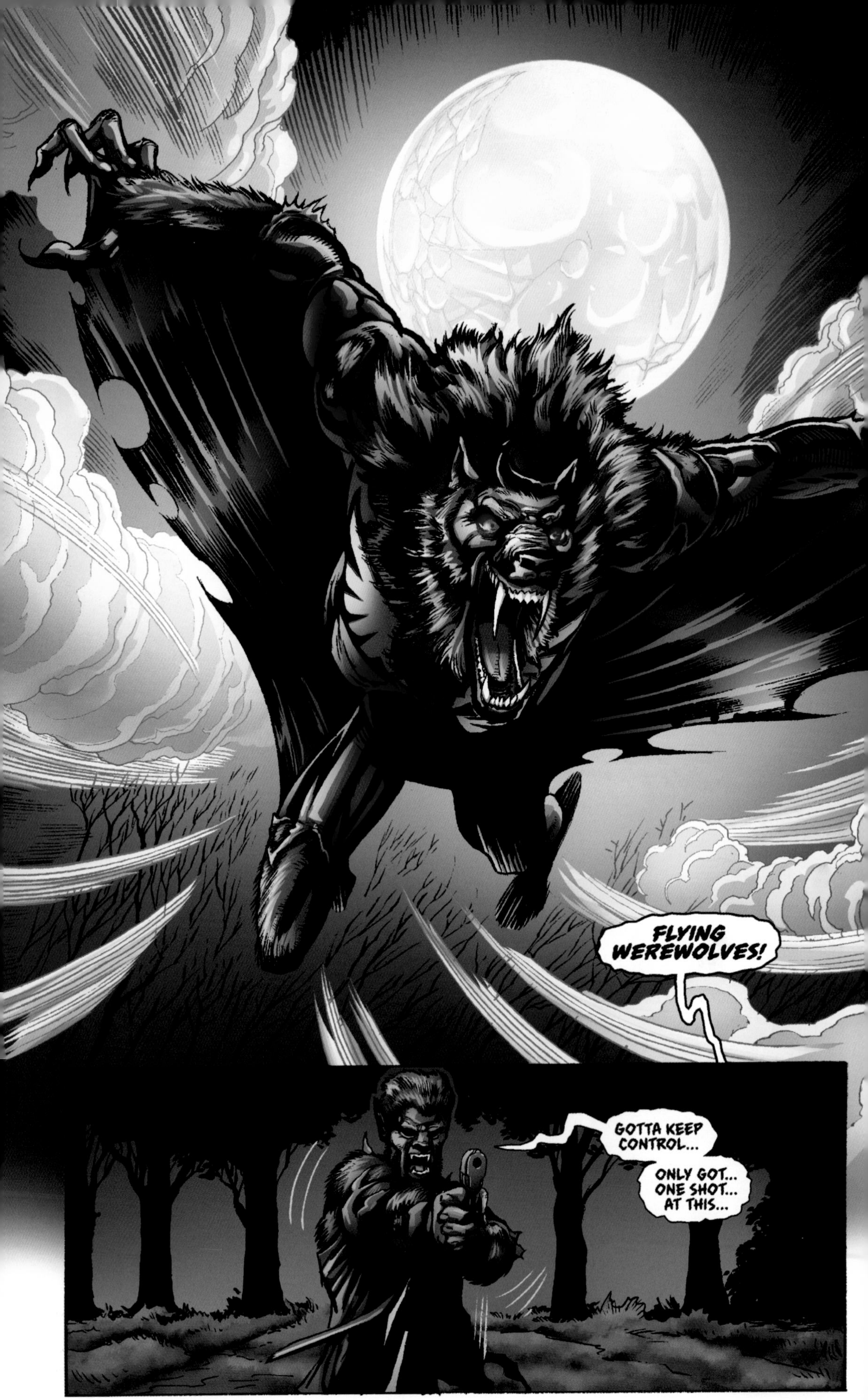
FLYING WEREWOLVES!
GOTTA KEEP CONTROL...
ONLY GOT... ONE SHOT... AT THIS...

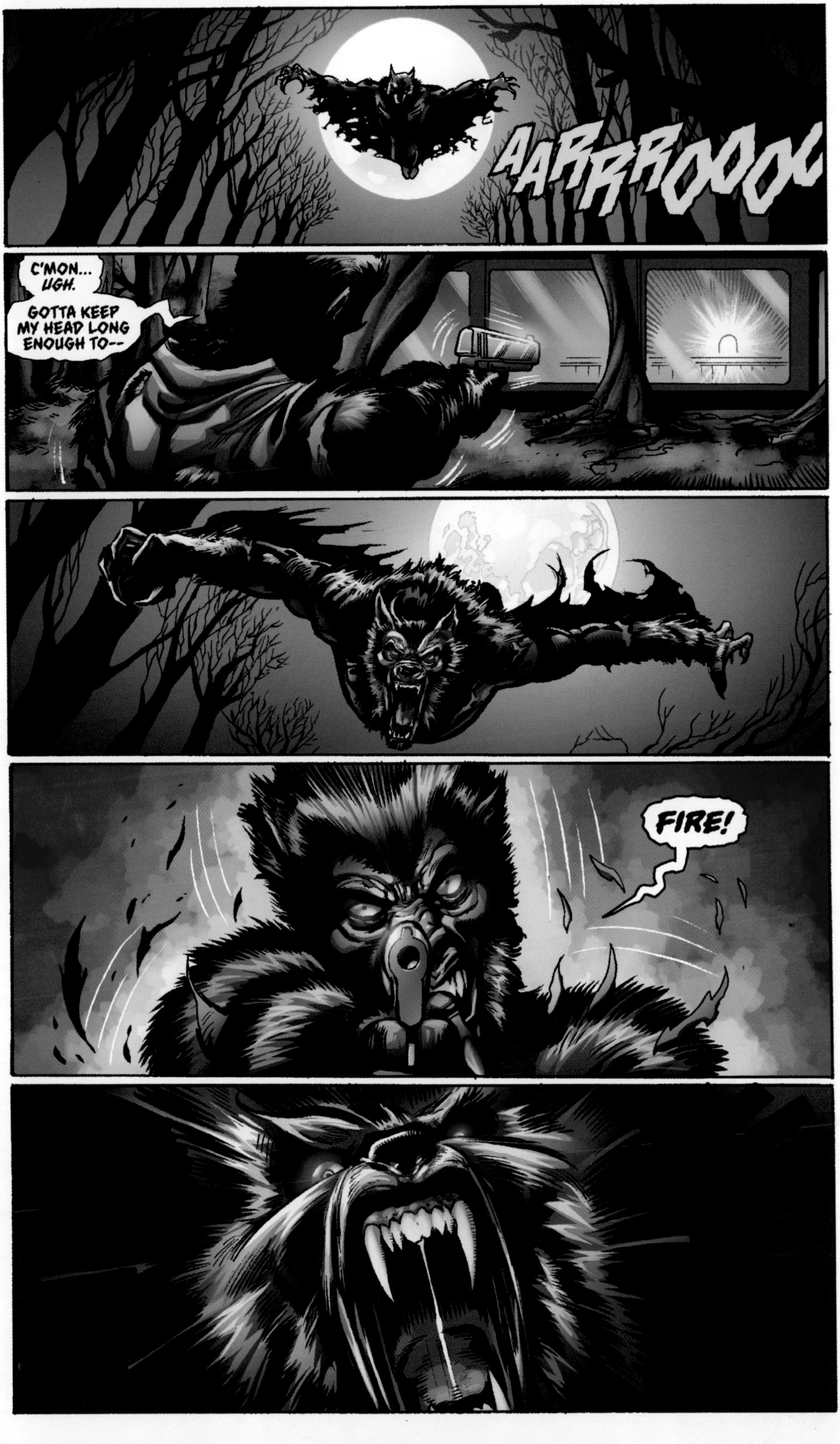
AARRROOOO
C'MON... UGH.
GOTTA KEEP MY HEAD LONG ENOUGH TO--
FIRE!

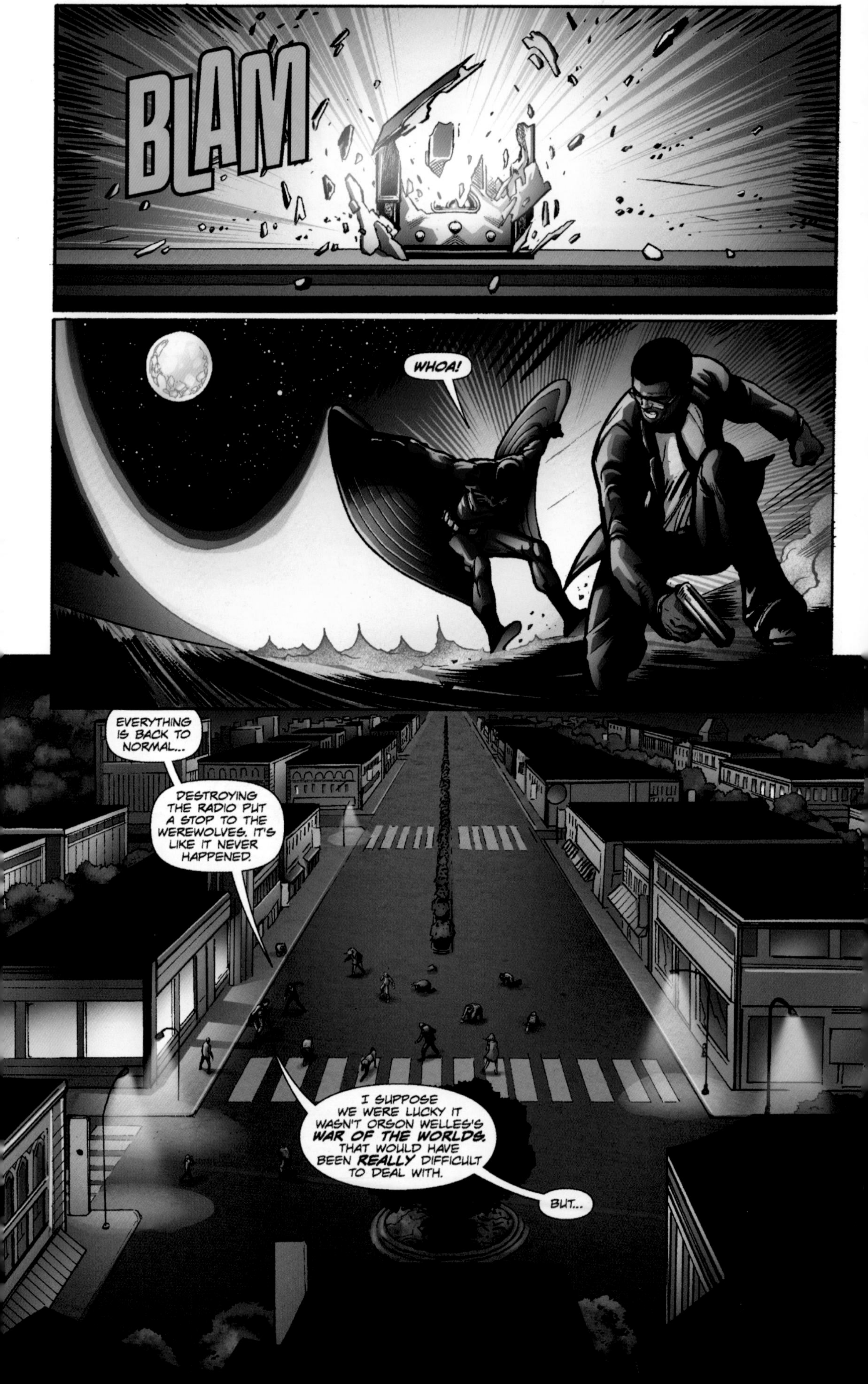
BLAM
WHOA!
EVERYTHING IS BACK TO NORMAL...
DESTROYING THE RADIO PUT A STOP TO THE WEREWOLVES. IT'S LIKE IT NEVER HAPPENED.
I SUPPOSE WE WERE LUCKY IT WASN'T ORSON WELLES'S **WAR OF THE WORLDS.** THAT WOULD HAVE BEEN **REALLY** DIFFICULT TO DEAL WITH.
BUT...

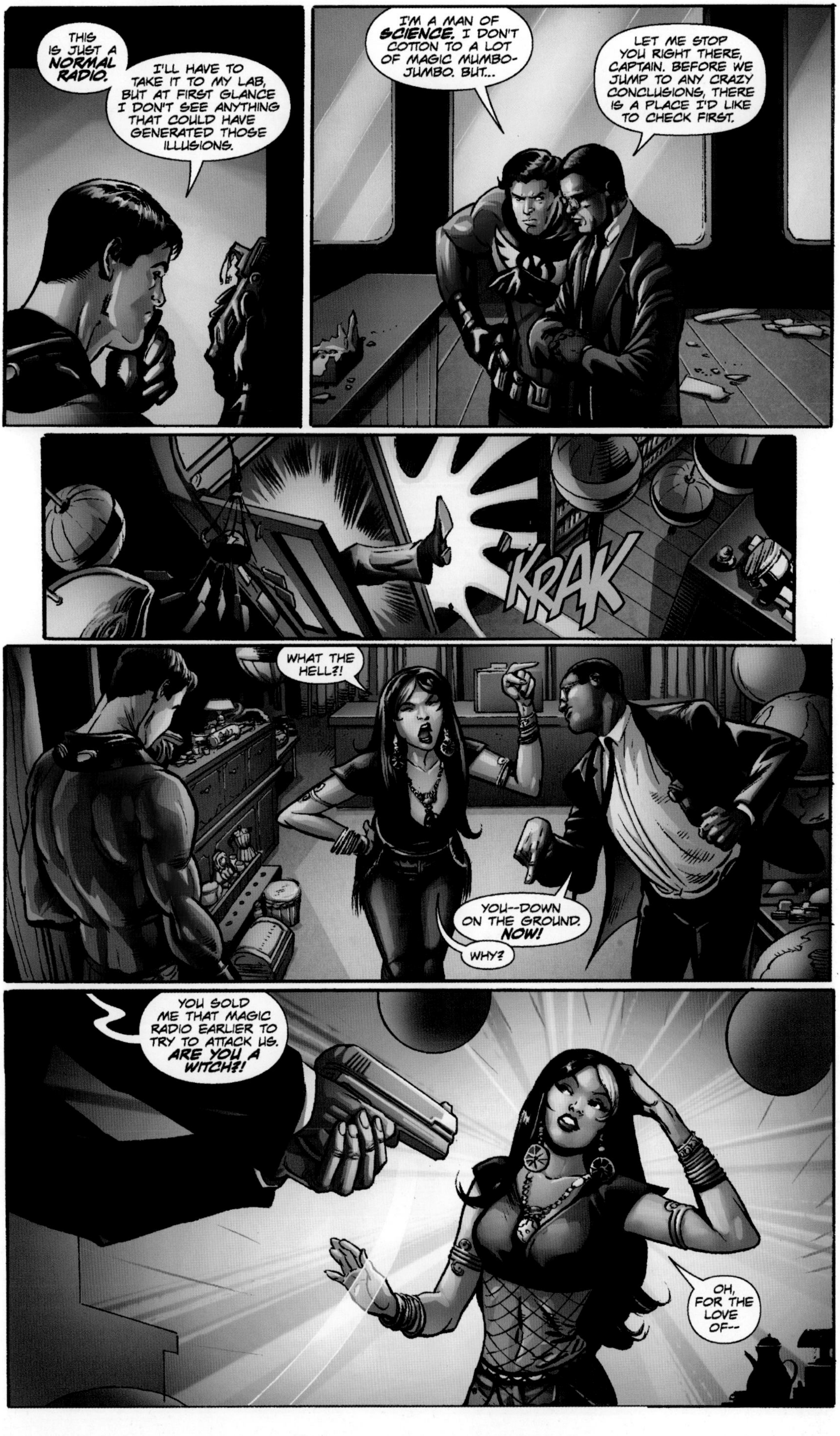
THIS IS JUST A NORMAL RADIO.
I'LL HAVE TO TAKE IT TO MY LAB, BUT AT FIRST GLANCE I DON'T SEE ANYTHING THAT COULD HAVE GENERATED THOSE ILLUSIONS.
I'M A MAN OF SCIENCE. I DON'T COTTON TO A LOT OF MAGIC MUMBO-JUMBO. BUT...
LET ME STOP YOU RIGHT THERE, CAPTAIN. BEFORE WE JUMP TO ANY CRAZY CONCLUSIONS, THERE IS A PLACE I'D LIKE TO CHECK FIRST.
KRAK
WHAT THE HELL?!
YOU--DOWN ON THE GROUND. NOW!
WHY?
YOU SOLD ME THAT MAGIC RADIO EARLIER TO TRY TO ATTACK US. ARE YOU A WITCH?!
OH, FOR THE LOVE OF--

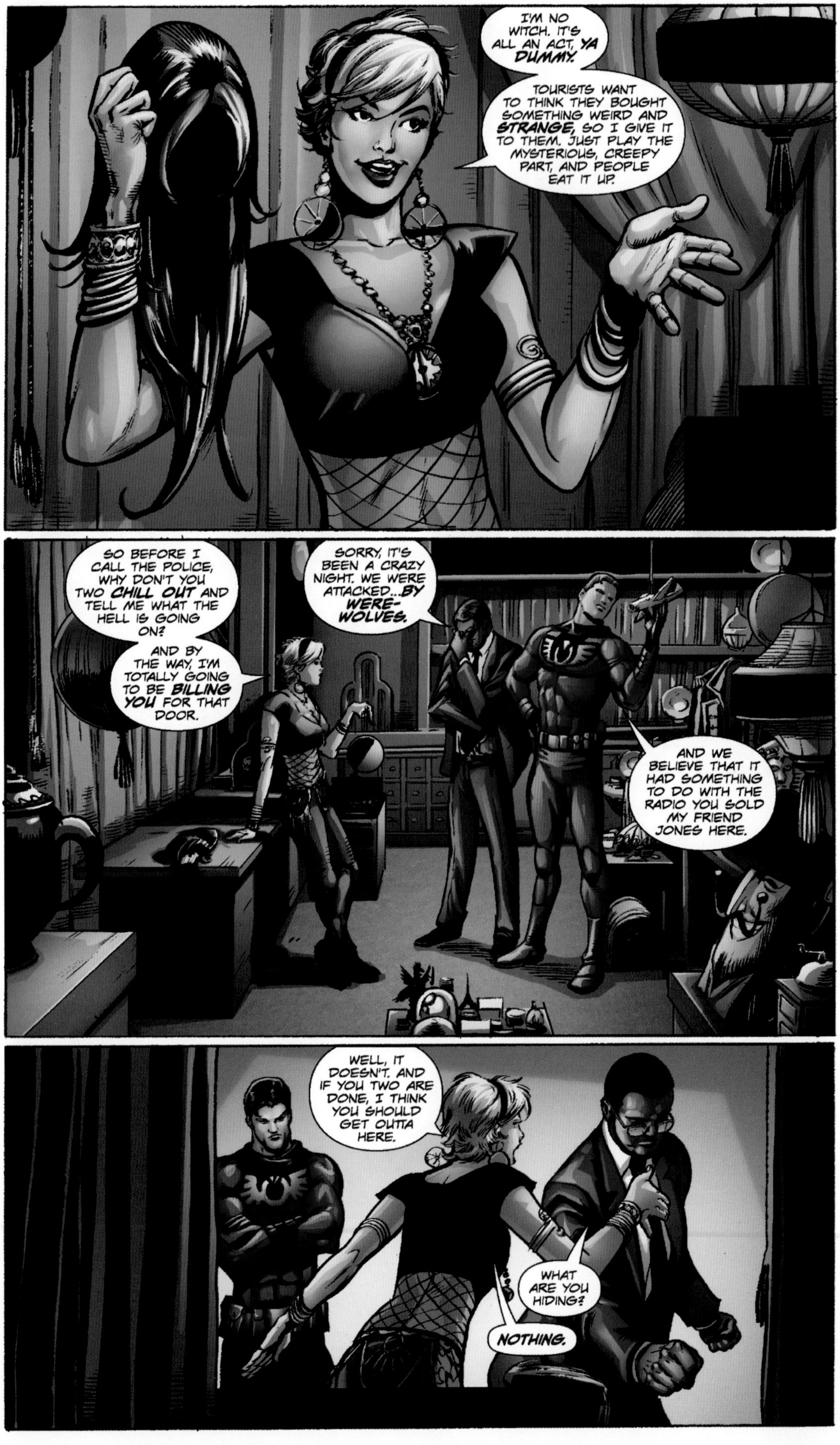
I'M NO WITCH. IT'S ALL AN ACT, YA DUMMY.
TOURISTS WANT TO THINK THEY BOUGHT SOMETHING WEIRD AND STRANGE, SO I GIVE IT TO THEM. JUST PLAY THE MYSTERIOUS, CREEPY PART, AND PEOPLE EAT IT UP.
SO BEFORE I CALL THE POLICE, WHY DON'T YOU TWO CHILL OUT AND TELL ME WHAT THE HELL IS GOING ON?
AND BY THE WAY, I'M TOTALLY GOING TO BE BILLING YOU FOR THAT DOOR.
SORRY, IT'S BEEN A CRAZY NIGHT. WE WERE ATTACKED...BY WERE-WOLVES.
AND WE BELIEVE THAT IT HAD SOMETHING TO DO WITH THE RADIO YOU SOLD MY FRIEND JONES HERE.
WELL, IT DOESN'T. AND IF YOU TWO ARE DONE, I THINK YOU SHOULD GET OUTTA HERE.
WHAT ARE YOU HIDING?
NOTHING.

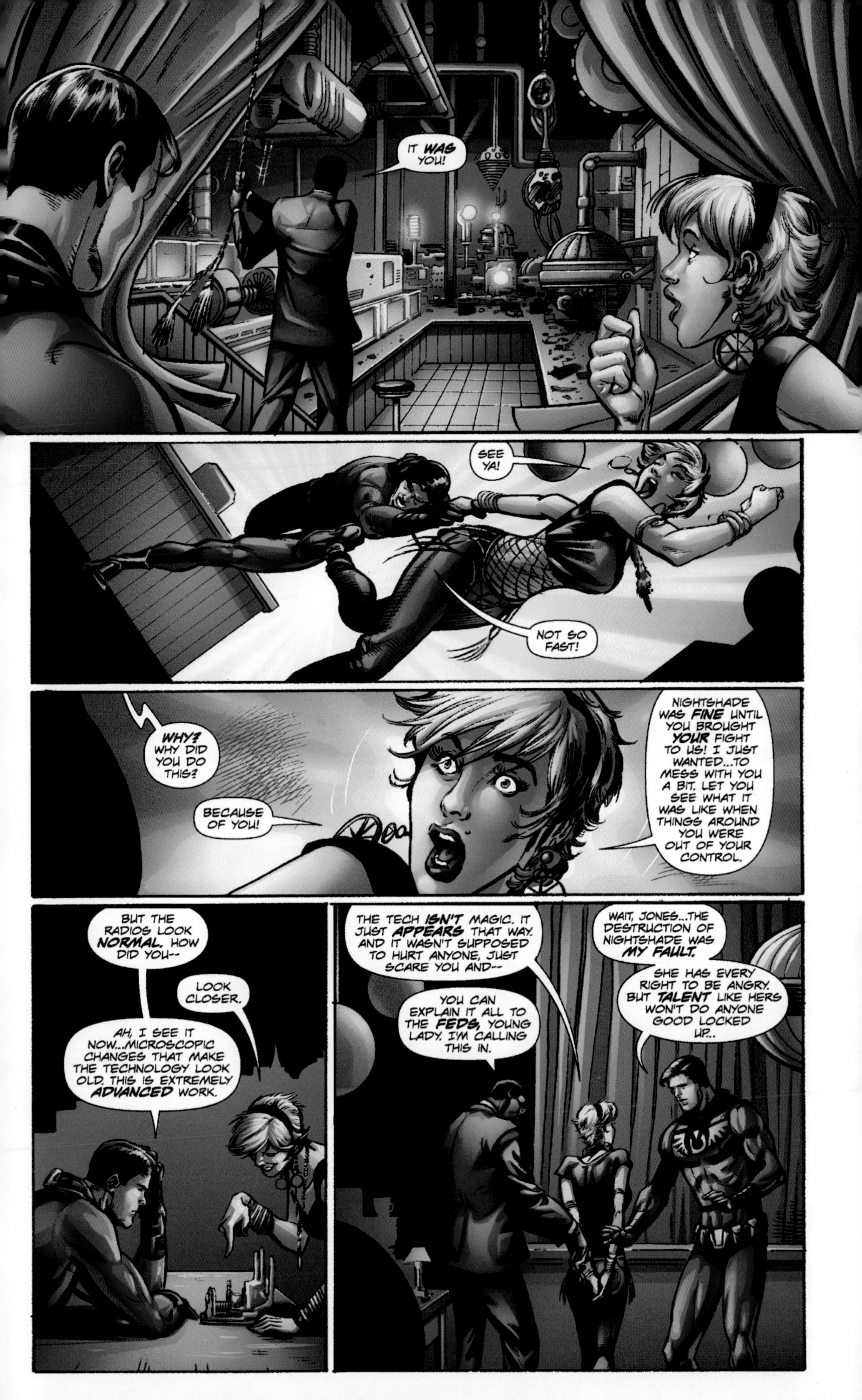
IT WAS YOU!
SEE YA!
NOT SO FAST!
WHY? WHY DID YOU DO THIS?
BECAUSE OF YOU!
NIGHTSHADE WAS FINE UNTIL YOU BROUGHT YOUR FIGHT TO US! I JUST WANTED...TO MESS WITH YOU A BIT. LET YOU SEE WHAT IT WAS LIKE WHEN THINGS AROUND YOU WERE OUT OF YOUR CONTROL.
BUT THE RADIOS LOOK NORMAL. HOW DID YOU--
LOOK CLOSER.
AH, I SEE IT NOW...MICROSCOPIC CHANGES THAT MAKE THE TECHNOLOGY LOOK OLD. THIS IS EXTREMELY ADVANCED WORK.
THE TECH ISN'T MAGIC. IT JUST APPEARS THAT WAY. AND IT WASN'T SUPPOSED TO HURT ANYONE, JUST SCARE YOU AND--
YOU CAN EXPLAIN IT ALL TO THE FEDS, YOUNG LADY. I'M CALLING THIS IN.
WAIT, JONES...THE DESTRUCTION OF NIGHTSHADE WAS MY FAULT.
SHE HAS EVERY RIGHT TO BE ANGRY. BUT TALENT LIKE HERS WON'T DO ANYONE GOOD LOCKED UP..

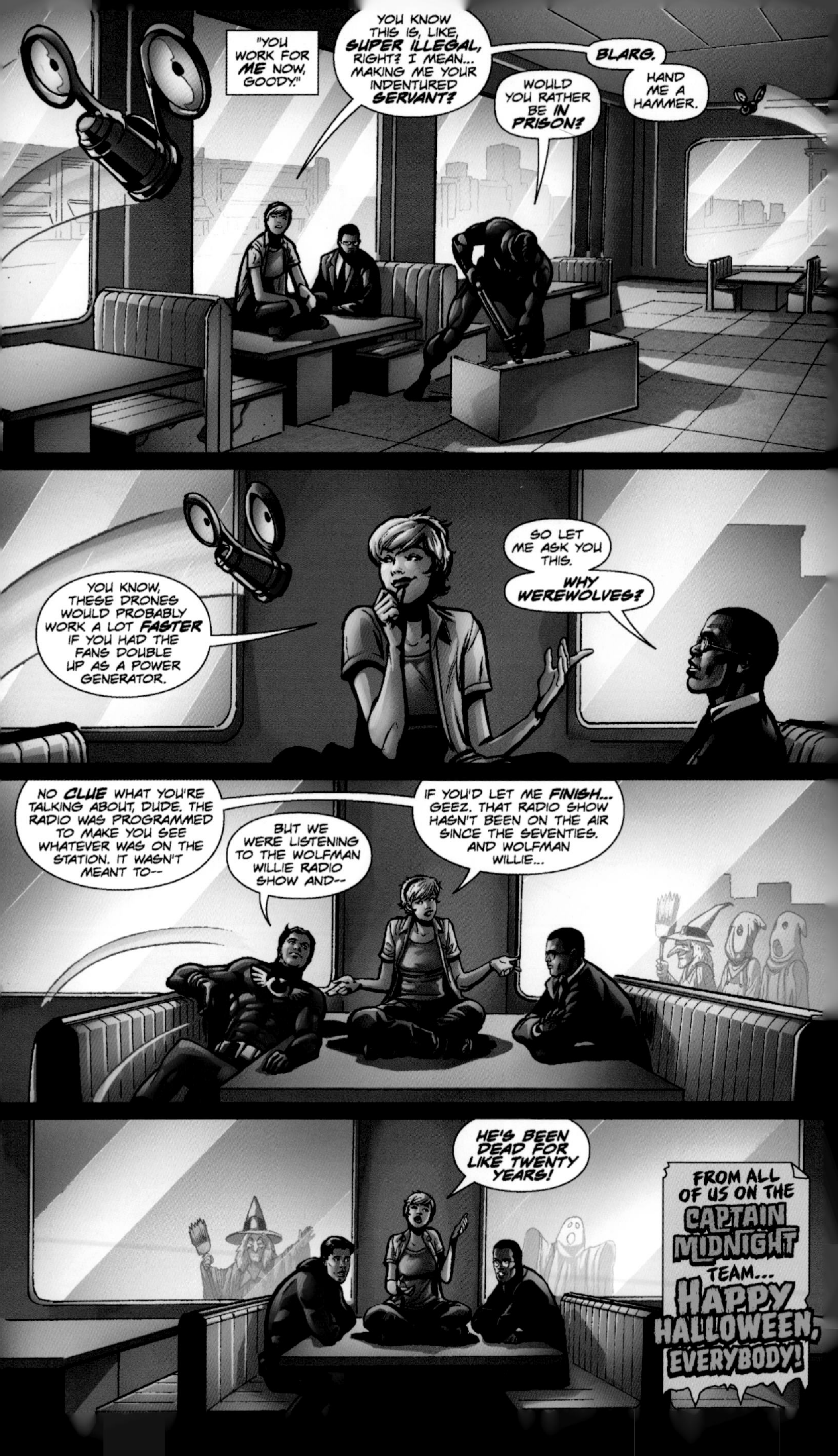
"YOU WORK FOR ME NOW, GOODY."
YOU KNOW THIS IS, LIKE, SUPER ILLEGAL, RIGHT? I MEAN... MAKING ME YOUR INDENTURED SERVANT?
WOULD YOU RATHER BE IN PRISON?
BLARG.
HAND ME A HAMMER.
YOU KNOW, THESE DRONES WOULD PROBABLY WORK A LOT FASTER IF YOU HAD THE FANS DOUBLE UP AS A POWER GENERATOR.
SO LET ME ASK YOU THIS.
WHY WEREWOLVES?
NO CLUE WHAT YOU'RE TALKING ABOUT, DUDE. THE RADIO WAS PROGRAMMED TO MAKE YOU SEE WHATEVER WAS ON THE STATION. IT WASN'T MEANT TO--
BUT WE WERE LISTENING TO THE WOLFMAN WILLIE RADIO SHOW AND--
IF YOU'D LET ME FINISH... GEEZ. THAT RADIO SHOW HASN'T BEEN ON THE AIR SINCE THE SEVENTIES. AND WOLFMAN WILLIE...
HE'S BEEN DEAD FOR LIKE TWENTY YEARS!
FROM ALL OF US ON THE CAPTAIN MIDNIGHT TEAM... HAPPY HALLOWEEN, EVERYBODY!

CHAPTER 2

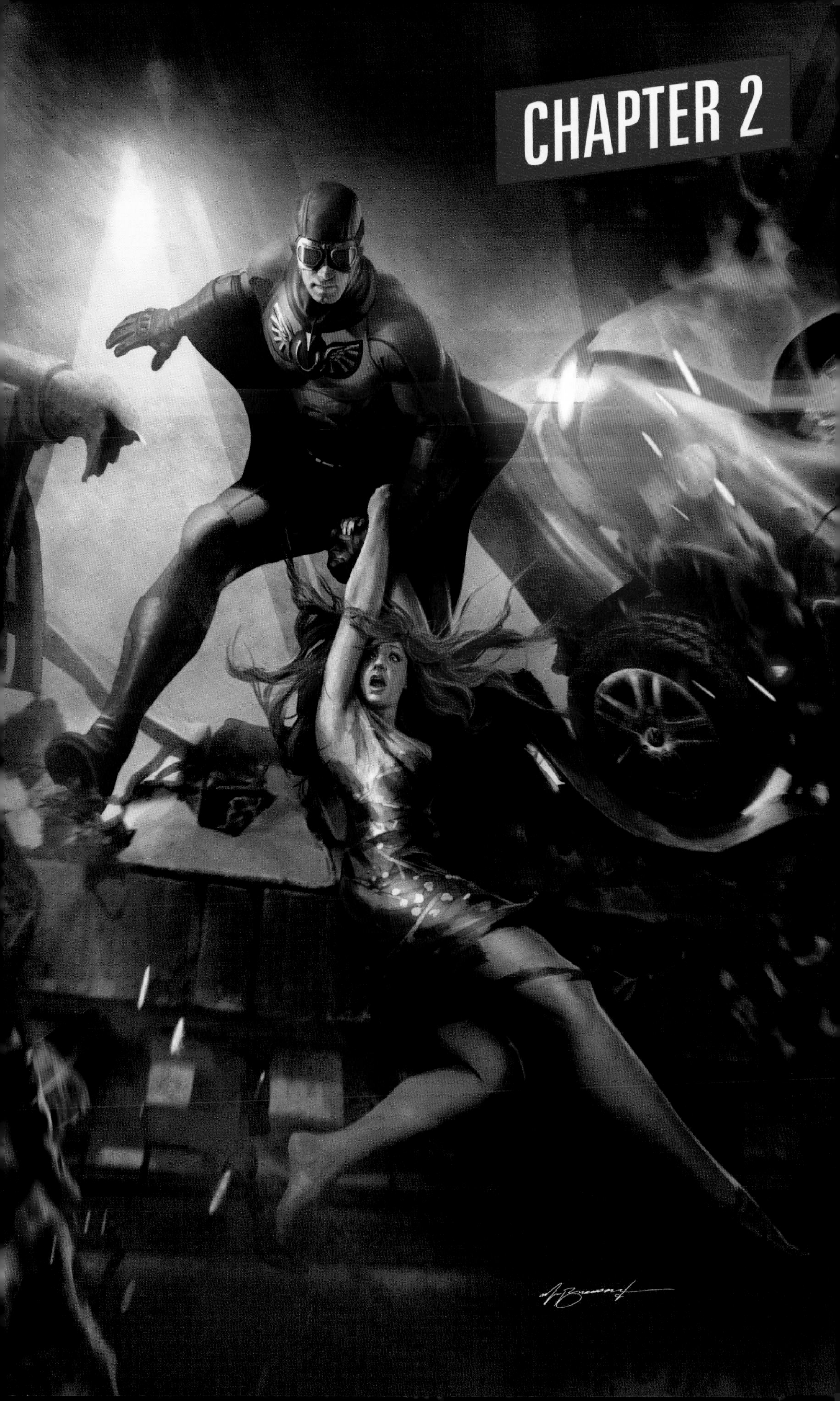

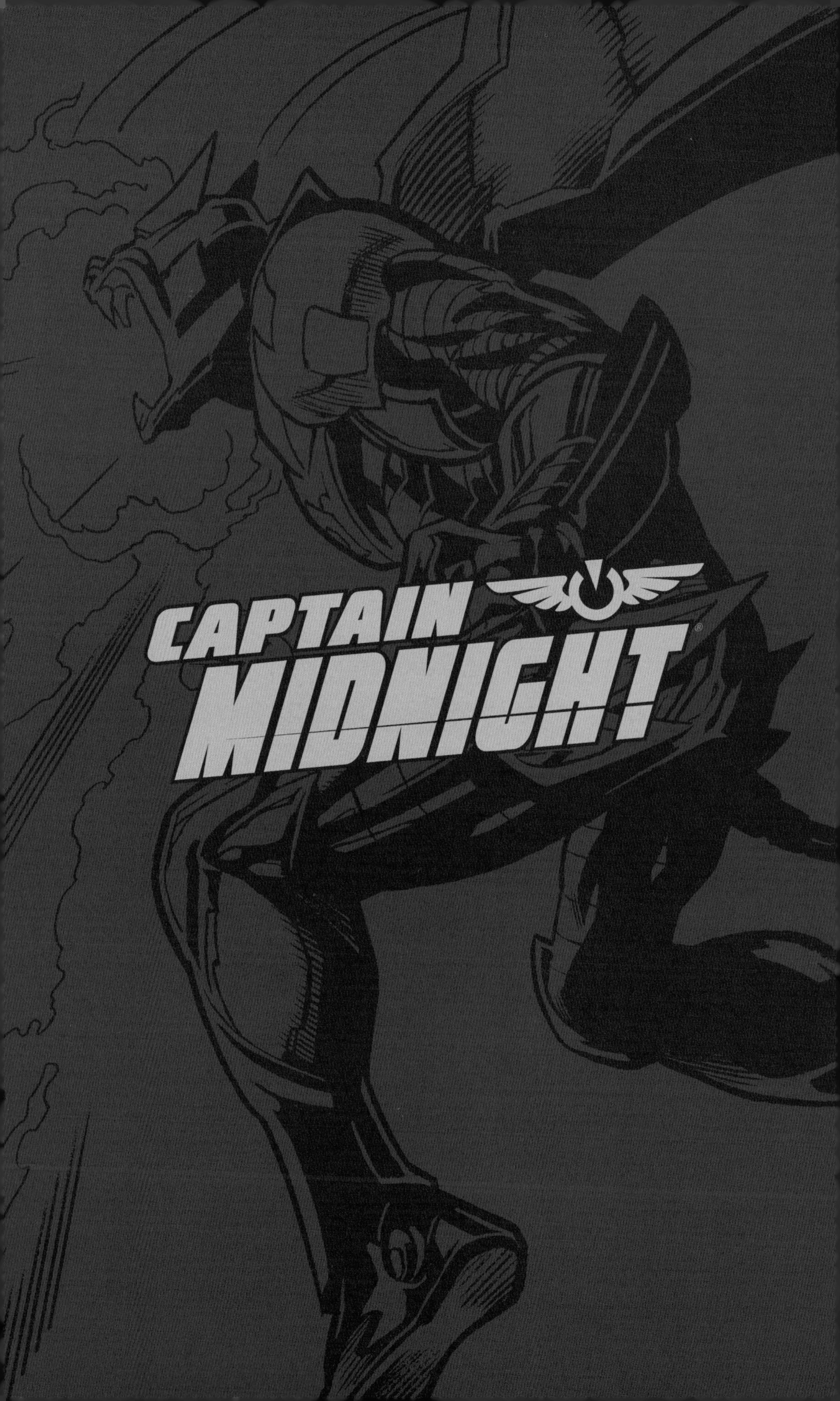
CAPTAIN
MIDNIGHT®

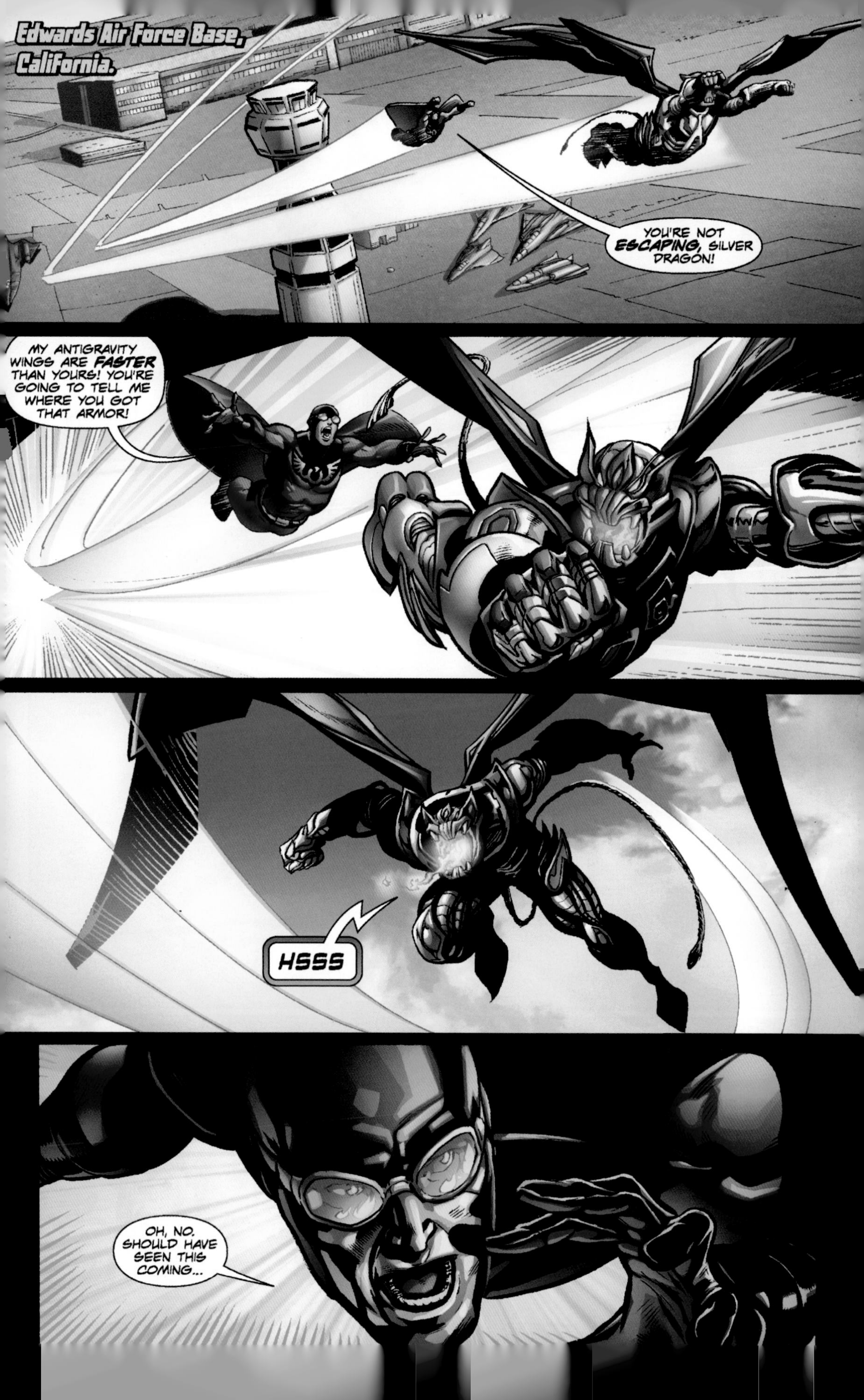
Edwards Air Force Base, California.
YOU'RE NOT ESCAPING, SILVER DRAGON!
MY ANTIGRAVITY WINGS ARE FASTER THAN YOURS! YOU'RE GOING TO TELL ME WHERE YOU GOT THAT ARMOR!
HSSS
OH, NO. SHOULD HAVE SEEN THIS COMING...

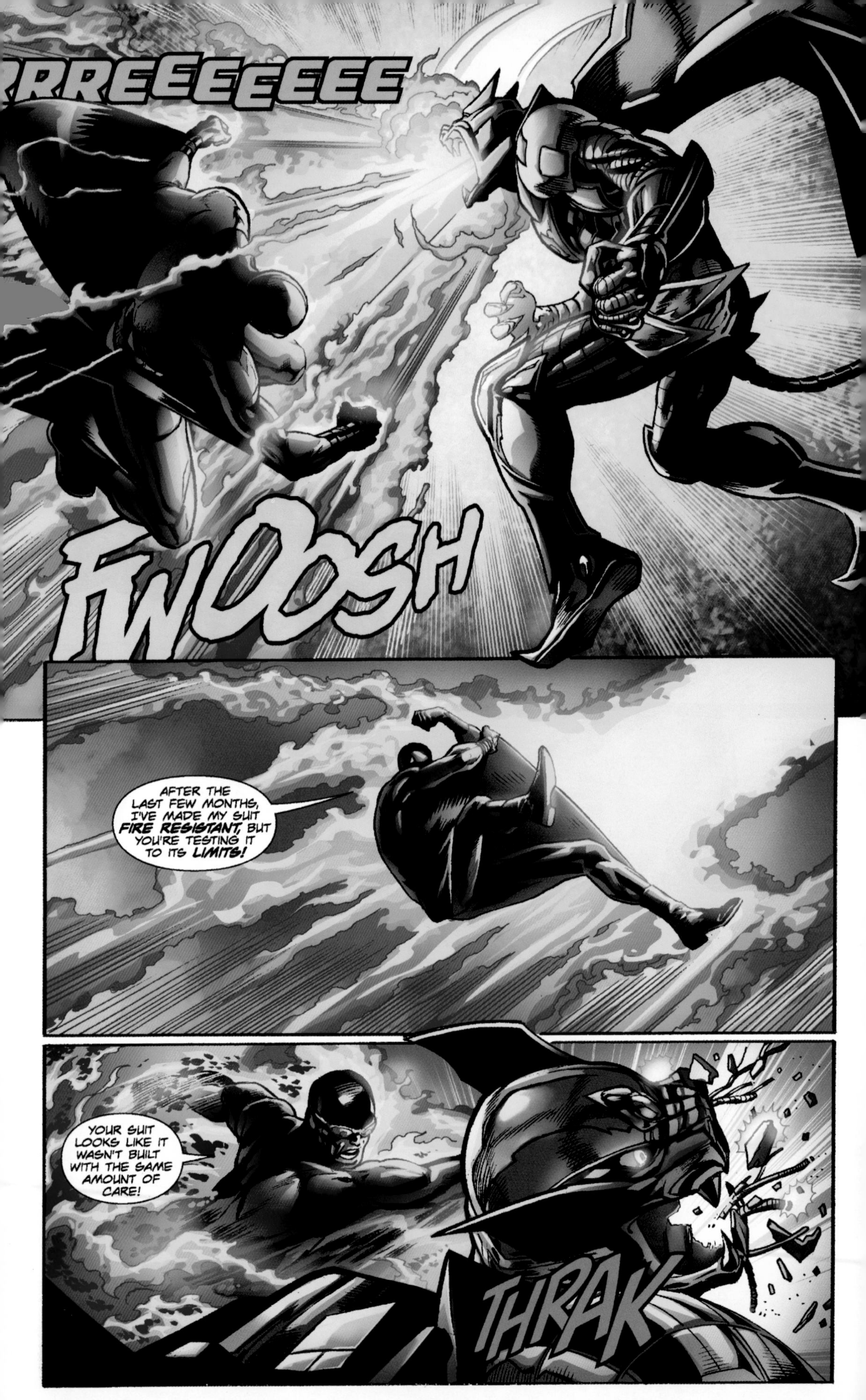
RRREEEEEEEE
FWOOSH
AFTER THE LAST FEW MONTHS, I'VE MADE MY SUIT FIRE RESISTANT, BUT YOU'RE TESTING IT TO ITS LIMITS!
YOUR SUIT LOOKS LIKE IT WASN'T BUILT WITH THE SAME AMOUNT OF CARE!
THRAK

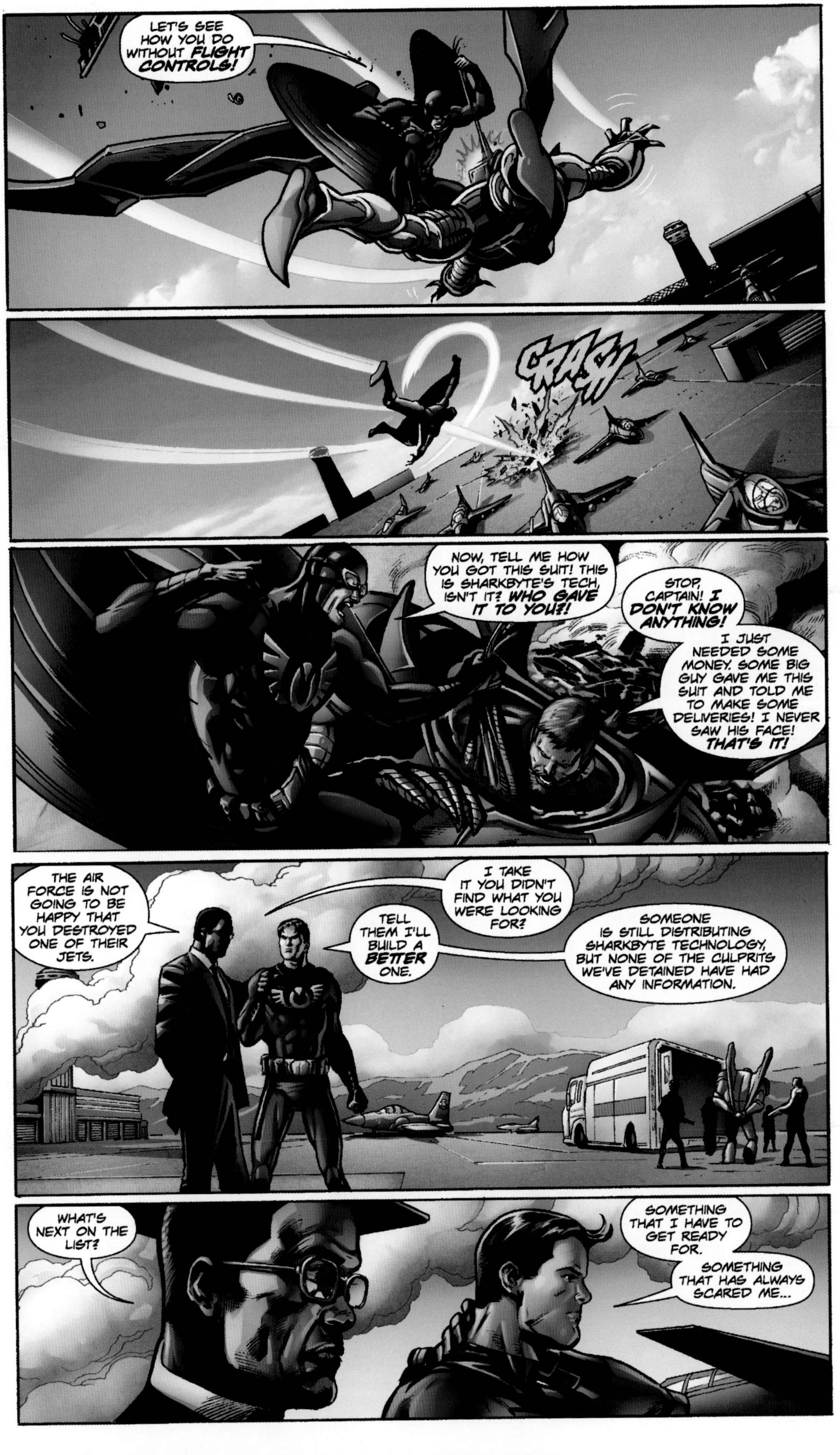

LET'S SEE HOW YOU DO WITHOUT FLIGHT CONTROLS!
CRASH
NOW, TELL ME HOW YOU GOT THIS SUIT! THIS IS SHARKBYTE'S TECH, ISN'T IT? WHO GAVE IT TO YOU?!
STOP, CAPTAIN! I DON'T KNOW ANYTHING!
I JUST NEEDED SOME MONEY. SOME BIG GUY GAVE ME THIS SUIT AND TOLD ME TO MAKE SOME DELIVERIES! I NEVER SAW HIS FACE! THAT'S IT!
THE AIR FORCE IS NOT GOING TO BE HAPPY THAT YOU DESTROYED ONE OF THEIR JETS.
TELL THEM I'LL BUILD A BETTER ONE.
I TAKE IT YOU DIDN'T FIND WHAT YOU WERE LOOKING FOR?
SOMEONE IS STILL DISTRIBUTING SHARKBYTE TECHNOLOGY, BUT NONE OF THE CULPRITS WE'VE DETAINED HAVE HAD ANY INFORMATION.
WHAT'S NEXT ON THE LIST?
SOMETHING THAT I HAVE TO GET READY FOR.
SOMETHING THAT HAS ALWAYS SCARED ME...

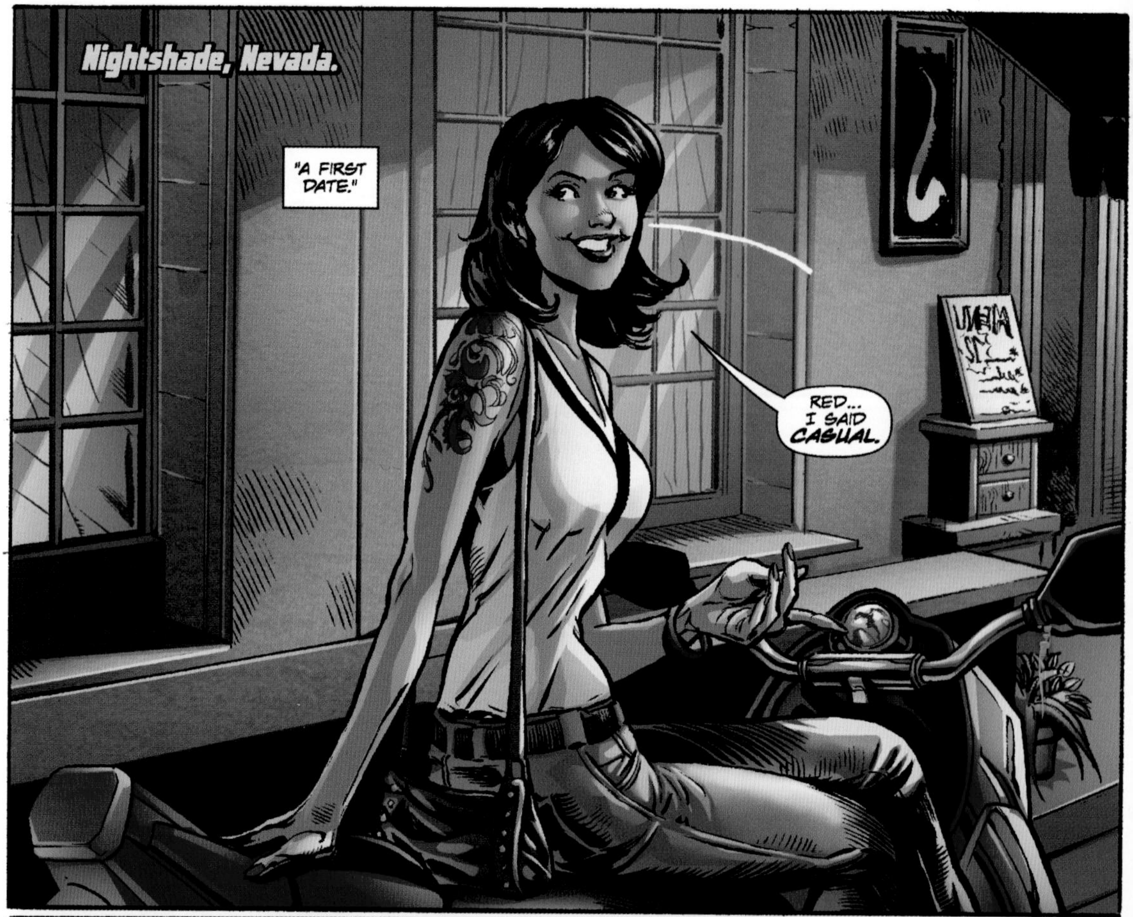
Nightshade, Nevada.
"A FIRST DATE."
RED... I SAID CASUAL.

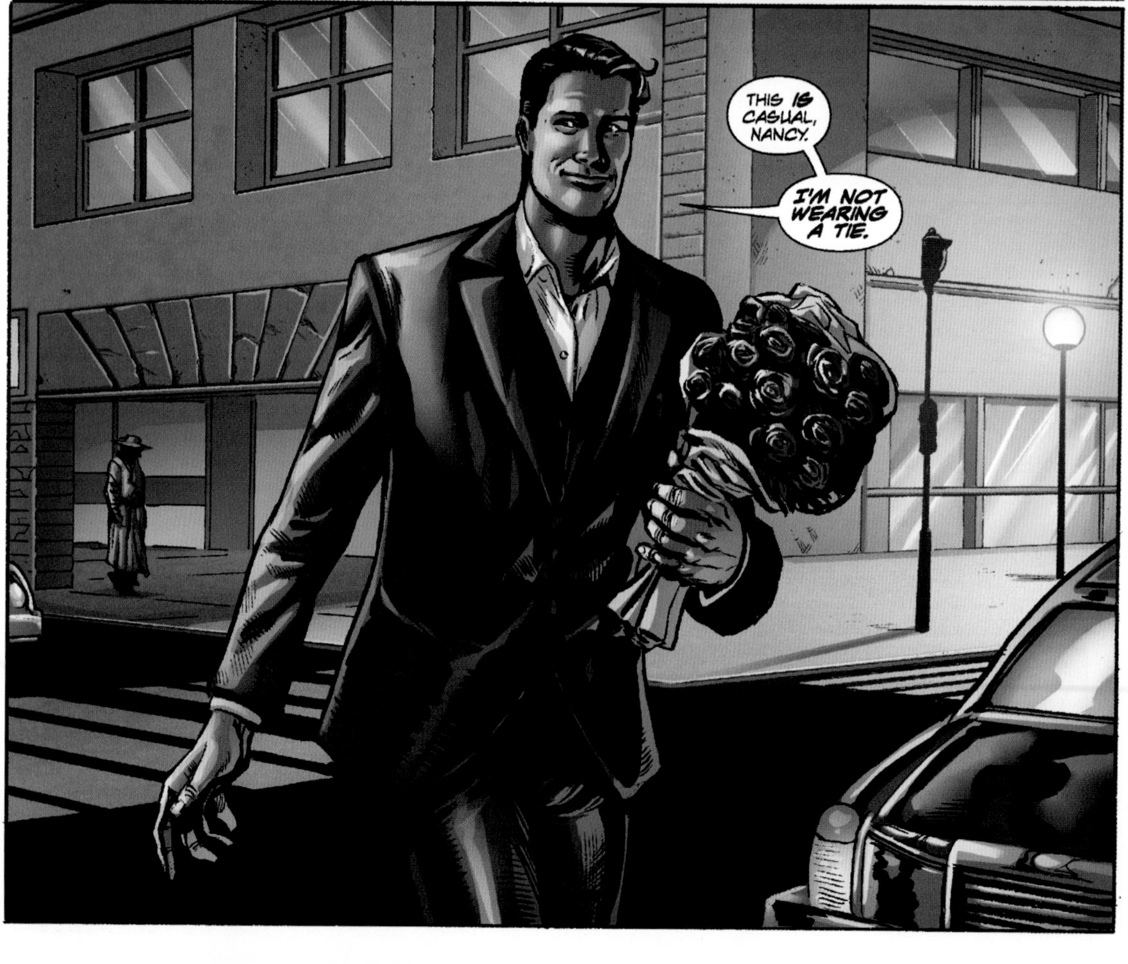
THIS IS CASUAL, NANCY.
I'M NOT WEARING A TIE.

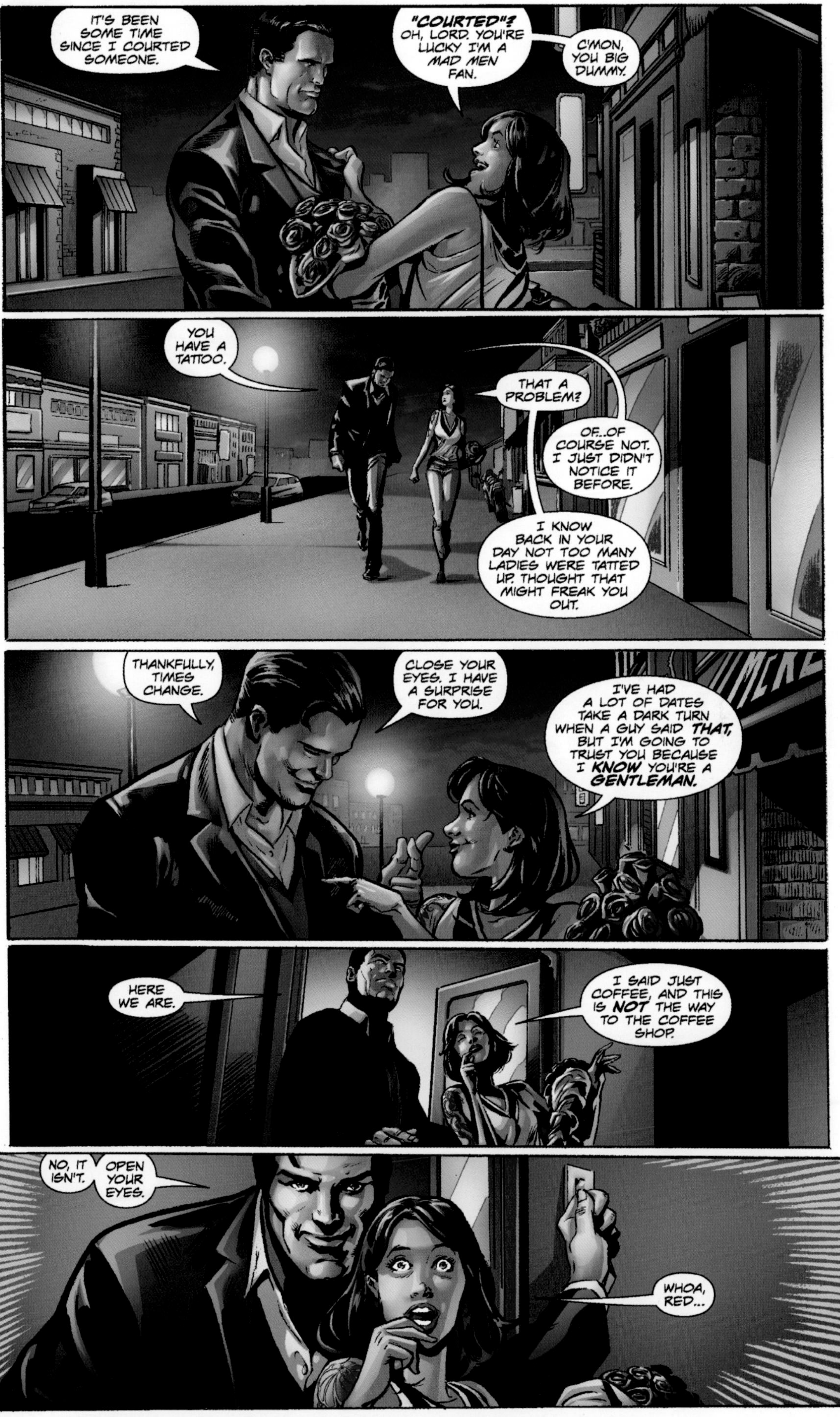
IT'S BEEN SOME TIME SINCE I COURTED SOMEONE.
"COURTED"? OH, LORD, YOU'RE LUCKY I'M A MAD MEN FAN.
C'MON, YOU BIG DUMMY.
YOU HAVE A TATTOO.
THAT A PROBLEM?
OF...OF COURSE NOT. I JUST DIDN'T NOTICE IT BEFORE.
I KNOW BACK IN YOUR DAY NOT TOO MANY LADIES WERE TATTED UP. THOUGHT THAT MIGHT FREAK YOU OUT.
THANKFULLY, TIMES CHANGE.
CLOSE YOUR EYES. I HAVE A SURPRISE FOR YOU.
I'VE HAD A LOT OF DATES TAKE A DARK TURN WHEN A GUY SAID THAT, BUT I'M GOING TO TRUST YOU BECAUSE I KNOW YOU'RE A GENTLEMAN.
HERE WE ARE.
I SAID JUST COFFEE, AND THIS IS NOT THE WAY TO THE COFFEE SHOP.
NO, IT ISN'T.
OPEN YOUR EYES.
WHOA, RED...

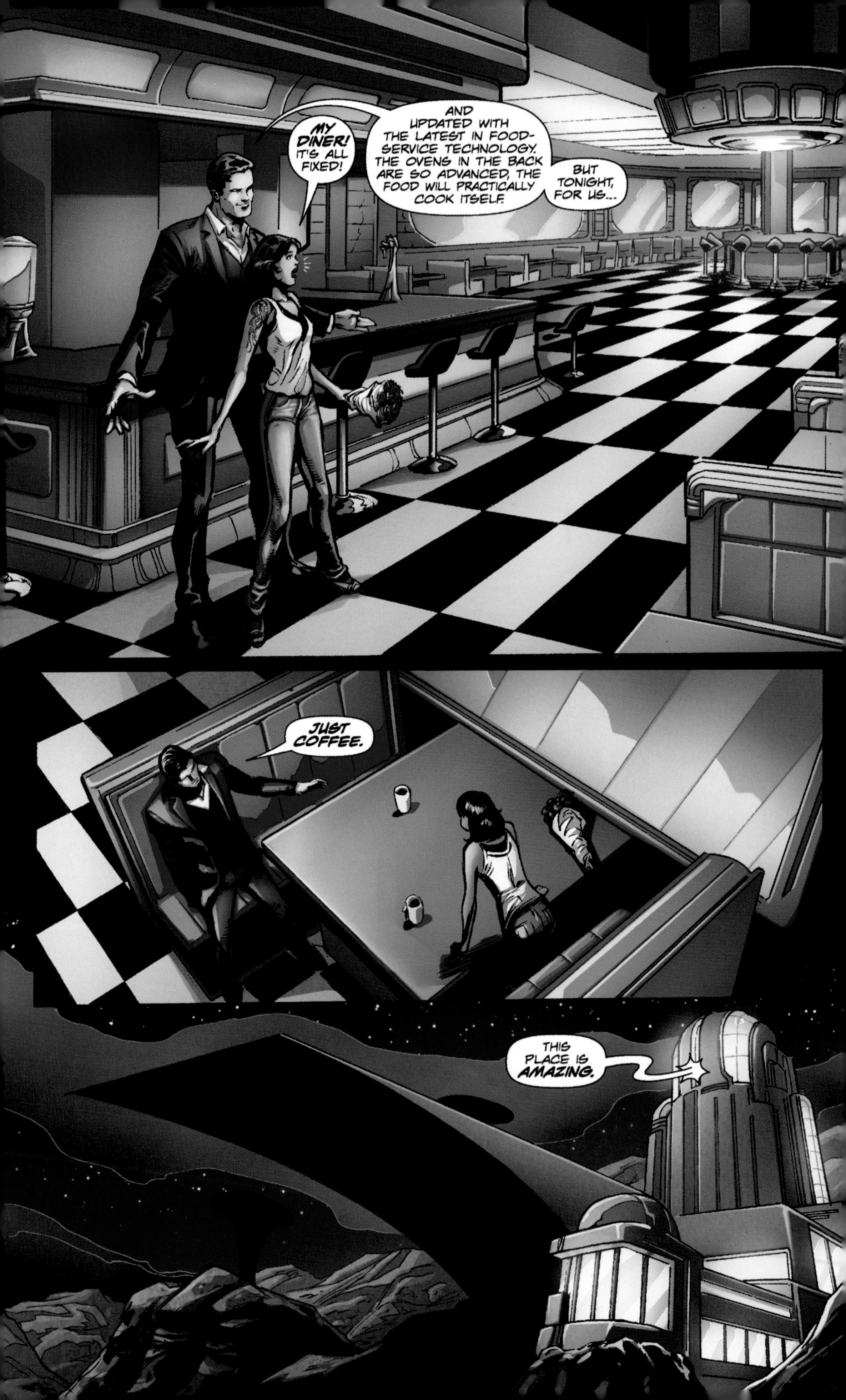
MY DINER! IT'S ALL FIXED!
AND UPDATED WITH THE LATEST IN FOOD-SERVICE TECHNOLOGY. THE OVENS IN THE BACK ARE SO ADVANCED, THE FOOD WILL PRACTICALLY COOK ITSELF.
BUT TONIGHT, FOR US...
JUST COFFEE.
THIS PLACE IS AMAZING.

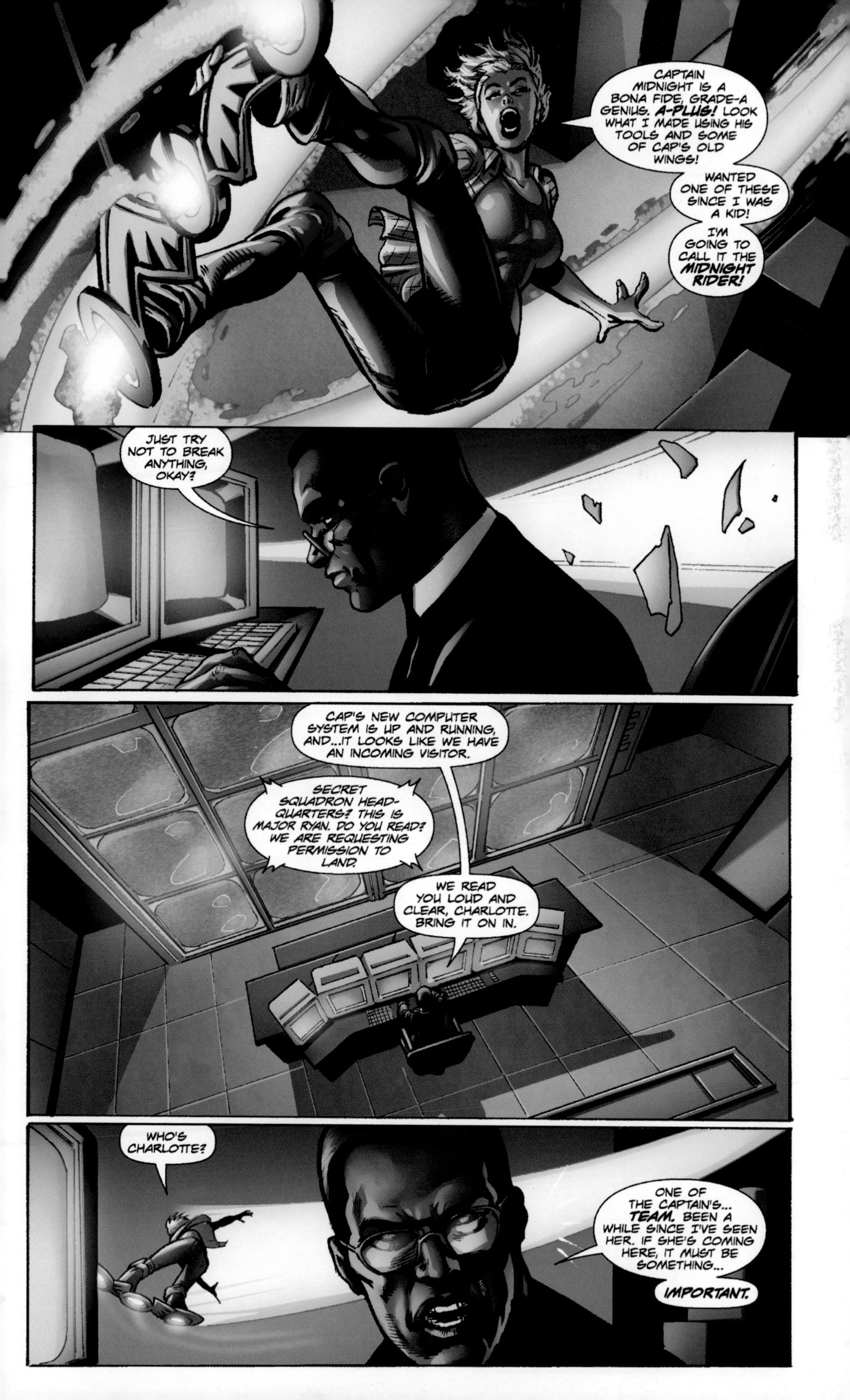
CAPTAIN MIDNIGHT IS A BONA FIDE, GRADE-A GENIUS. A-PLUS! LOOK WHAT I MADE USING HIS TOOLS AND SOME OF CAP'S OLD WINGS!
WANTED ONE OF THESE SINCE I WAS A KID!
I'M GOING TO CALL IT THE MIDNIGHT RIDER!
JUST TRY NOT TO BREAK ANYTHING, OKAY?
CAP'S NEW COMPUTER SYSTEM IS UP AND RUNNING, AND...IT LOOKS LIKE WE HAVE AN INCOMING VISITOR.
SECRET SQUADRON HEAD-QUARTERS? THIS IS MAJOR RYAN. DO YOU READ? WE ARE REQUESTING PERMISSION TO LAND.
WE READ YOU LOUD AND CLEAR, CHARLOTTE. BRING IT ON IN.
WHO'S CHARLOTTE?
ONE OF THE CAPTAIN'S... TEAM. BEEN A WHILE SINCE I'VE SEEN HER. IF SHE'S COMING HERE, IT MUST BE SOMETHING...
IMPORTANT.

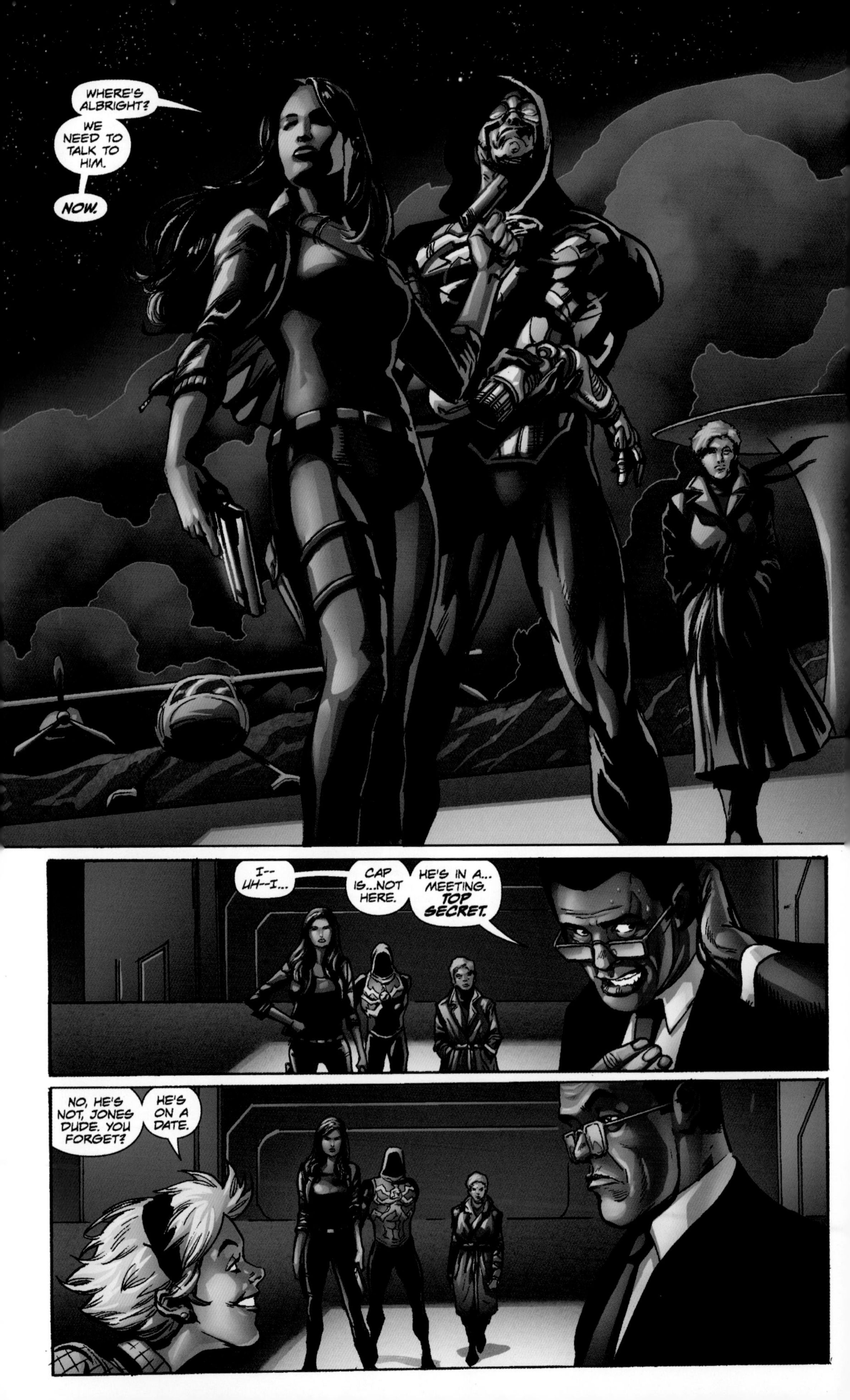
WHERE'S ALBRIGHT?
WE NEED TO TALK TO HIM.
NOW.
I-- UH--I...
CAP IS...NOT HERE.
HE'S IN A... MEETING. TOP SECRET.
NO, HE'S NOT, JONES DUDE. YOU FORGET?
HE'S ON A DATE.

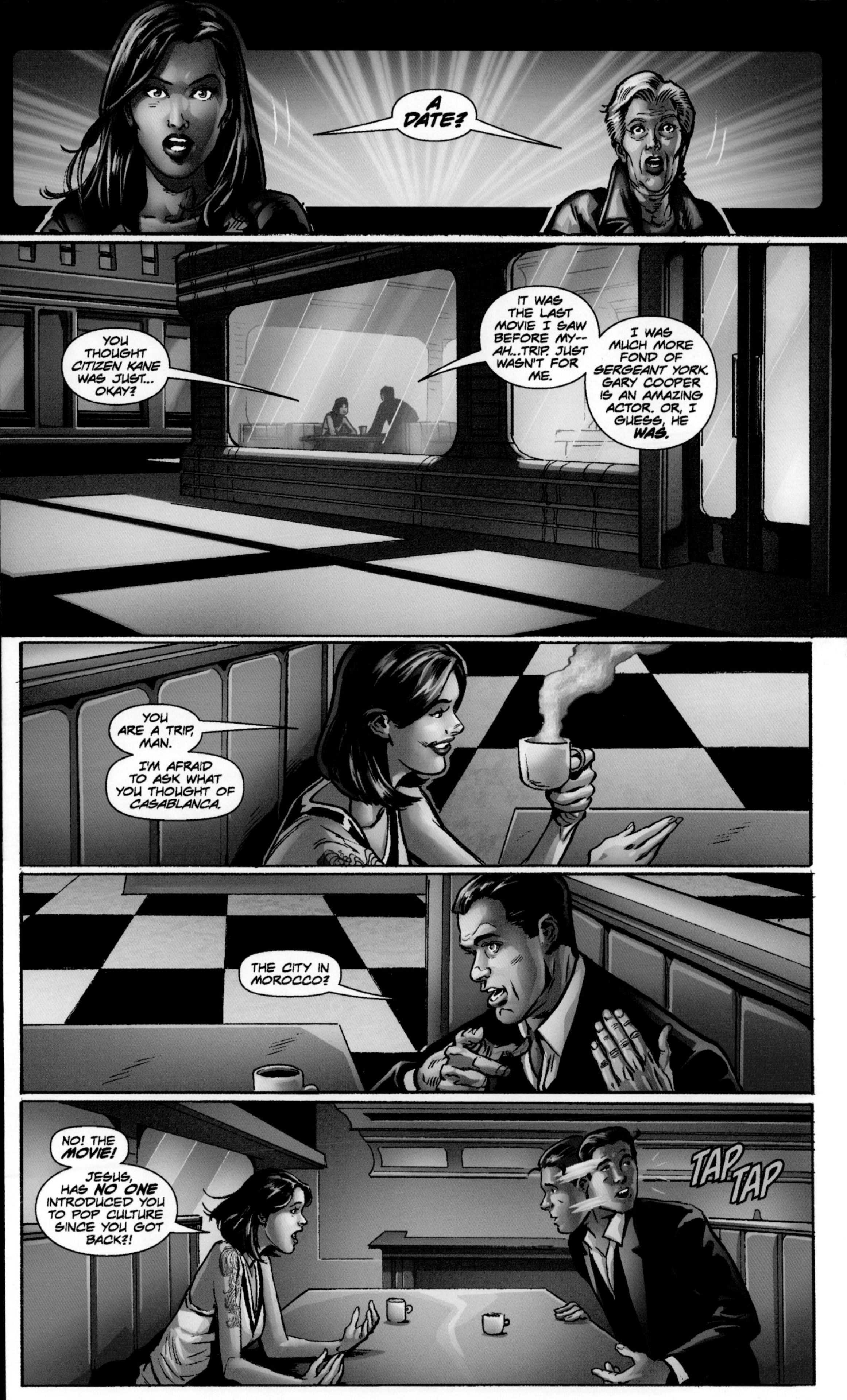
A DATE?
YOU THOUGHT CITIZEN KANE WAS JUST... OKAY?
IT WAS THE LAST MOVIE I SAW BEFORE MY-- AH...TRIP. JUST WASN'T FOR ME.
I WAS MUCH MORE FOND OF SERGEANT YORK. GARY COOPER IS AN AMAZING ACTOR. OR, I GUESS, HE WAS.
YOU ARE A TRIP, MAN.
I'M AFRAID TO ASK WHAT YOU THOUGHT OF CASABLANCA.
THE CITY IN MOROCCO?
NO! THE MOVIE!
JESUS, HAS NO ONE INTRODUCED YOU TO POP CULTURE SINCE YOU GOT BACK?!
TAP TAP

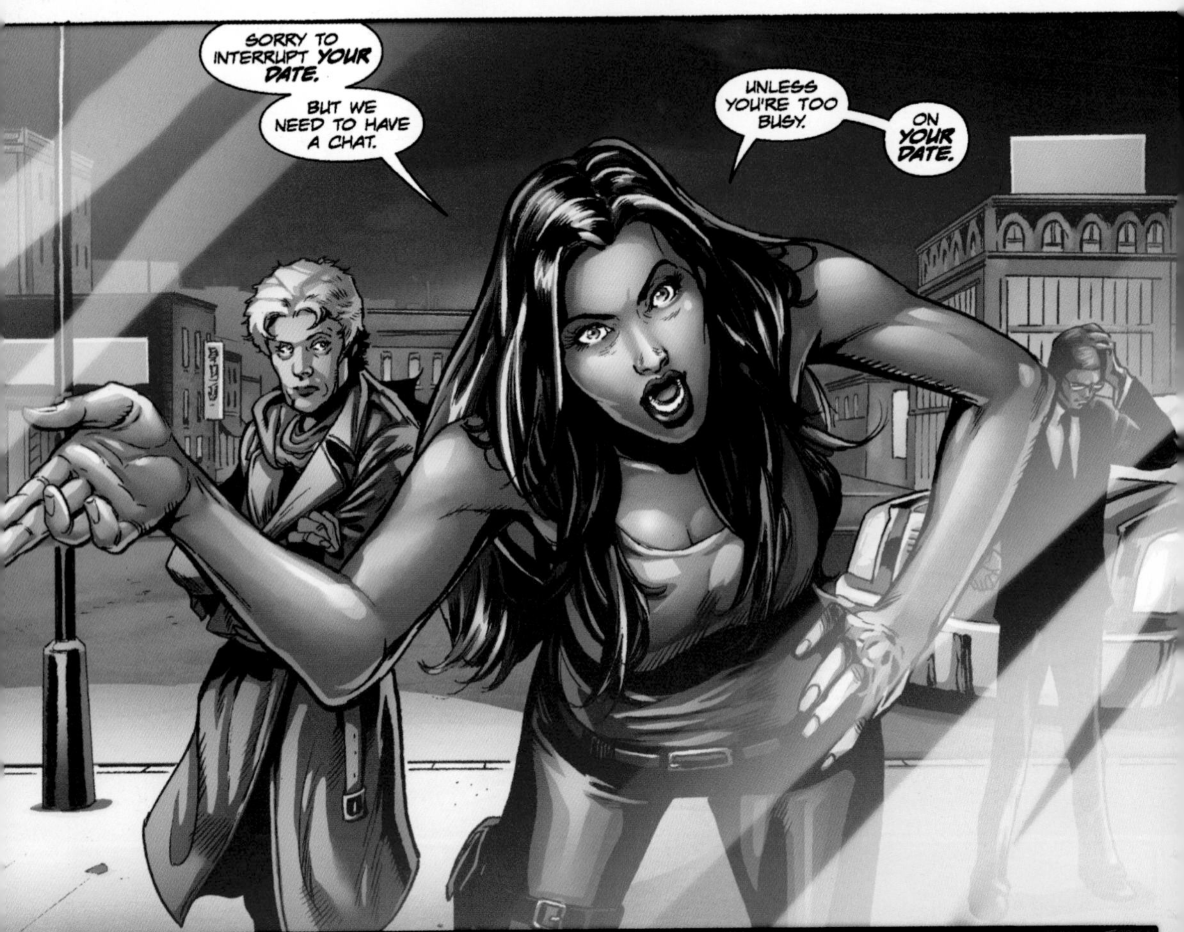
SORRY TO INTERRUPT YOUR DATE.
BUT WE NEED TO HAVE A CHAT.
UNLESS YOU'RE TOO BUSY.
ON YOUR DATE.

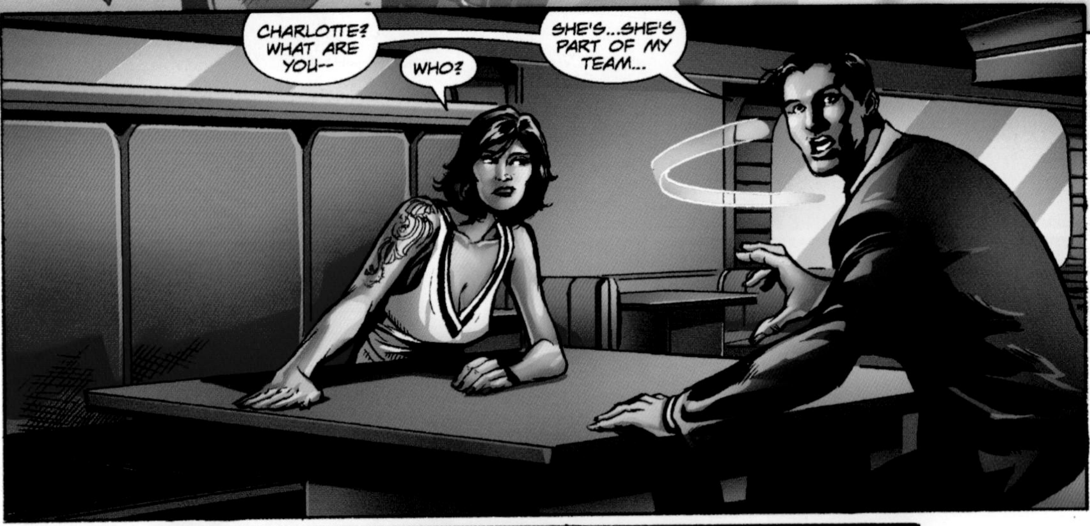
CHARLOTTE? WHAT ARE YOU--
WHO?
SHE'S...SHE'S PART OF MY TEAM...

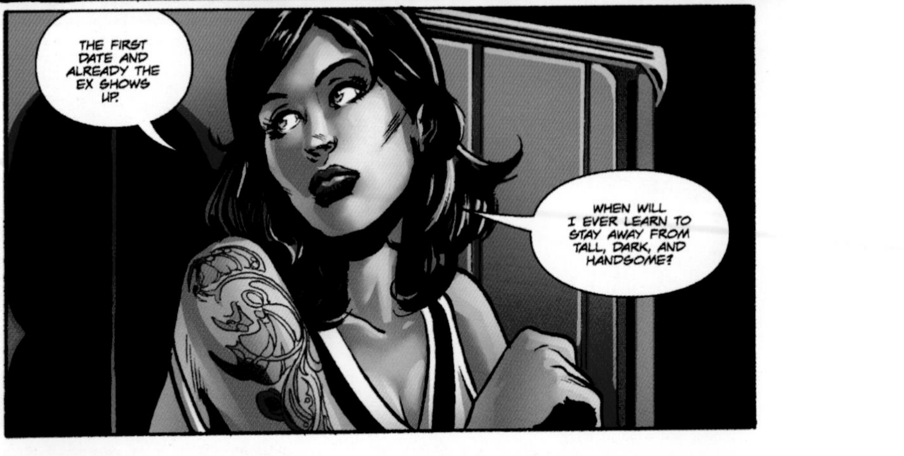
THE FIRST DATE AND ALREADY THE EX SHOWS UP.
WHEN WILL I EVER LEARN TO STAY AWAY FROM TALL, DARK, AND HANDSOME?

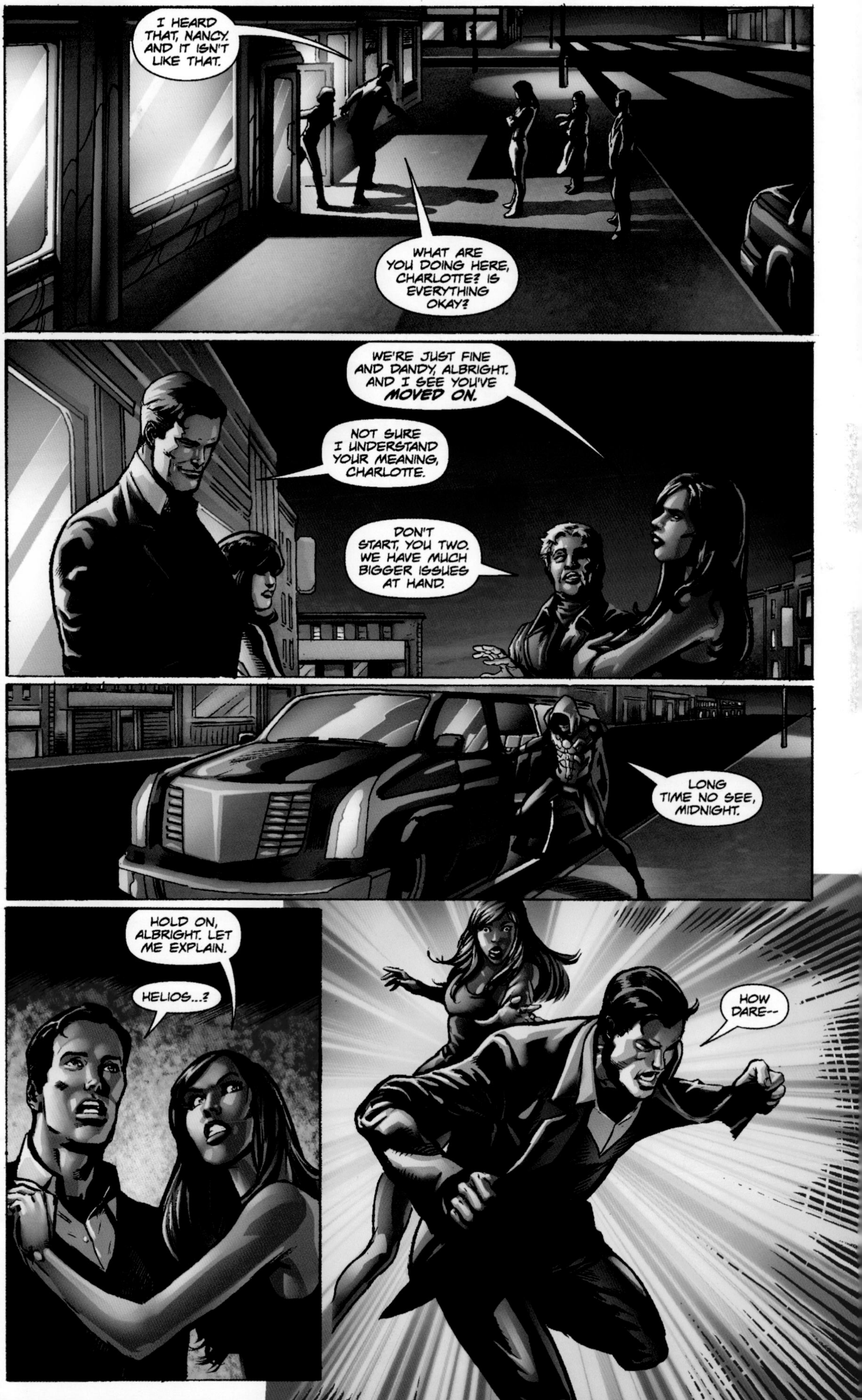
I HEARD THAT, NANCY. AND IT ISN'T LIKE THAT.
WHAT ARE YOU DOING HERE, CHARLOTTE? IS EVERYTHING OKAY?
WE'RE JUST FINE AND DANDY, ALBRIGHT. AND I SEE YOU'VE MOVED ON.
NOT SURE I UNDERSTAND YOUR MEANING, CHARLOTTE.
DON'T START, YOU TWO. WE HAVE MUCH BIGGER ISSUES AT HAND.
LONG TIME NO SEE, MIDNIGHT.
HOLD ON, ALBRIGHT. LET ME EXPLAIN.
HELIOS...?
HOW DARE--

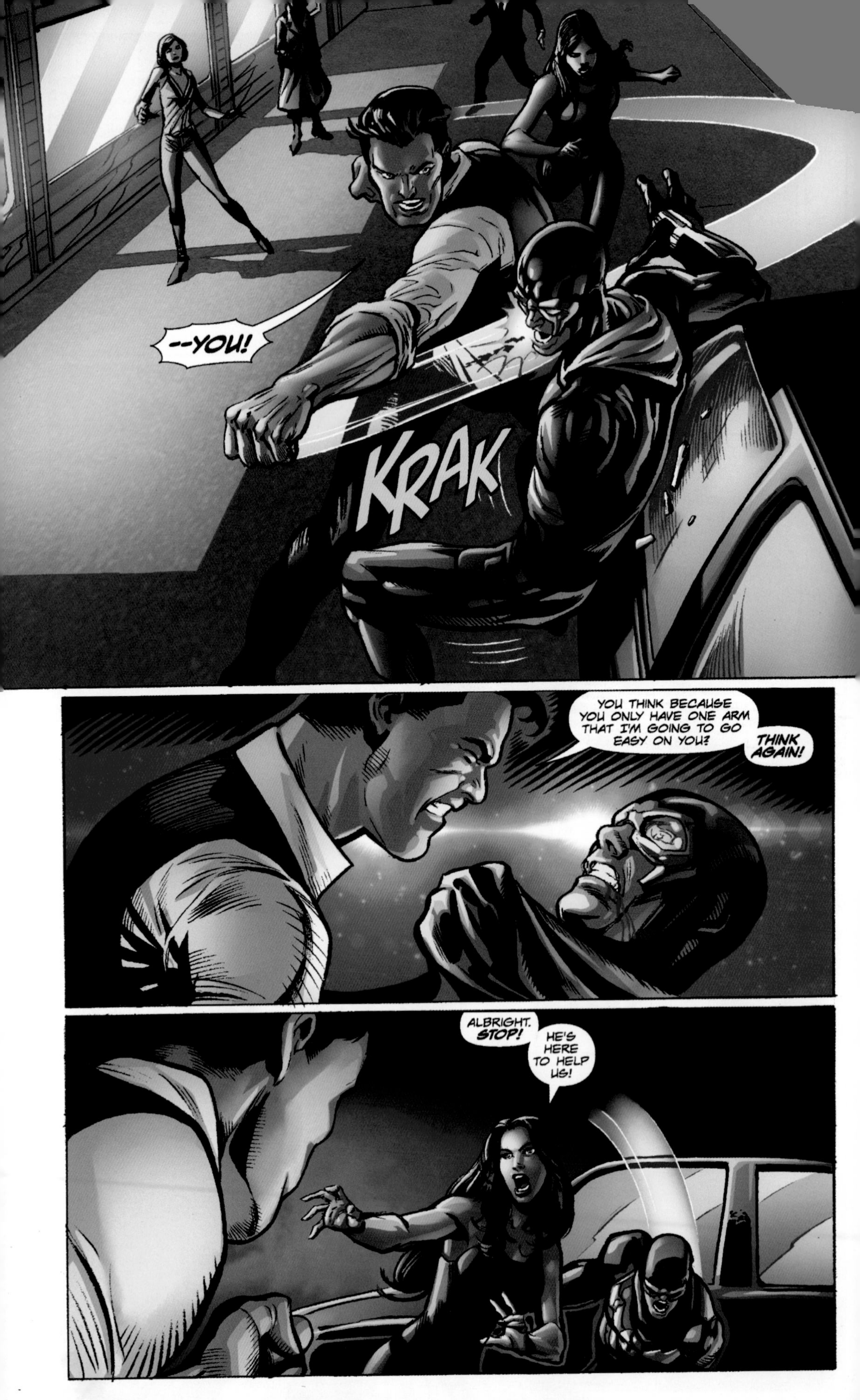
--YOU!
KRAK
YOU THINK BECAUSE YOU ONLY HAVE ONE ARM THAT I'M GOING TO GO EASY ON YOU?
THINK AGAIN!
ALBRIGHT. STOP!
HE'S HERE TO HELP US!

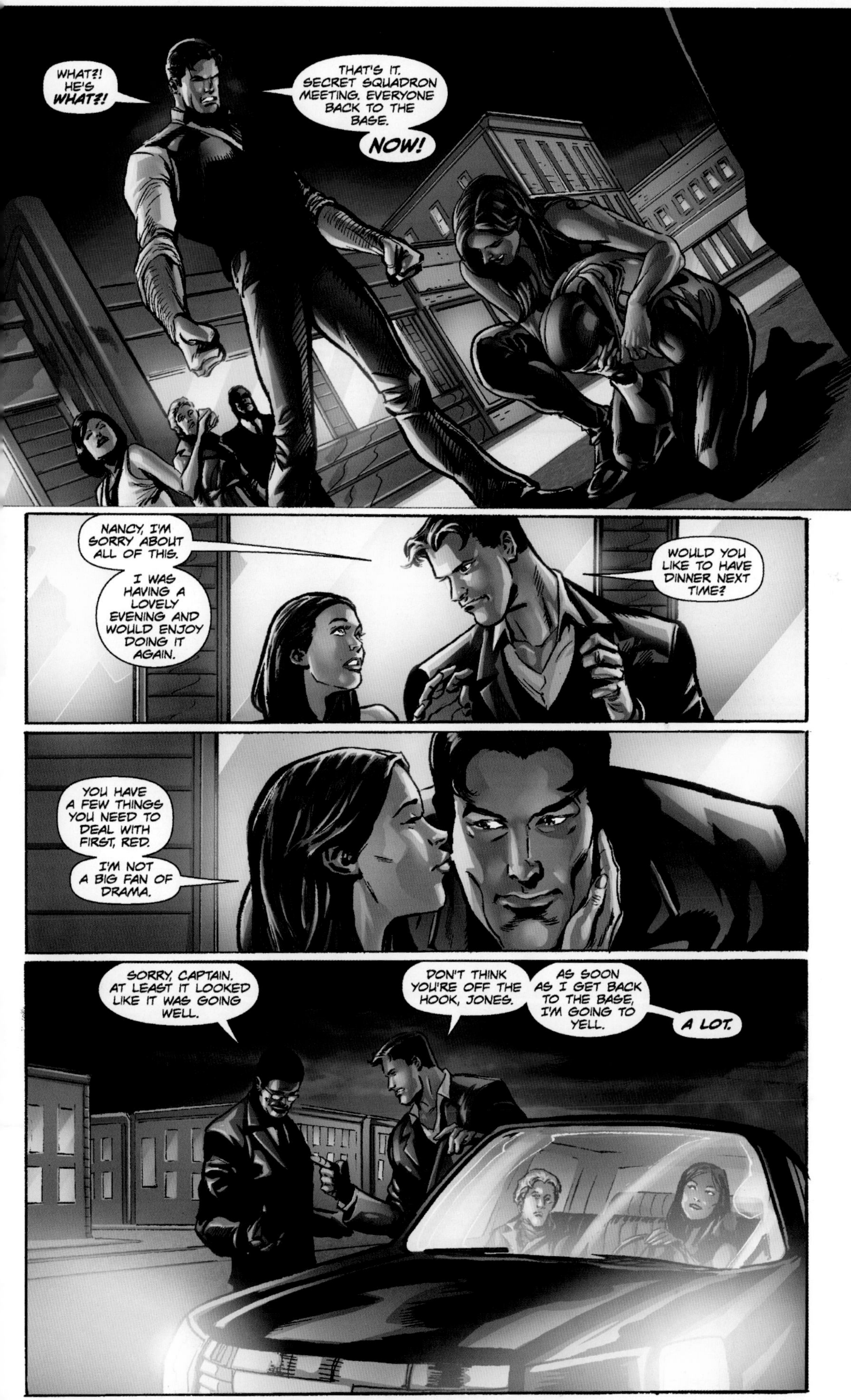
WHAT?! HE'S WHAT?!
THAT'S IT. SECRET SQUADRON MEETING. EVERYONE BACK TO THE BASE.
NOW!
NANCY, I'M SORRY ABOUT ALL OF THIS.
I WAS HAVING A LOVELY EVENING AND WOULD ENJOY DOING IT AGAIN.
WOULD YOU LIKE TO HAVE DINNER NEXT TIME?
YOU HAVE A FEW THINGS YOU NEED TO DEAL WITH FIRST, RED.
I'M NOT A BIG FAN OF DRAMA.
SORRY, CAPTAIN. AT LEAST IT LOOKED LIKE IT WAS GOING WELL.
DON'T THINK YOU'RE OFF THE HOOK, JONES.
AS SOON AS I GET BACK TO THE BASE, I'M GOING TO YELL.
A LOT.

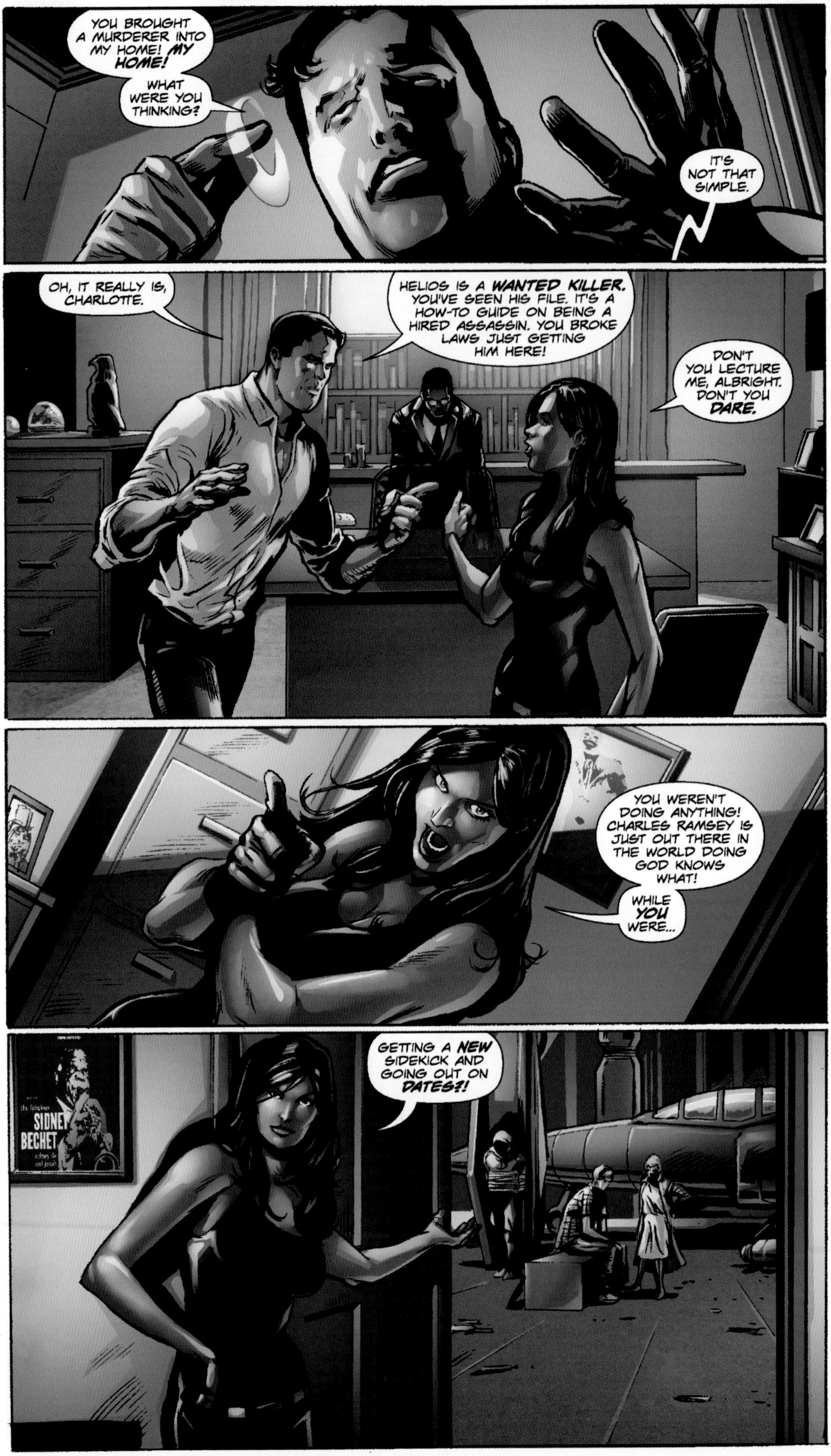
YOU BROUGHT A MURDERER INTO MY HOME! MY HOME!
WHAT WERE YOU THINKING?
IT'S NOT THAT SIMPLE.
OH, IT REALLY IS, CHARLOTTE.
HELIOS IS A WANTED KILLER. YOU'VE SEEN HIS FILE. IT'S A HOW-TO GUIDE ON BEING A HIRED ASSASSIN. YOU BROKE LAWS JUST GETTING HIM HERE!
DON'T YOU LECTURE ME, ALBRIGHT. DON'T YOU DARE.
YOU WEREN'T DOING ANYTHING! CHARLES RAMSEY IS JUST OUT THERE IN THE WORLD DOING GOD KNOWS WHAT!
WHILE YOU WERE...
GETTING A NEW SIDEKICK AND GOING OUT ON DATES?!
the fabulous
SIDNEY BECHET

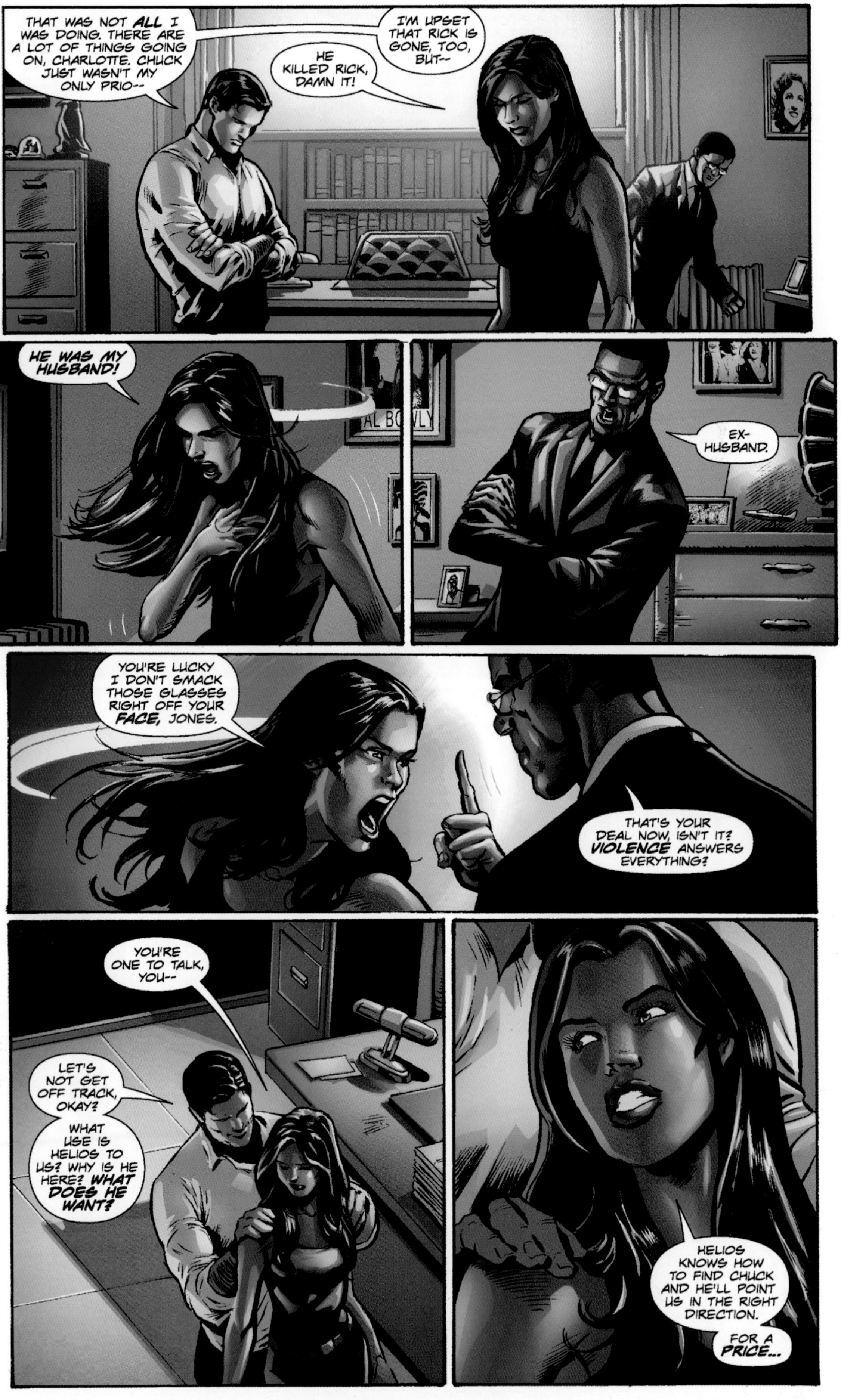

THAT WAS NOT ALL I WAS DOING. THERE ARE A LOT OF THINGS GOING ON, CHARLOTTE. CHUCK JUST WASN'T MY ONLY PRIO--
I'M UPSET THAT RICK IS GONE, TOO, BUT--
HE KILLED RICK, DAMN IT!
HE WAS MY HUSBAND!
AL BOWLY
EX-HUSBAND.
YOU'RE LUCKY I DON'T SMACK THOSE GLASSES RIGHT OFF YOUR FACE, JONES.
THAT'S YOUR DEAL NOW, ISN'T IT? VIOLENCE ANSWERS EVERYTHING?
YOU'RE ONE TO TALK, YOU--
LET'S NOT GET OFF TRACK, OKAY?
WHAT USE IS HELIOS TO US? WHY IS HE HERE? WHAT DOES HE WANT?
HELIOS KNOWS HOW TO FIND CHUCK AND HE'LL POINT US IN THE RIGHT DIRECTION.
FOR A PRICE...

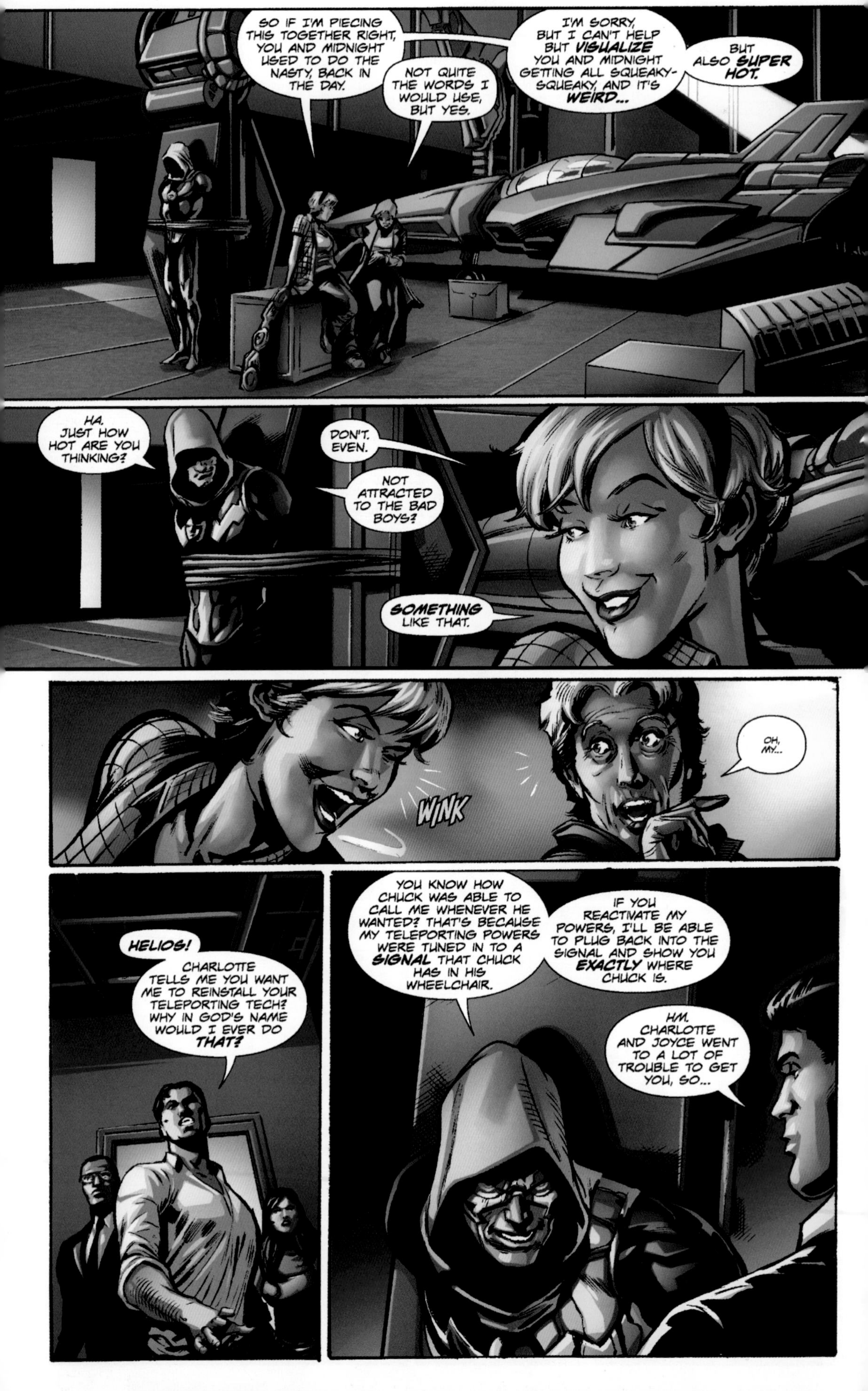
SO IF I'M PIECING THIS TOGETHER RIGHT, YOU AND MIDNIGHT USED TO DO THE NASTY, BACK IN THE DAY.
NOT QUITE THE WORDS I WOULD USE, BUT YES.
I'M SORRY, BUT I CAN'T HELP BUT VISUALIZE YOU AND MIDNIGHT GETTING ALL SQUEAKY-SQUEAKY, AND IT'S WEIRD...
BUT ALSO SUPER HOT.
HA. JUST HOW HOT ARE YOU THINKING?
DON'T. EVEN.
NOT ATTRACTED TO THE BAD BOYS?
SOMETHING LIKE THAT.
WINK
OH, MY...
HELIOS!
CHARLOTTE TELLS ME YOU WANT ME TO REINSTALL YOUR TELEPORTING TECH? WHY IN GOD'S NAME WOULD I EVER DO THAT?
YOU KNOW HOW CHUCK WAS ABLE TO CALL ME WHENEVER HE WANTED? THAT'S BECAUSE MY TELEPORTING POWERS WERE TUNED IN TO A SIGNAL THAT CHUCK HAS IN HIS WHEELCHAIR.
IF YOU REACTIVATE MY POWERS, I'LL BE ABLE TO PLUG BACK INTO THE SIGNAL AND SHOW YOU EXACTLY WHERE CHUCK IS.
HM. CHARLOTTE AND JOYCE WENT TO A LOT OF TROUBLE TO GET YOU, SO...

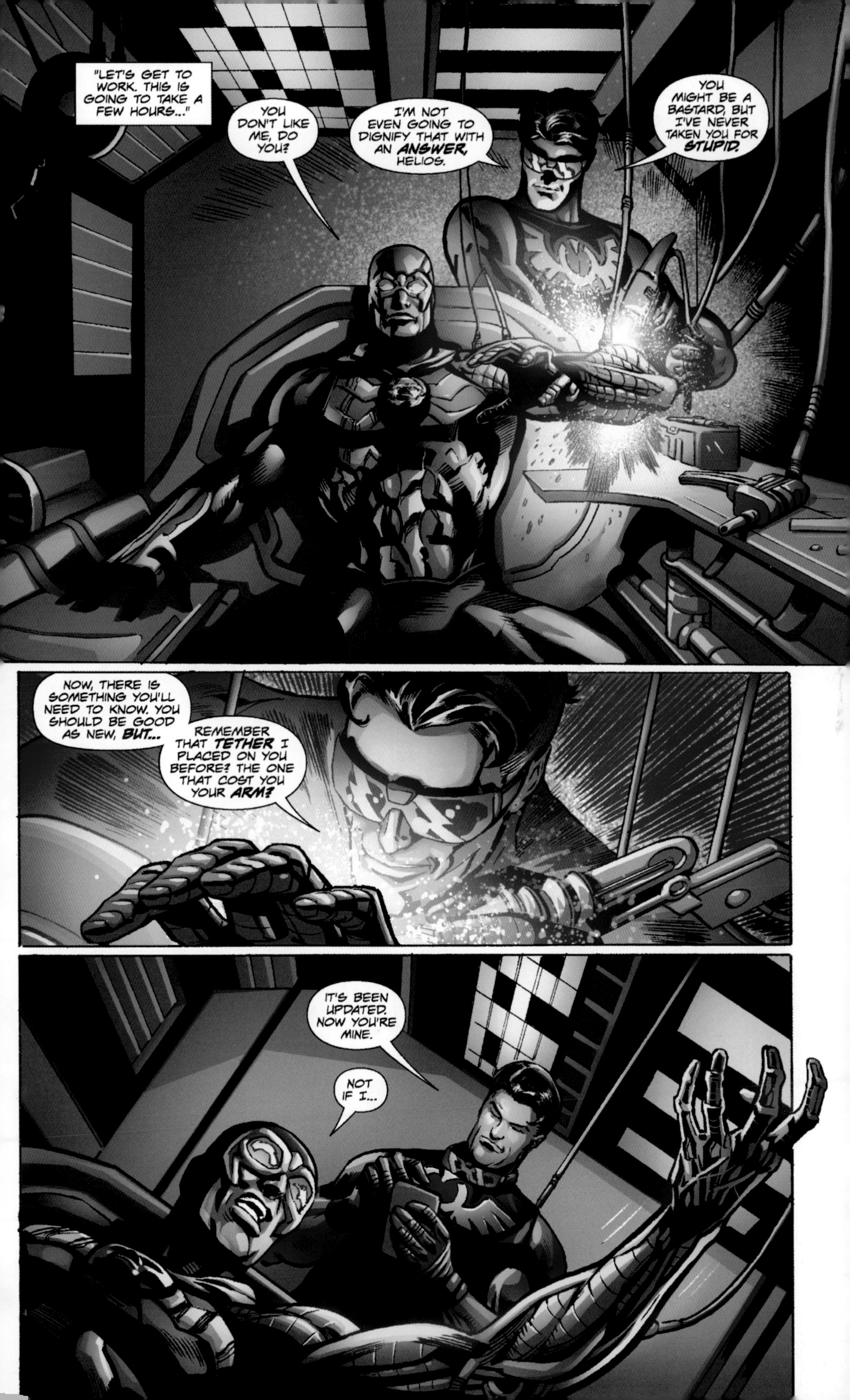
"LET'S GET TO WORK. THIS IS GOING TO TAKE A FEW HOURS..."
YOU DON'T LIKE ME, DO YOU?
I'M NOT EVEN GOING TO DIGNIFY THAT WITH AN ANSWER, HELIOS.
YOU MIGHT BE A BASTARD, BUT I'VE NEVER TAKEN YOU FOR STUPID.
NOW, THERE IS SOMETHING YOU'LL NEED TO KNOW. YOU SHOULD BE GOOD AS NEW, BUT...
REMEMBER THAT TETHER I PLACED ON YOU BEFORE? THE ONE THAT COST YOU YOUR ARM?
IT'S BEEN UPDATED. NOW YOU'RE MINE.
NOT IF I...

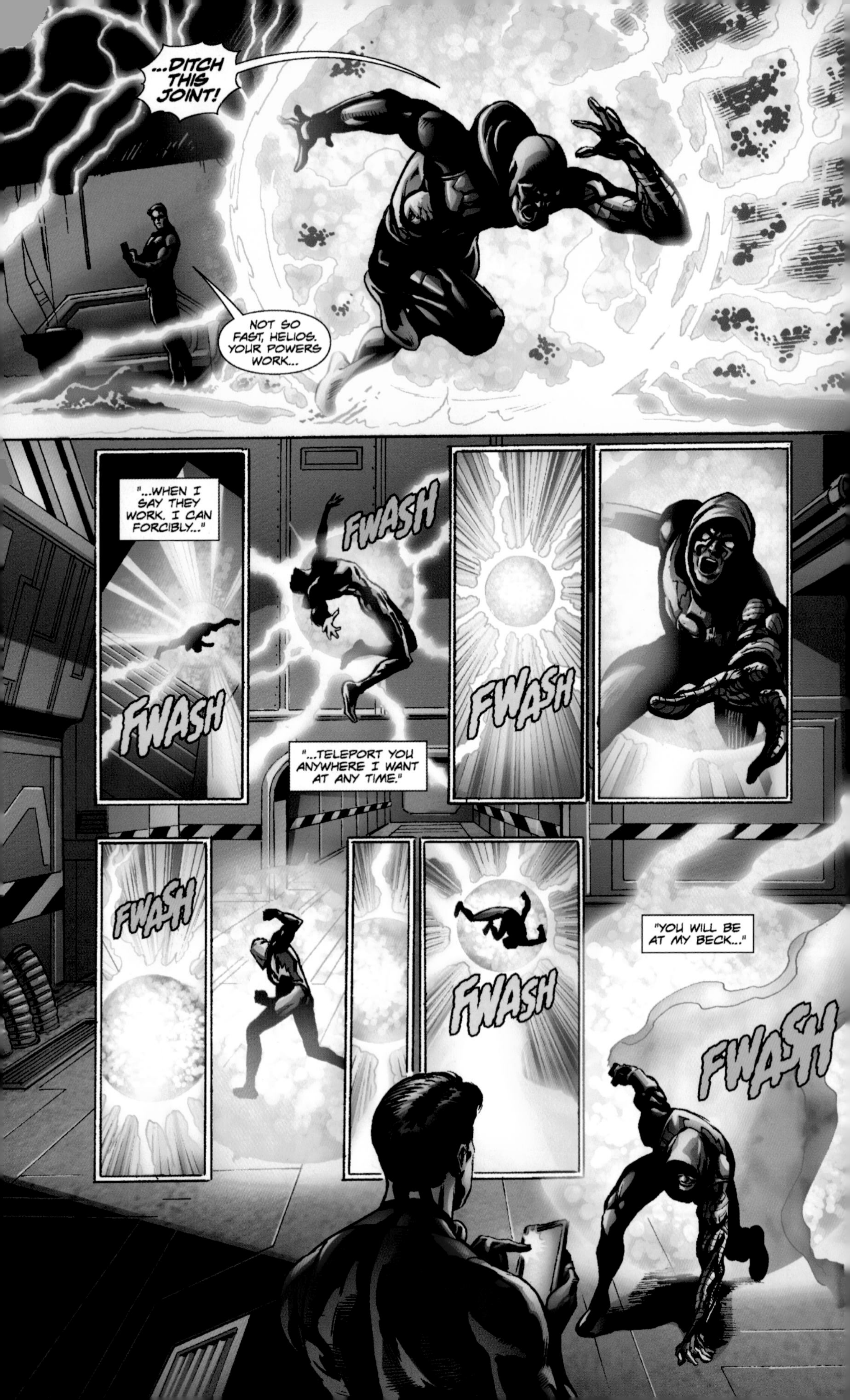
...DITCH THIS JOINT!
NOT SO FAST, HELIOS. YOUR POWERS WORK...
"...WHEN I SAY THEY WORK. I CAN FORCIBLY..."
FWASH
FWASH
"...TELEPORT YOU ANYWHERE I WANT AT ANY TIME."
FWASH
FWASH
FWASH
"YOU WILL BE AT MY BECK..."
FWASH

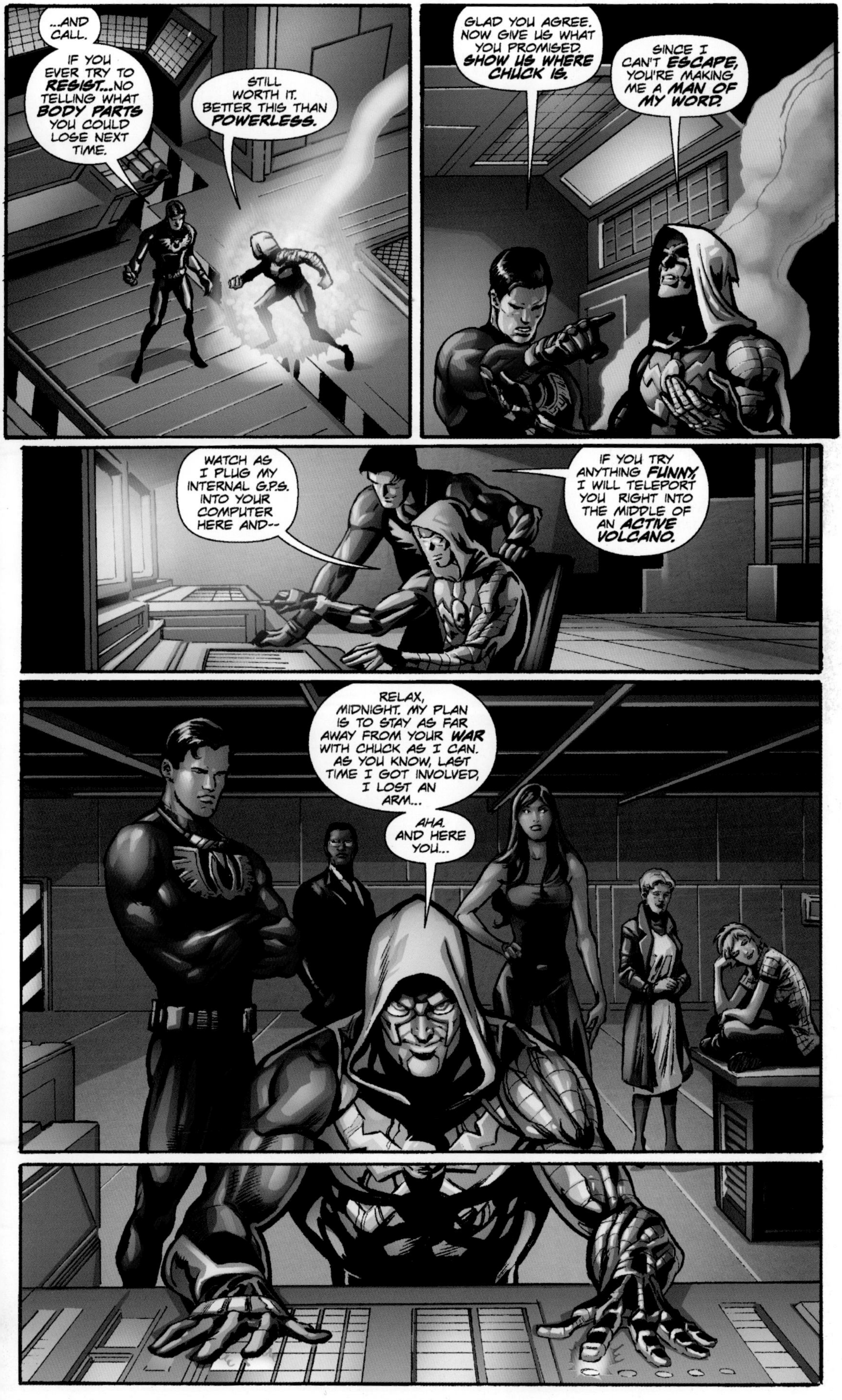

...AND CALL.
IF YOU EVER TRY TO RESIST...NO TELLING WHAT BODY PARTS YOU COULD LOSE NEXT TIME.
STILL WORTH IT. BETTER THIS THAN POWERLESS.
GLAD YOU AGREE. NOW GIVE US WHAT YOU PROMISED. SHOW US WHERE CHUCK IS.
SINCE I CAN'T ESCAPE, YOU'RE MAKING ME A MAN OF MY WORD.
WATCH AS I PLUG MY INTERNAL G.P.S. INTO YOUR COMPUTER HERE AND--
IF YOU TRY ANYTHING FUNNY, I WILL TELEPORT YOU RIGHT INTO THE MIDDLE OF AN ACTIVE VOLCANO.
RELAX, MIDNIGHT. MY PLAN IS TO STAY AS FAR AWAY FROM YOUR WAR WITH CHUCK AS I CAN. AS YOU KNOW, LAST TIME I GOT INVOLVED, I LOST AN ARM...
AHA. AND HERE YOU...

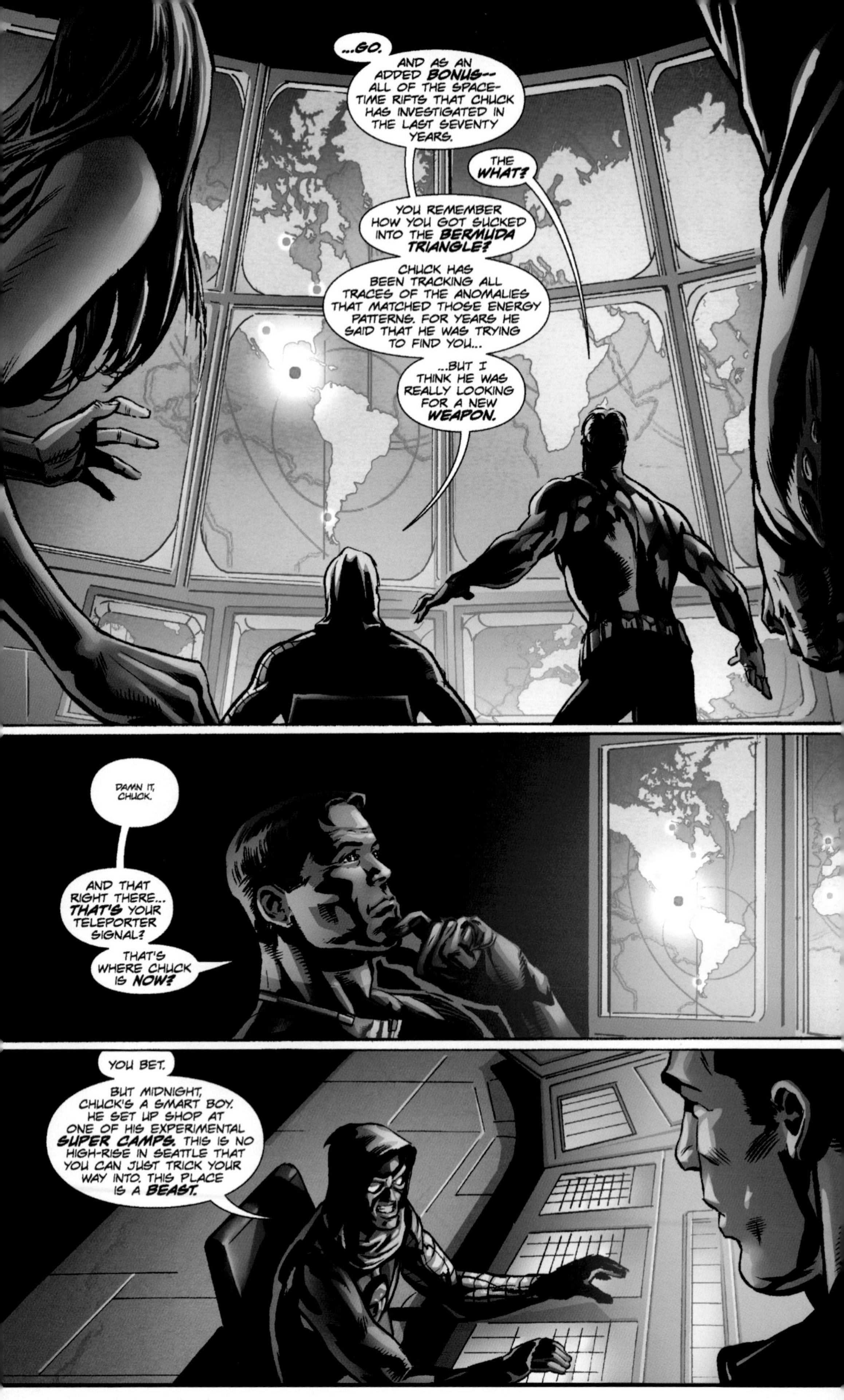
...GO.
AND AS AN ADDED BONUS-- ALL OF THE SPACE-TIME RIFTS THAT CHUCK HAS INVESTIGATED IN THE LAST SEVENTY YEARS.
THE WHAT?
YOU REMEMBER HOW YOU GOT SUCKED INTO THE BERMUDA TRIANGLE?
CHUCK HAS BEEN TRACKING ALL TRACES OF THE ANOMALIES THAT MATCHED THOSE ENERGY PATTERNS. FOR YEARS HE SAID THAT HE WAS TRYING TO FIND YOU...
...BUT I THINK HE WAS REALLY LOOKING FOR A NEW WEAPON.
DAMN IT, CHUCK.
AND THAT RIGHT THERE... THAT'S YOUR TELEPORTER SIGNAL?
THAT'S WHERE CHUCK IS NOW?
YOU BET.
BUT MIDNIGHT, CHUCK'S A SMART BOY. HE SET UP SHOP AT ONE OF HIS EXPERIMENTAL SUPER CAMPS. THIS IS NO HIGH-RISE IN SEATTLE THAT YOU CAN JUST TRICK YOUR WAY INTO. THIS PLACE IS A BEAST.

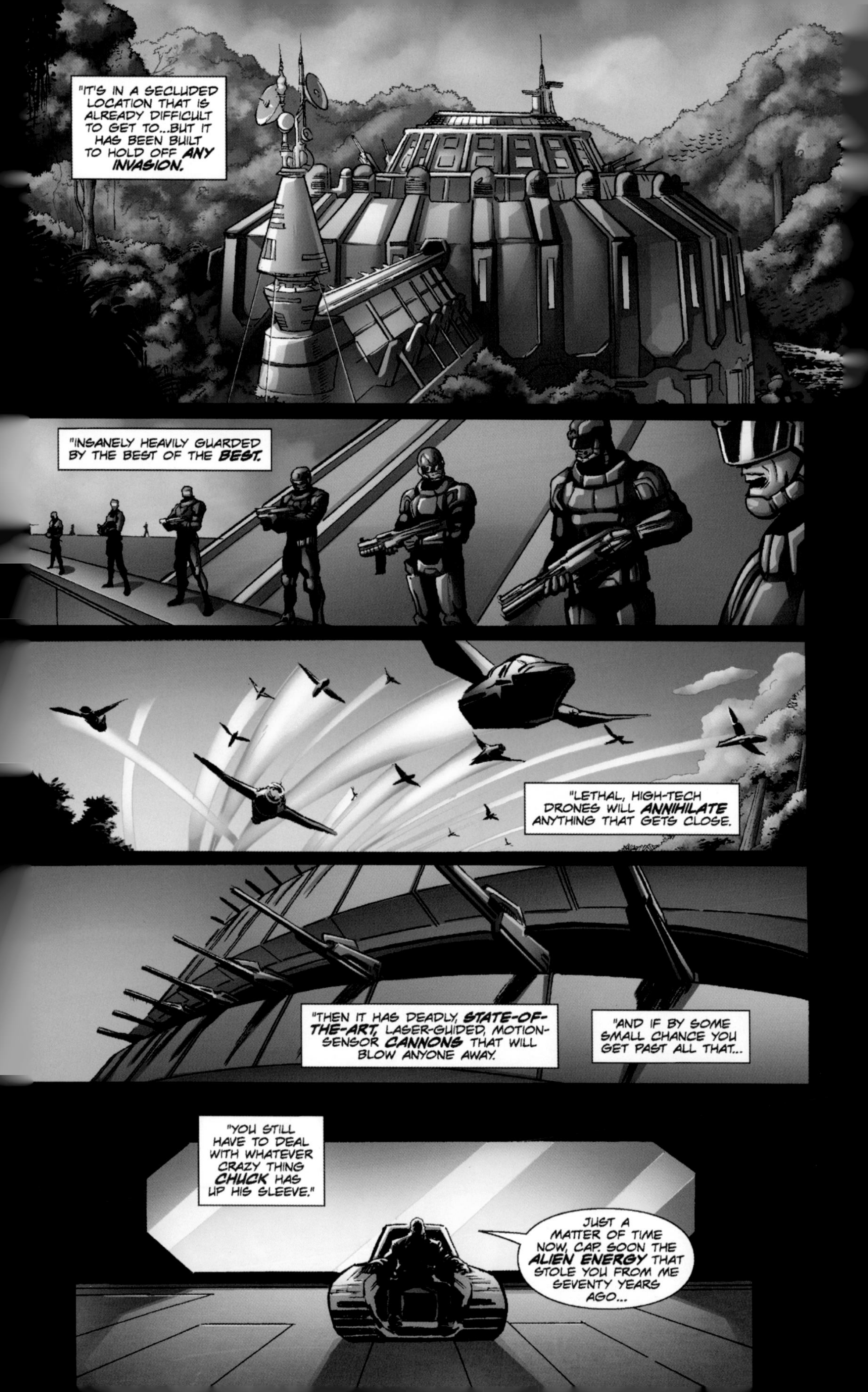
"IT'S IN A SECLUDED LOCATION THAT IS ALREADY DIFFICULT TO GET TO...BUT IT HAS BEEN BUILT TO HOLD OFF ANY INVASION.
"INSANELY HEAVILY GUARDED BY THE BEST OF THE BEST.
"LETHAL, HIGH-TECH DRONES WILL ANNIHILATE ANYTHING THAT GETS CLOSE.
"THEN IT HAS DEADLY, STATE-OF-THE-ART, LASER-GUIDED, MOTION-SENSOR CANNONS THAT WILL BLOW ANYONE AWAY.
"AND IF BY SOME SMALL CHANCE YOU GET PAST ALL THAT...
"YOU STILL HAVE TO DEAL WITH WHATEVER CRAZY THING CHUCK HAS UP HIS SLEEVE."
JUST A MATTER OF TIME NOW, CAP. SOON THE ALIEN ENERGY THAT STOLE YOU FROM ME SEVENTY YEARS AGO...

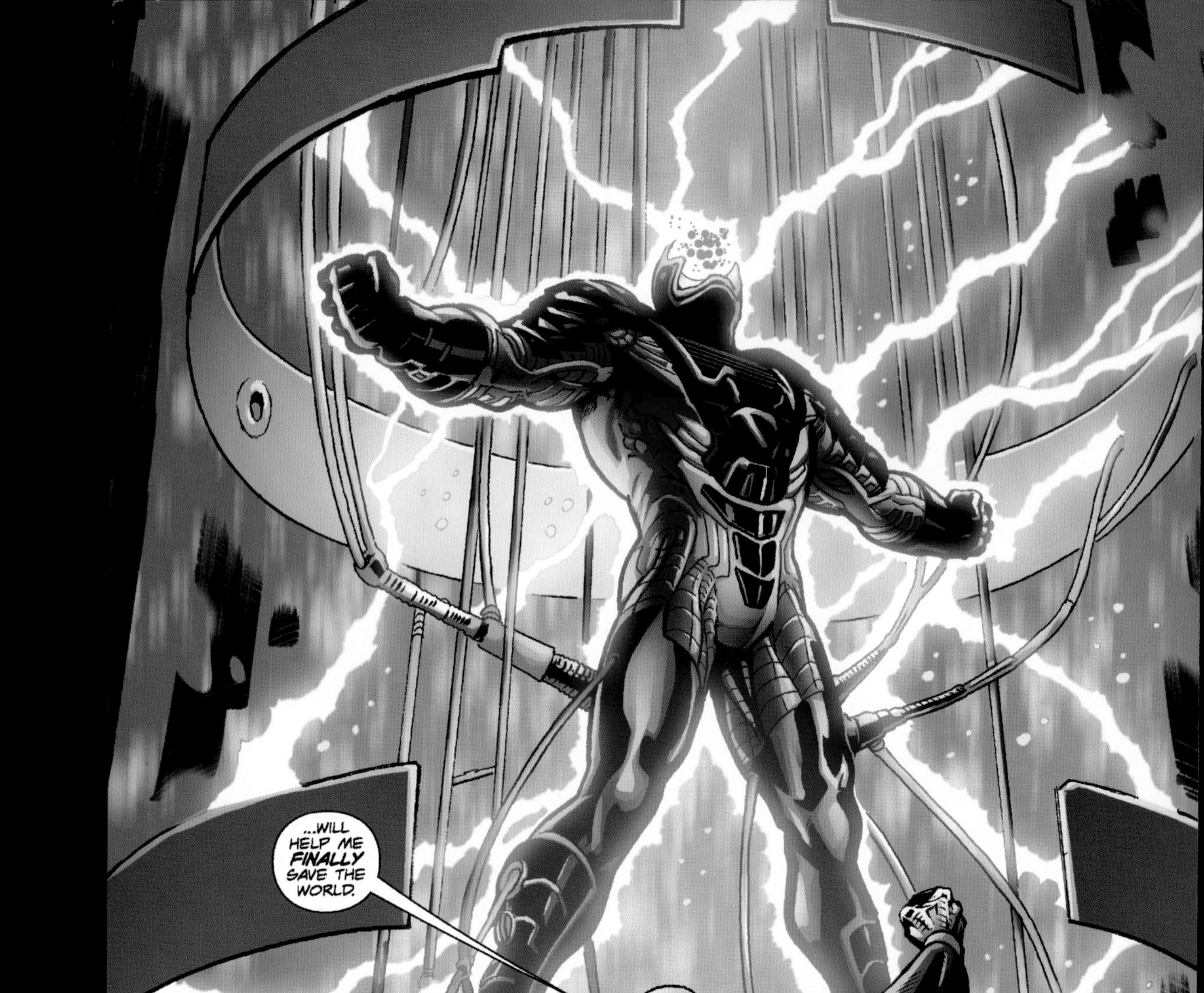
...WILL HELP ME FINALLY SAVE THE WORLD.

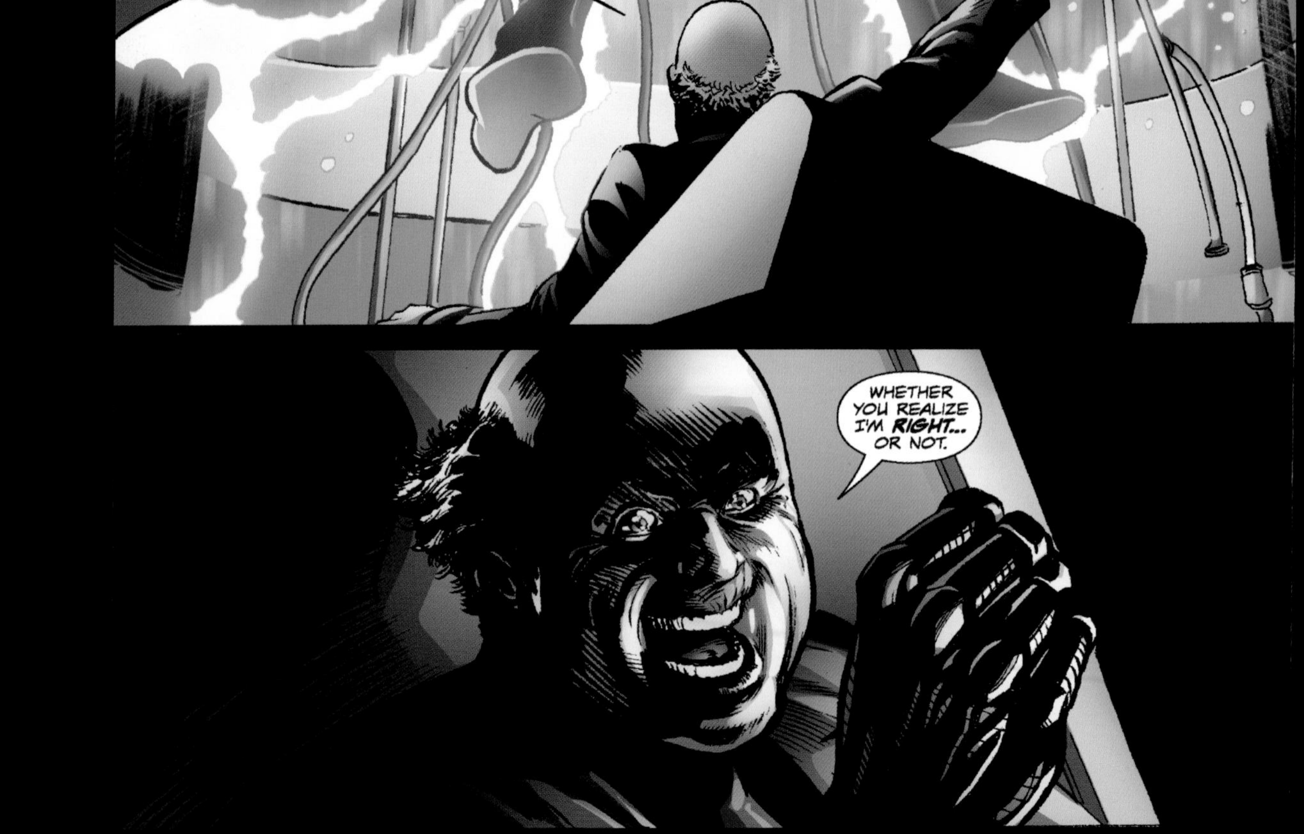
WHETHER YOU REALIZE I'M RIGHT... OR NOT.

CHAPTER 3

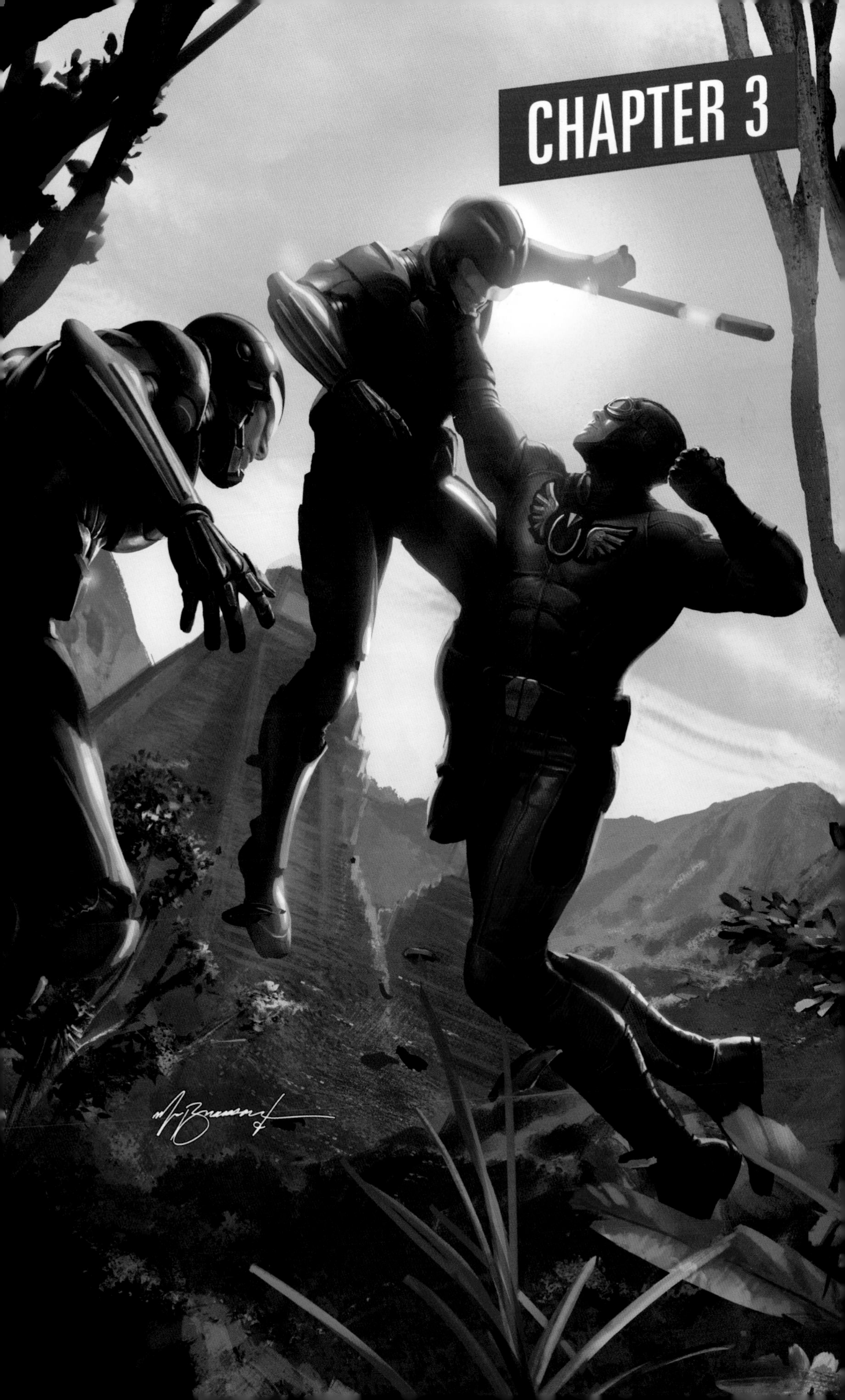

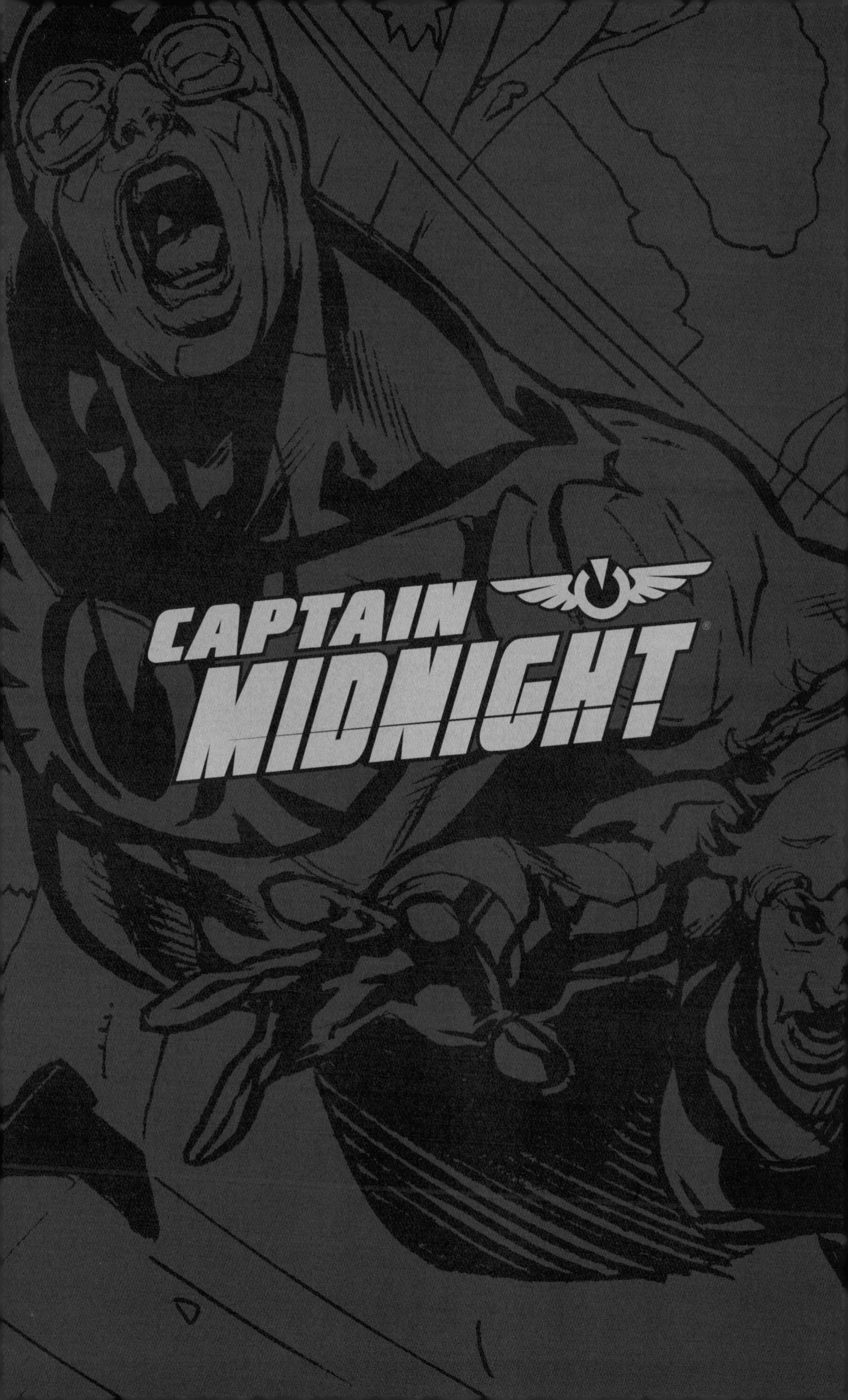
CAPTAIN
MIDNIGHT

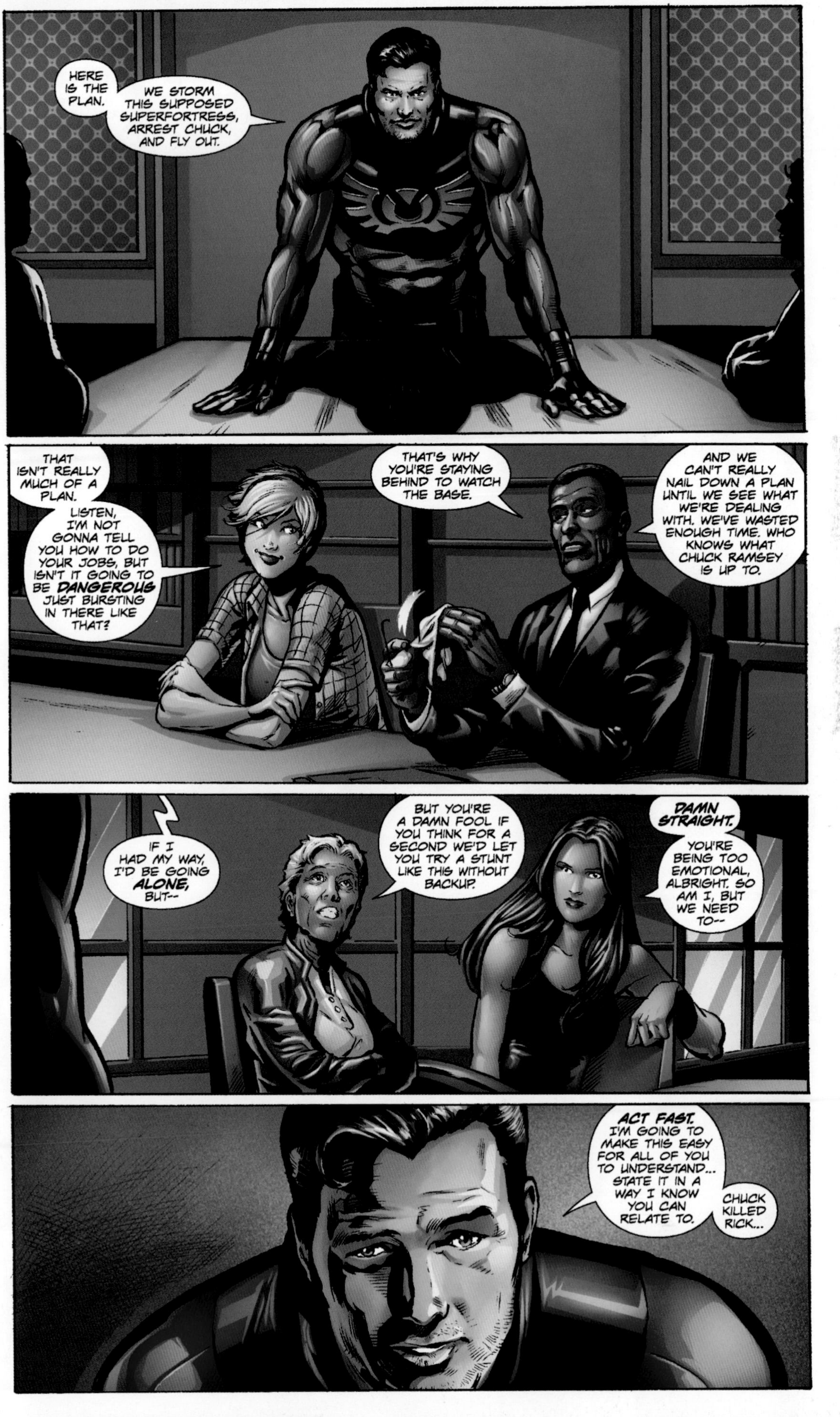
HERE IS THE PLAN.
WE STORM THIS SUPPOSED SUPERFORTRESS, ARREST CHUCK, AND FLY OUT.
THAT ISN'T REALLY MUCH OF A PLAN.
LISTEN, I'M NOT GONNA TELL YOU HOW TO DO YOUR JOBS, BUT ISN'T IT GOING TO BE DANGEROUS JUST BURSTING IN THERE LIKE THAT?
THAT'S WHY YOU'RE STAYING BEHIND TO WATCH THE BASE.
AND WE CAN'T REALLY NAIL DOWN A PLAN UNTIL WE SEE WHAT WE'RE DEALING WITH. WE'VE WASTED ENOUGH TIME. WHO KNOWS WHAT CHUCK RAMSEY IS UP TO.
IF I HAD MY WAY, I'D BE GOING ALONE, BUT--
BUT YOU'RE A DAMN FOOL IF YOU THINK FOR A SECOND WE'D LET YOU TRY A STUNT LIKE THIS WITHOUT BACKUP.
DAMN STRAIGHT.
YOU'RE BEING TOO EMOTIONAL, ALBRIGHT. SO AM I, BUT WE NEED TO--
ACT FAST.
I'M GOING TO MAKE THIS EASY FOR ALL OF YOU TO UNDERSTAND... STATE IT IN A WAY I KNOW YOU CAN RELATE TO.
CHUCK KILLED RICK...

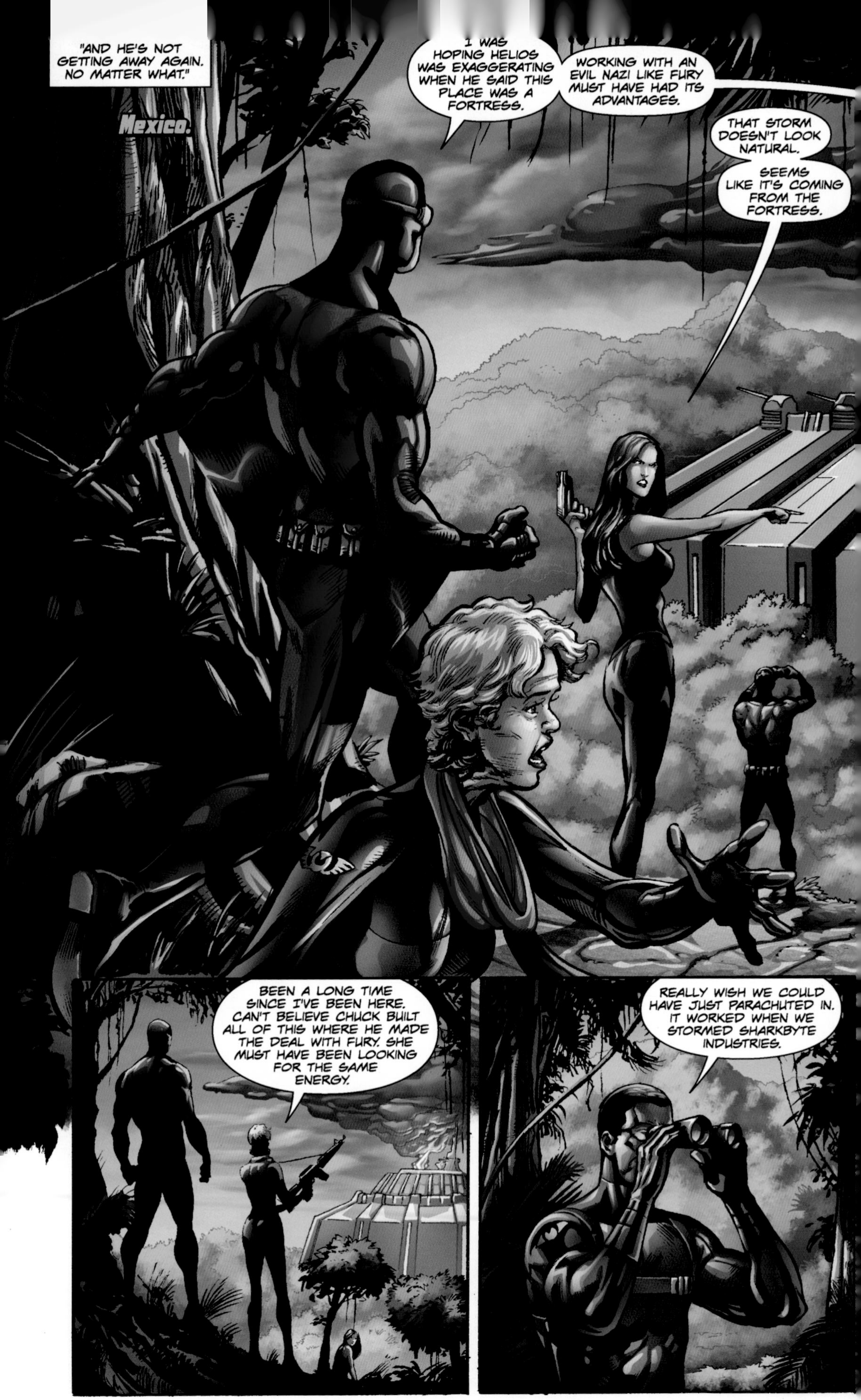
"AND HE'S NOT GETTING AWAY AGAIN. NO MATTER WHAT."
Mexico.
I WAS HOPING HELIOS WAS EXAGGERATING WHEN HE SAID THIS PLACE WAS A FORTRESS.
WORKING WITH AN EVIL NAZI LIKE FURY MUST HAVE HAD ITS ADVANTAGES.
THAT STORM DOESN'T LOOK NATURAL.
SEEMS LIKE IT'S COMING FROM THE FORTRESS.
BEEN A LONG TIME SINCE I'VE BEEN HERE. CAN'T BELIEVE CHUCK BUILT ALL OF THIS WHERE HE MADE THE DEAL WITH FURY. SHE MUST HAVE BEEN LOOKING FOR THE SAME ENERGY.
REALLY WISH WE COULD HAVE JUST PARACHUTED IN. IT WORKED WHEN WE STORMED SHARKBYTE INDUSTRIES.

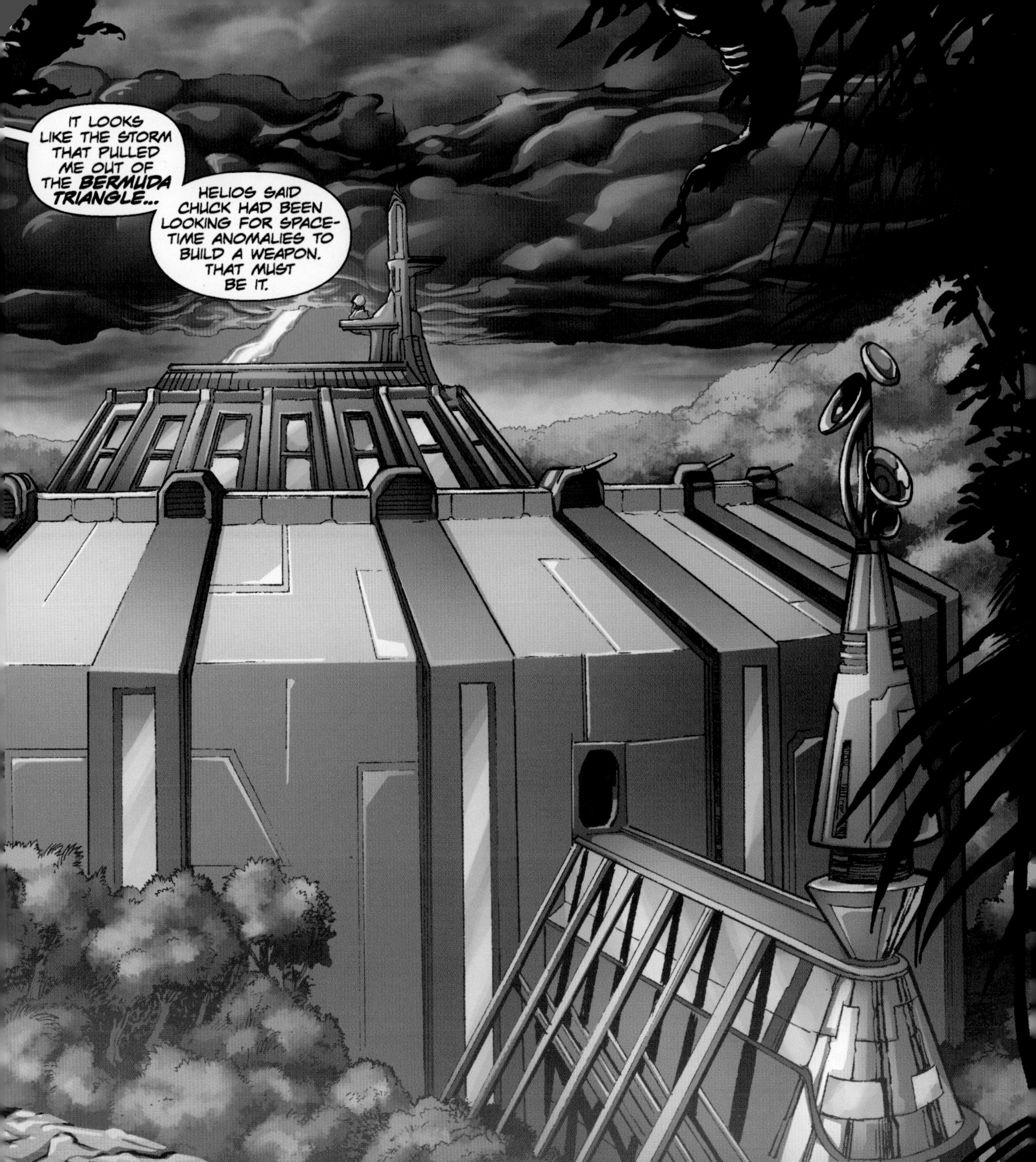
IT LOOKS LIKE THE STORM THAT PULLED ME OUT OF THE BERMUDA TRIANGLE...
HELIOS SAID CHUCK HAD BEEN LOOKING FOR SPACE-TIME ANOMALIES TO BUILD A WEAPON. THAT MUST BE IT.

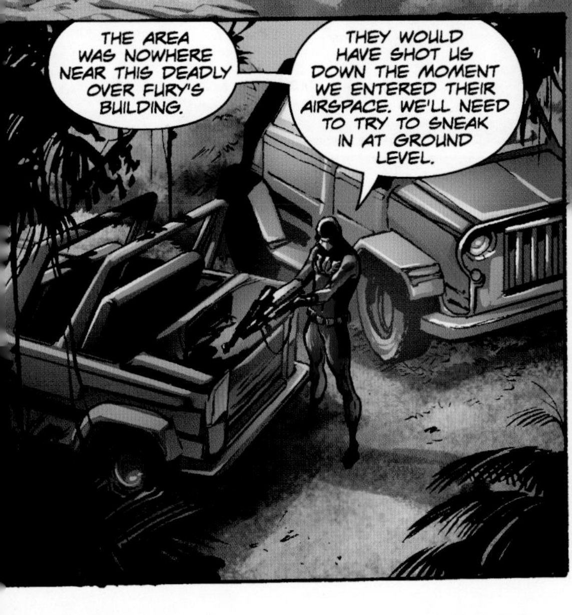
THE AREA WAS NOWHERE NEAR THIS DEADLY OVER FURY'S BUILDING.
THEY WOULD HAVE SHOT US DOWN THE MOMENT WE ENTERED THEIR AIRSPACE. WE'LL NEED TO TRY TO SNEAK IN AT GROUND LEVEL.

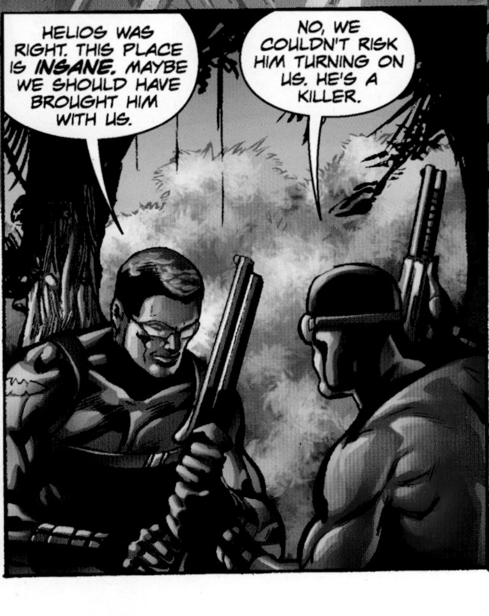
HELIOS WAS RIGHT. THIS PLACE IS INSANE. MAYBE WE SHOULD HAVE BROUGHT HIM WITH US.
NO, WE COULDN'T RISK HIM TURNING ON US. HE'S A KILLER.

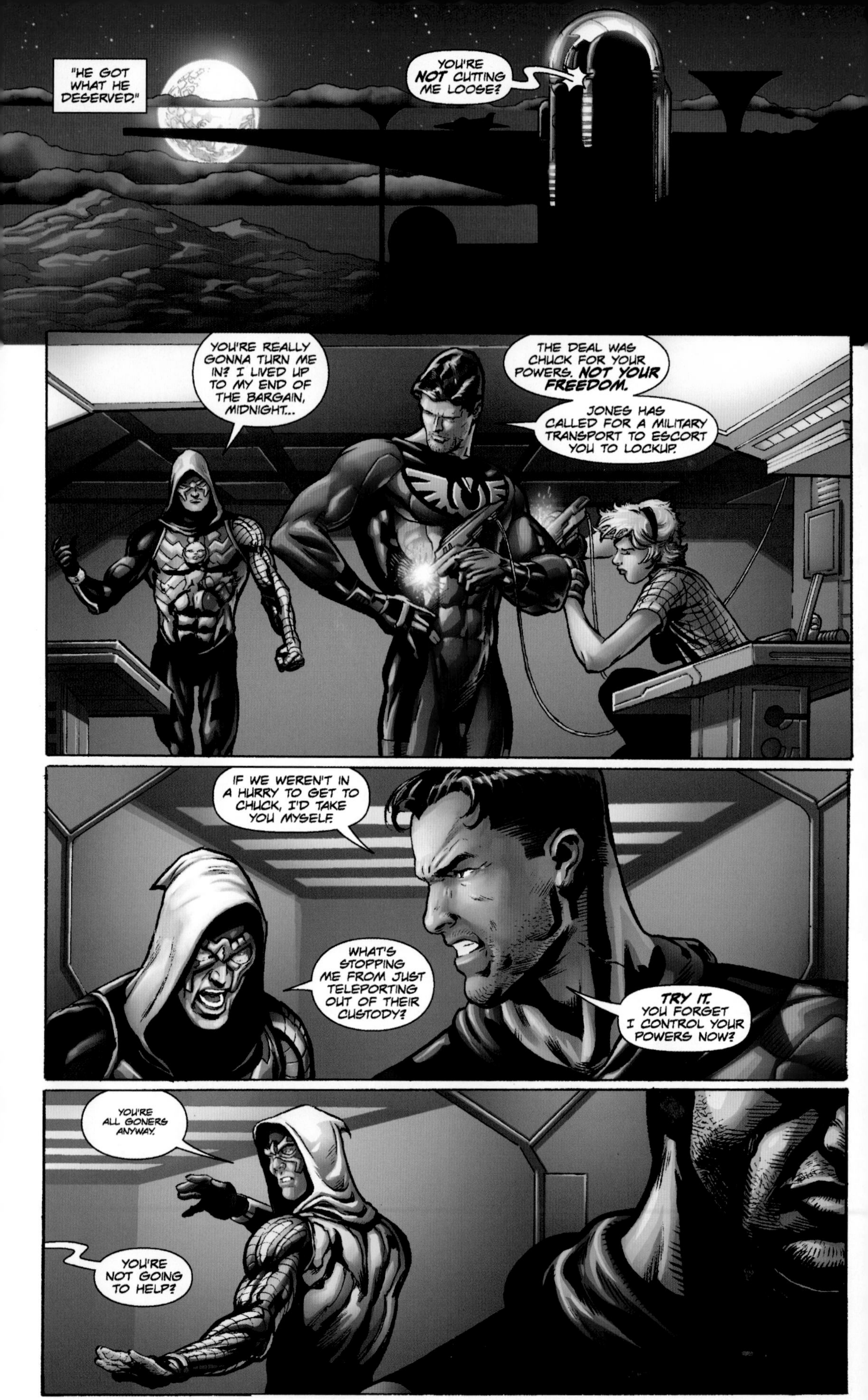
"HE GOT WHAT HE DESERVED."
YOU'RE **NOT** CUTTING ME LOOSE?
YOU'RE REALLY GONNA TURN ME IN? I LIVED UP TO MY END OF THE BARGAIN, MIDNIGHT...
THE DEAL WAS CHUCK FOR YOUR POWERS. **NOT YOUR FREEDOM.**
JONES HAS CALLED FOR A MILITARY TRANSPORT TO ESCORT YOU TO LOCKUP.
IF WE WEREN'T IN A HURRY TO GET TO CHUCK, I'D TAKE YOU MYSELF.
WHAT'S STOPPING ME FROM JUST TELEPORTING OUT OF THEIR CUSTODY?
TRY IT. YOU FORGET I CONTROL YOUR POWERS NOW?
YOU'RE ALL GONERS ANYWAY.
YOU'RE NOT GOING TO HELP?

CHUCK IS JUST AS MUCH YOUR PROBLEM AS OURS. HE'S SENT MEN TO KILL YOU. YOU DON'T WANT A LITTLE REVENGE?

SO NOW YOU TRUST ME?

NOT AT ALL, BUT I KNOW WE COULD USE YOUR SKILLS. YOU'D BE AN ASSET TO THE MISSION.

TOO BAD IT'S NOT THAT EASY. AND BESIDES...

I KNOW WHEN I'M NOT WANTED.

SO ON THAT NOTE-- GOOD LUCK, CHAR-BEAR. HAVE FUN GOING UP AGAINST A CRAZY OLD MAN.

WHAT DID YOU CALL ME...?

HELIOS!

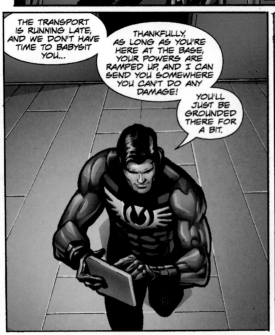

THE TRANSPORT IS RUNNING LATE, AND WE DON'T HAVE TIME TO BABYSIT YOU...

THANKFULLY, AS LONG AS YOU'RE HERE AT THE BASE, YOUR POWERS ARE RAMPED UP, AND I CAN SEND YOU SOMEWHERE YOU CAN'T DO ANY DAMAGE!

YOU'LL JUST BE GROUNDED THERE FOR A BIT.

WAIT, MIDNIGHT...!

FWASH

WHERE DID YOU SEND HIM?

SOMEPLACE... WARM.

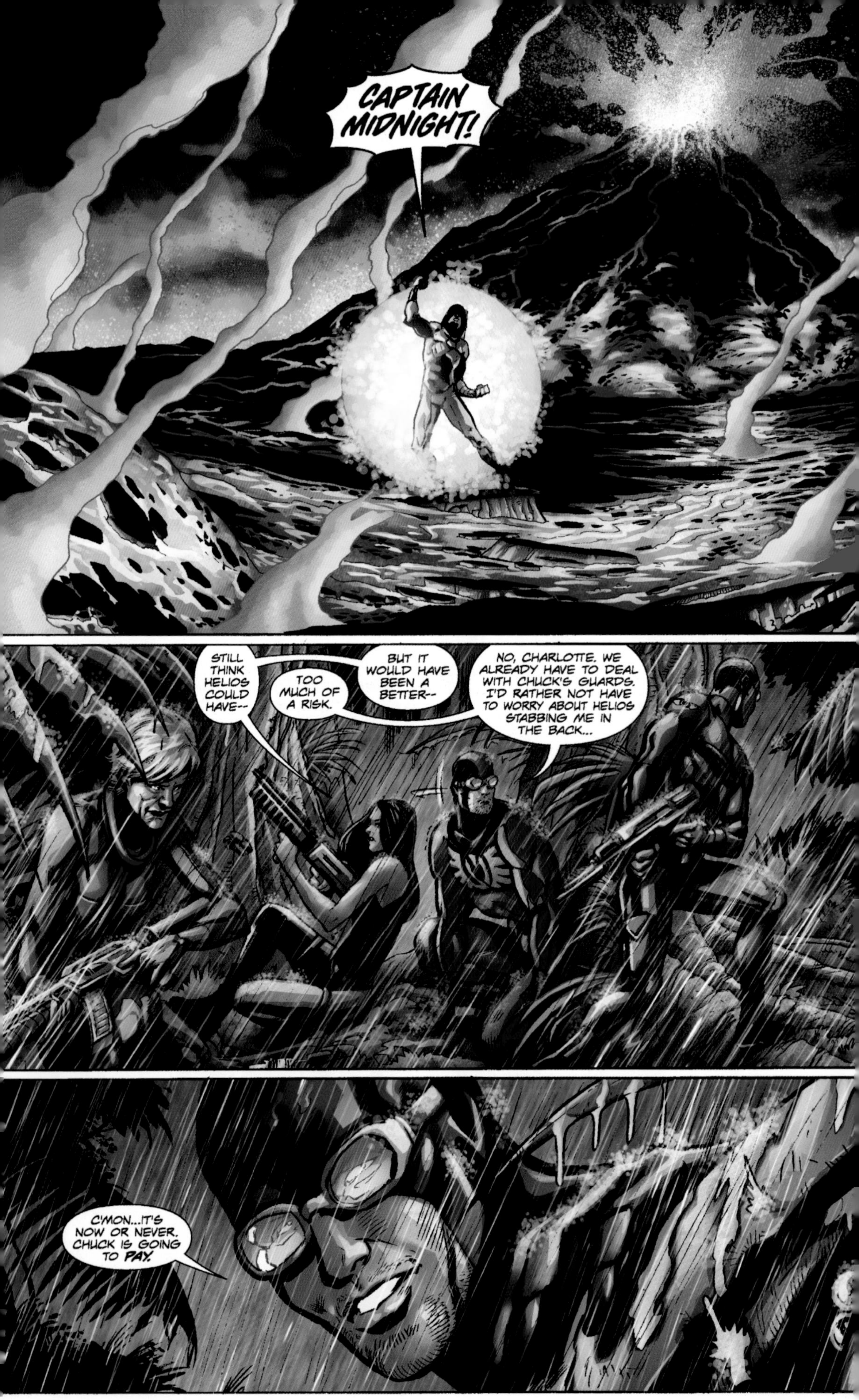
CAPTAIN MIDNIGHT!
STILL THINK HELIOS COULD HAVE--
TOO MUCH OF A RISK.
BUT IT WOULD HAVE BEEN A BETTER--
NO, CHARLOTTE. WE ALREADY HAVE TO DEAL WITH CHUCK'S GUARDS. I'D RATHER NOT HAVE TO WORRY ABOUT HELIOS STABBING ME IN THE BACK...
C'MON...IT'S NOW OR NEVER. CHUCK IS GOING TO PAY.

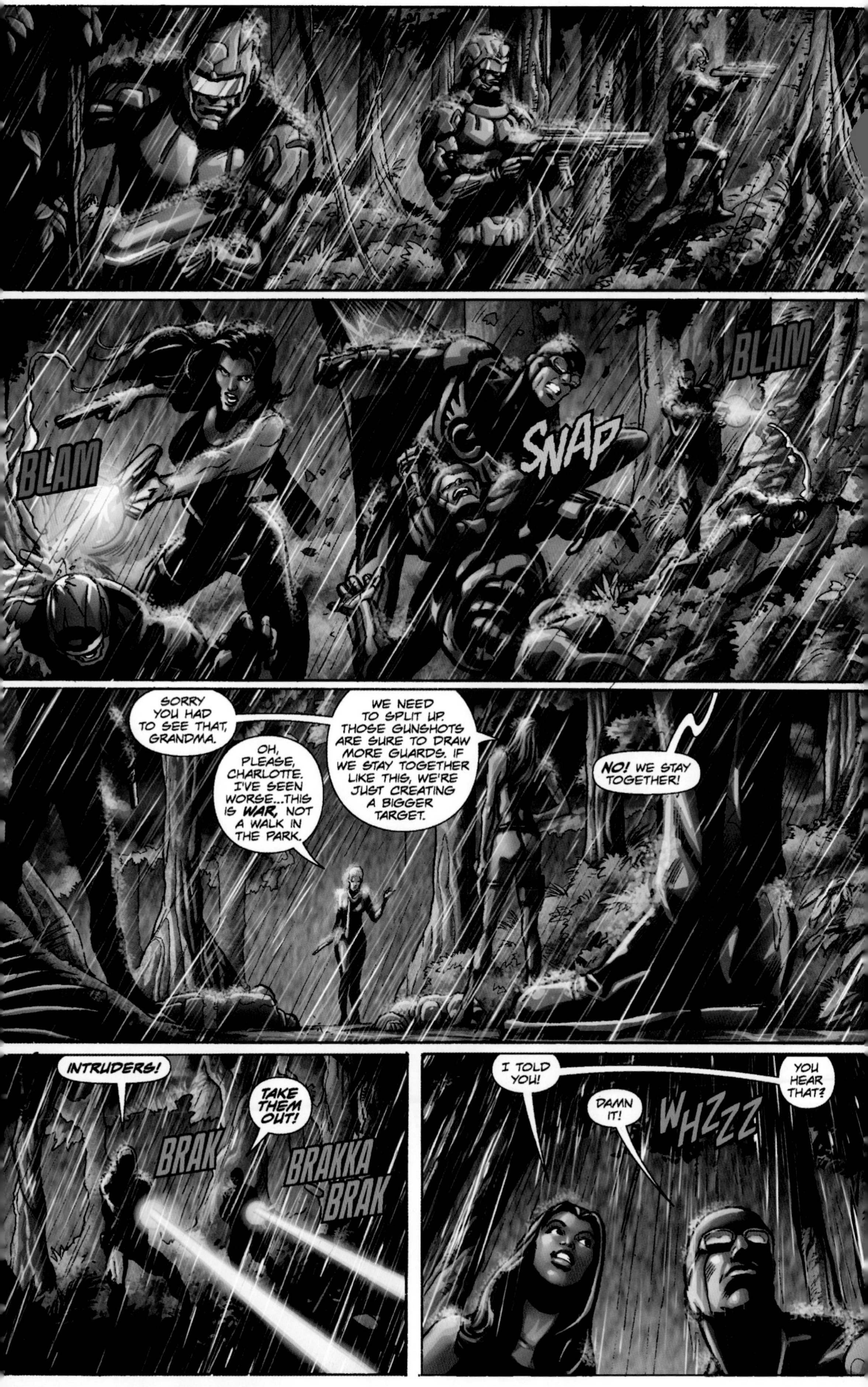
BLAM
SNAP
BLAM
SORRY YOU HAD TO SEE THAT, GRANDMA.
OH, PLEASE, CHARLOTTE. I'VE SEEN WORSE...THIS IS **WAR,** NOT A WALK IN THE PARK.
WE NEED TO SPLIT UP. THOSE GUNSHOTS ARE SURE TO DRAW MORE GUARDS. IF WE STAY TOGETHER LIKE THIS, WE'RE JUST CREATING A BIGGER TARGET.
NO! WE STAY TOGETHER!
INTRUDERS!
BRAK
TAKE THEM OUT!
BRAKKA BRAK
I TOLD YOU!
DAMN IT!
WHZZZ
YOU HEAR THAT?

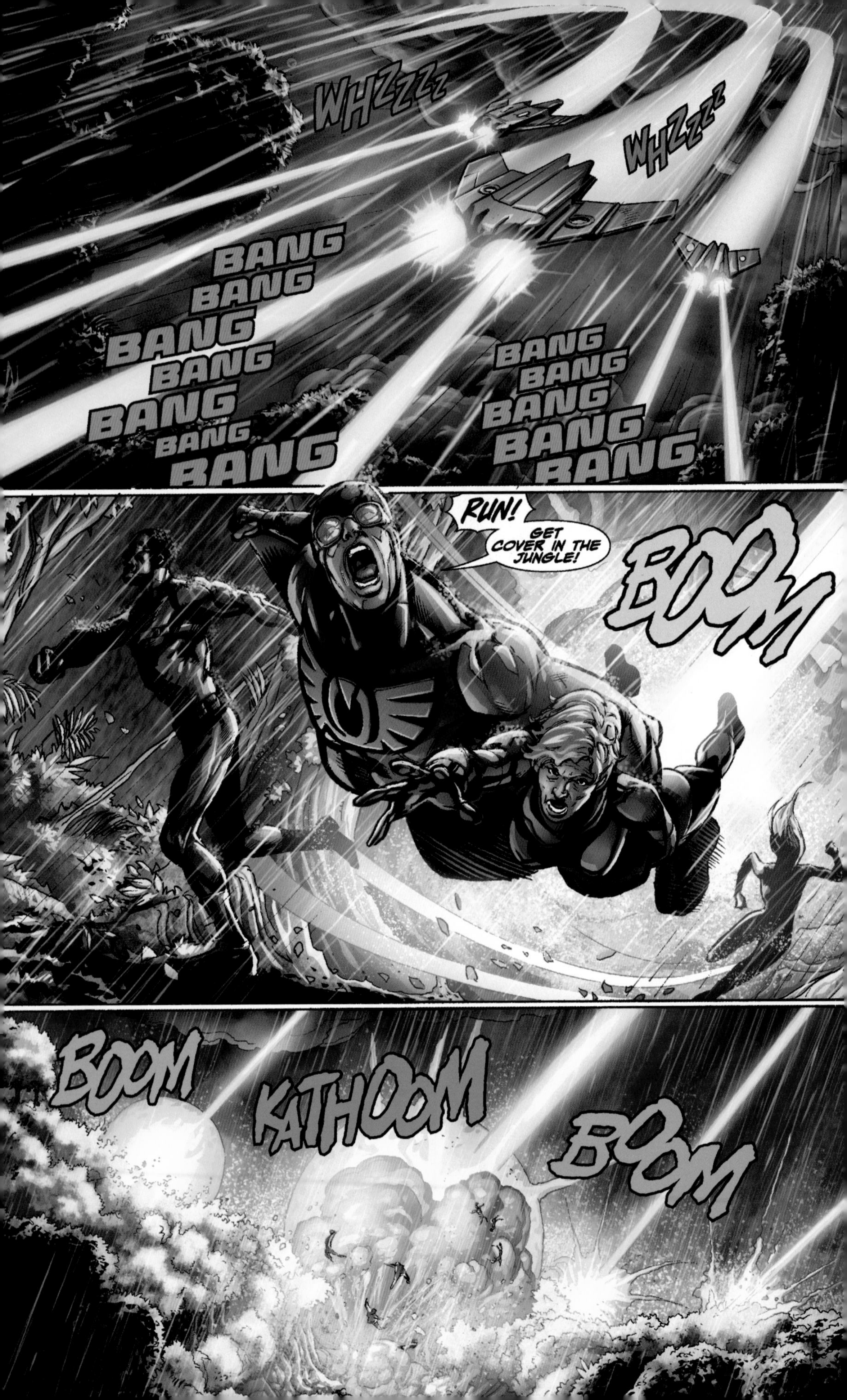
WHZZZZ
WHZZZZ
BANG BANG BANG BANG BANG BANG BANG
BANG BANG BANG BANG BANG
RUN!
GET COVER IN THE JUNGLE!
BOOM
BOOM
KATHOOM
BOOM

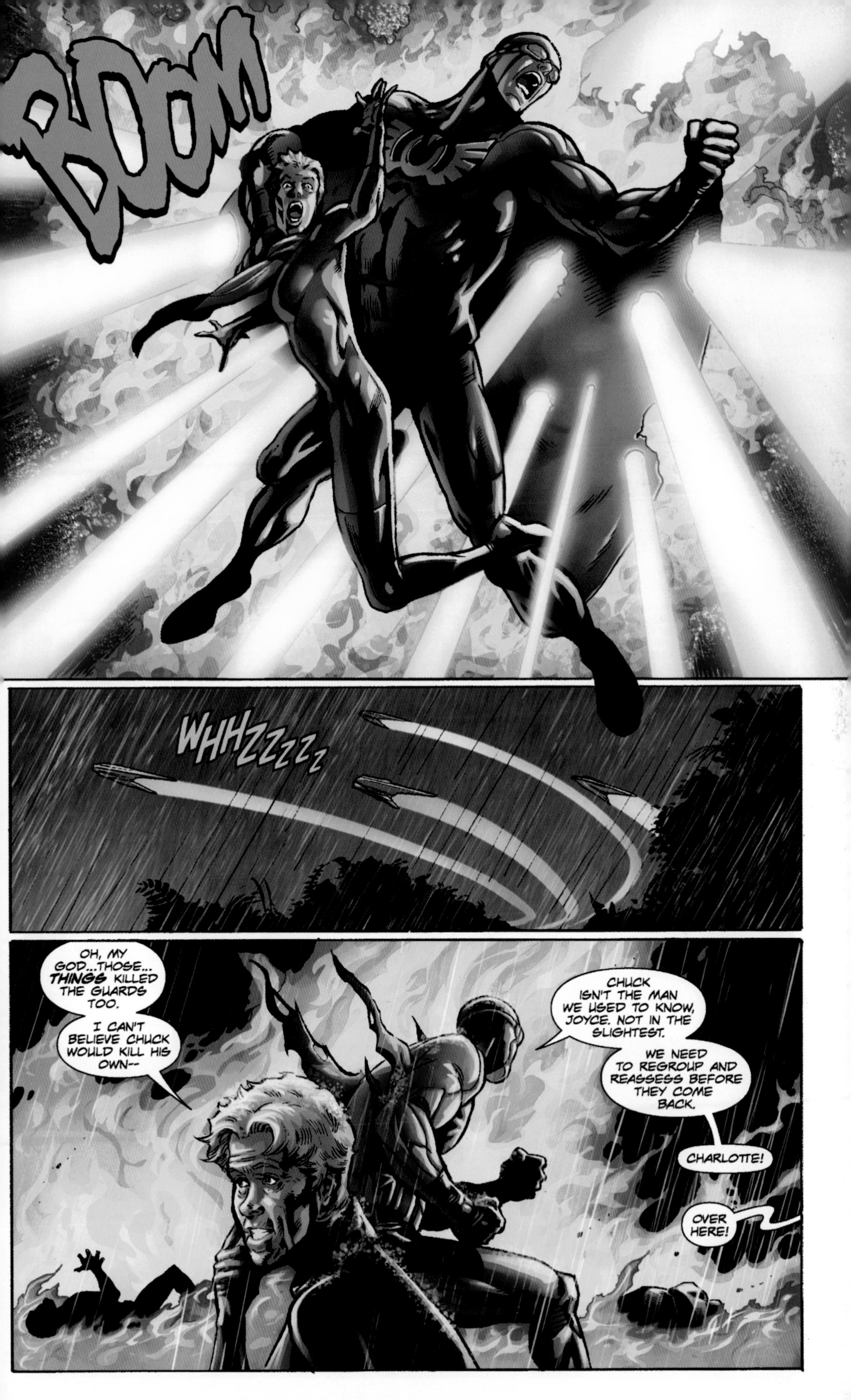
BOOM
WHHZZZZZ
OH, MY GOD...THOSE... THINGS KILLED THE GUARDS TOO.
I CAN'T BELIEVE CHUCK WOULD KILL HIS OWN--
CHUCK ISN'T THE MAN WE USED TO KNOW, JOYCE. NOT IN THE SLIGHTEST.
WE NEED TO REGROUP AND REASSESS BEFORE THEY COME BACK.
CHARLOTTE!
OVER HERE!

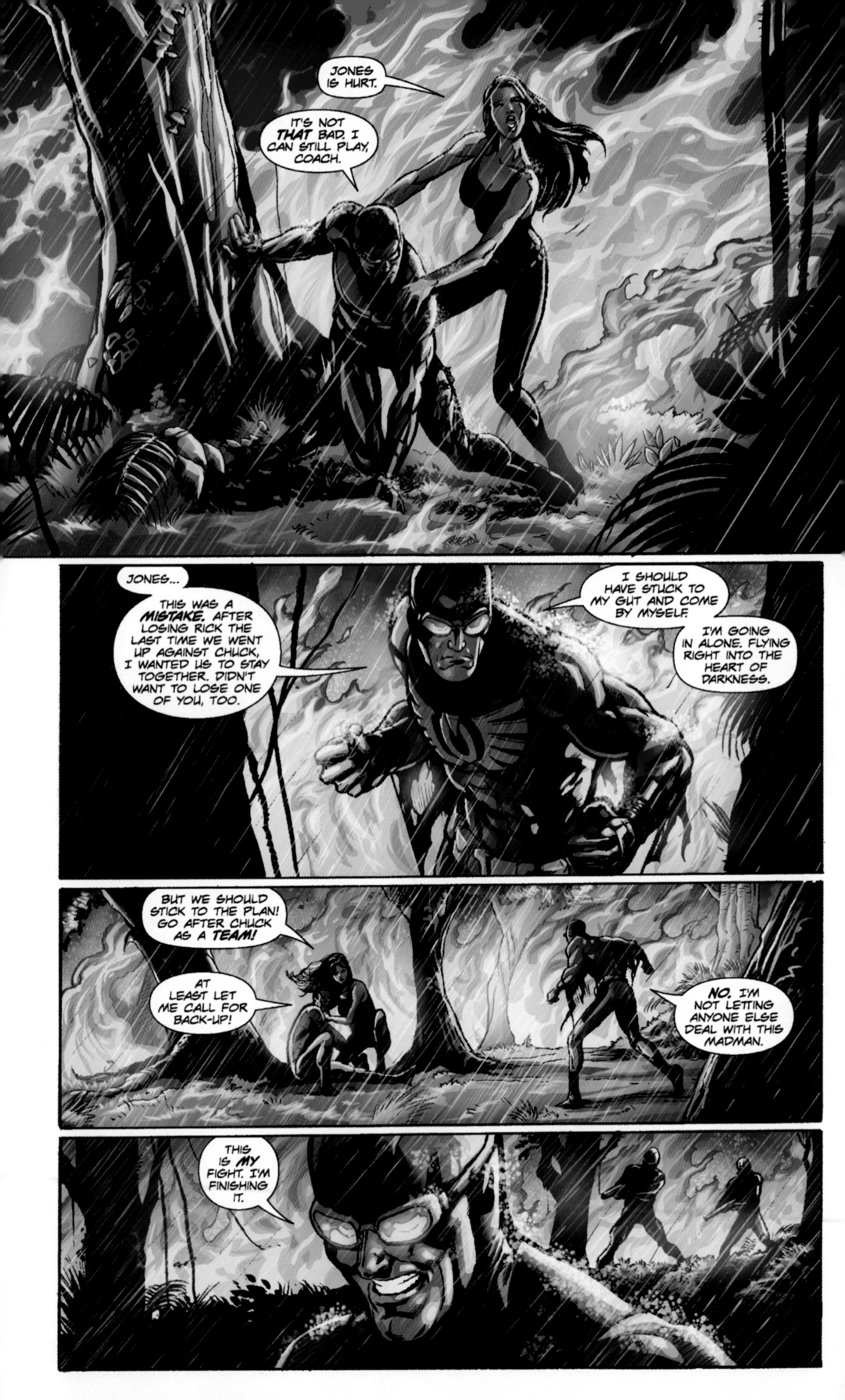

JONES IS HURT.
IT'S NOT THAT BAD. I CAN STILL PLAY, COACH.
JONES...
THIS WAS A MISTAKE. AFTER LOSING RICK THE LAST TIME WE WENT UP AGAINST CHUCK, I WANTED US TO STAY TOGETHER. DIDN'T WANT TO LOSE ONE OF YOU, TOO.
I SHOULD HAVE STUCK TO MY GUT AND COME BY MYSELF.
I'M GOING IN ALONE. FLYING RIGHT INTO THE HEART OF DARKNESS.
BUT WE SHOULD STICK TO THE PLAN! GO AFTER CHUCK AS A TEAM!
AT LEAST LET ME CALL FOR BACK-UP!
NO. I'M NOT LETTING ANYONE ELSE DEAL WITH THIS MADMAN.
THIS IS MY FIGHT. I'M FINISHING IT.

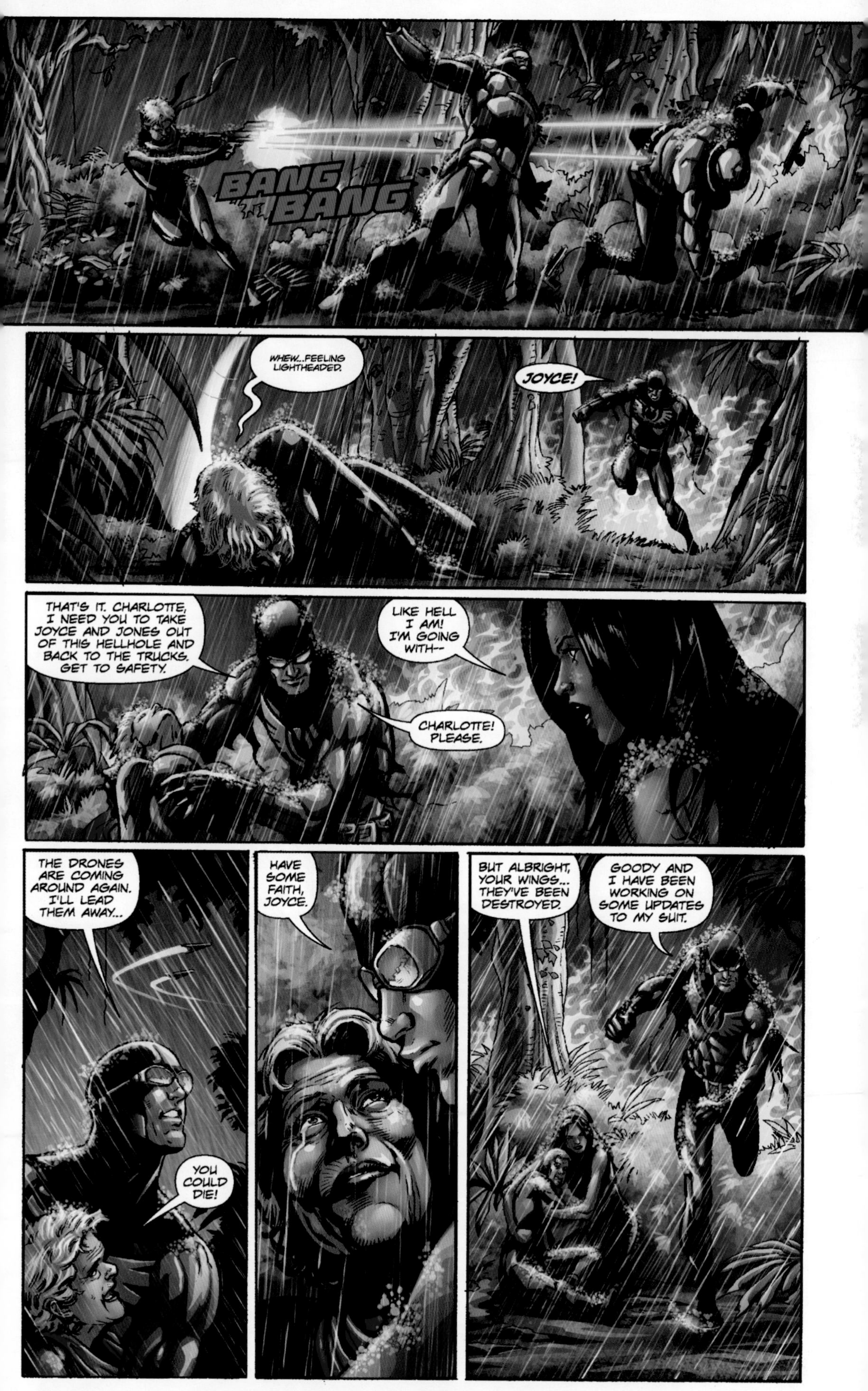

BANG BANG
WHEW...FEELING LIGHTHEADED.
JOYCE!
THAT'S IT. CHARLOTTE, I NEED YOU TO TAKE JOYCE AND JONES OUT OF THIS HELLHOLE AND BACK TO THE TRUCKS. GET TO SAFETY.
LIKE HELL I AM! I'M GOING WITH--
CHARLOTTE! PLEASE.
THE DRONES ARE COMING AROUND AGAIN. I'LL LEAD THEM AWAY...
YOU COULD DIE!
HAVE SOME FAITH, JOYCE.
BUT ALBRIGHT, YOUR WINGS... THEY'VE BEEN DESTROYED.
GOODY AND I HAVE BEEN WORKING ON SOME UPDATES TO MY SUIT.

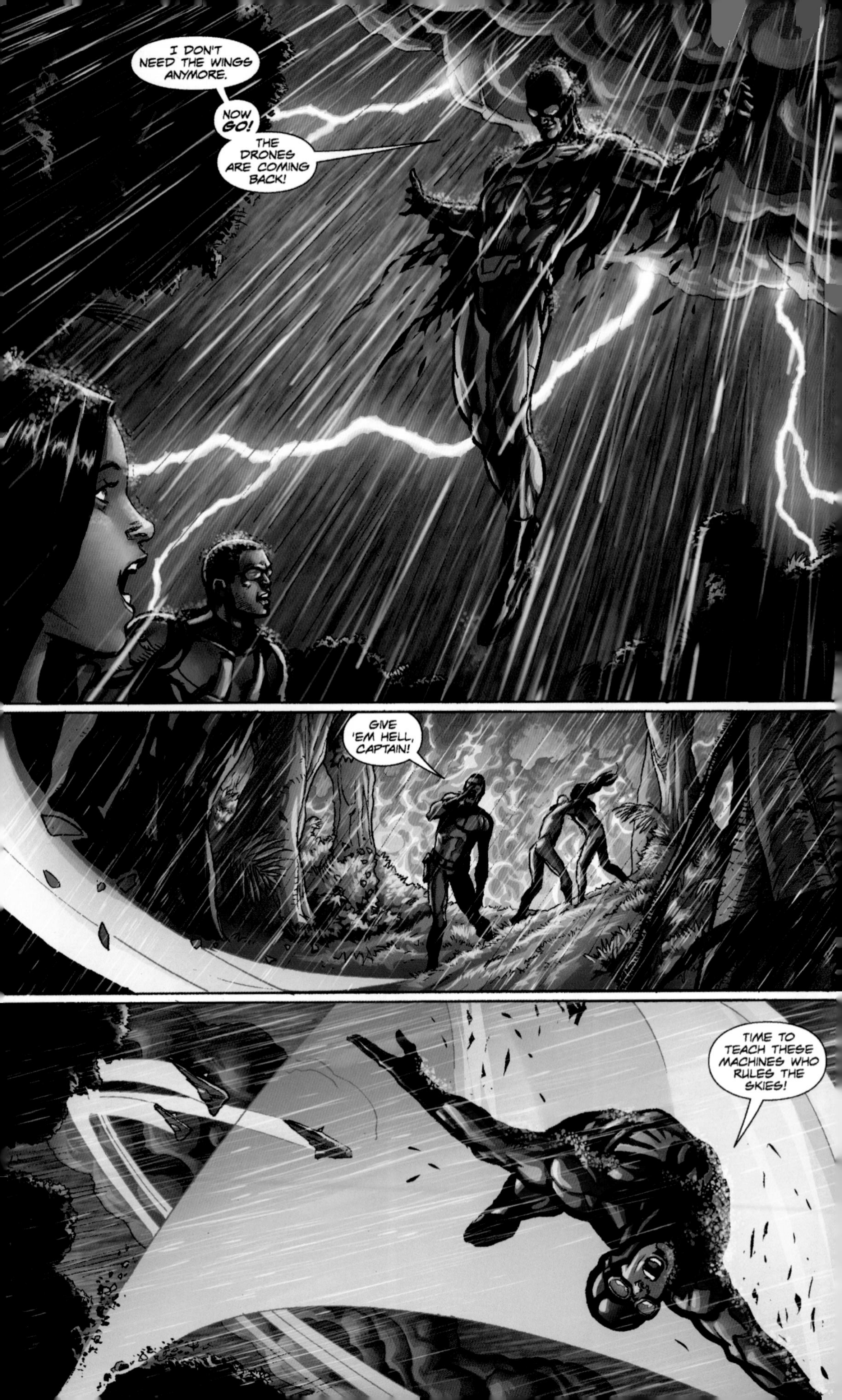

I DON'T NEED THE WINGS ANYMORE.
NOW GO!
THE DRONES ARE COMING BACK!
GIVE 'EM HELL, CAPTAIN!
TIME TO TEACH THESE MACHINES WHO RULES THE SKIES!

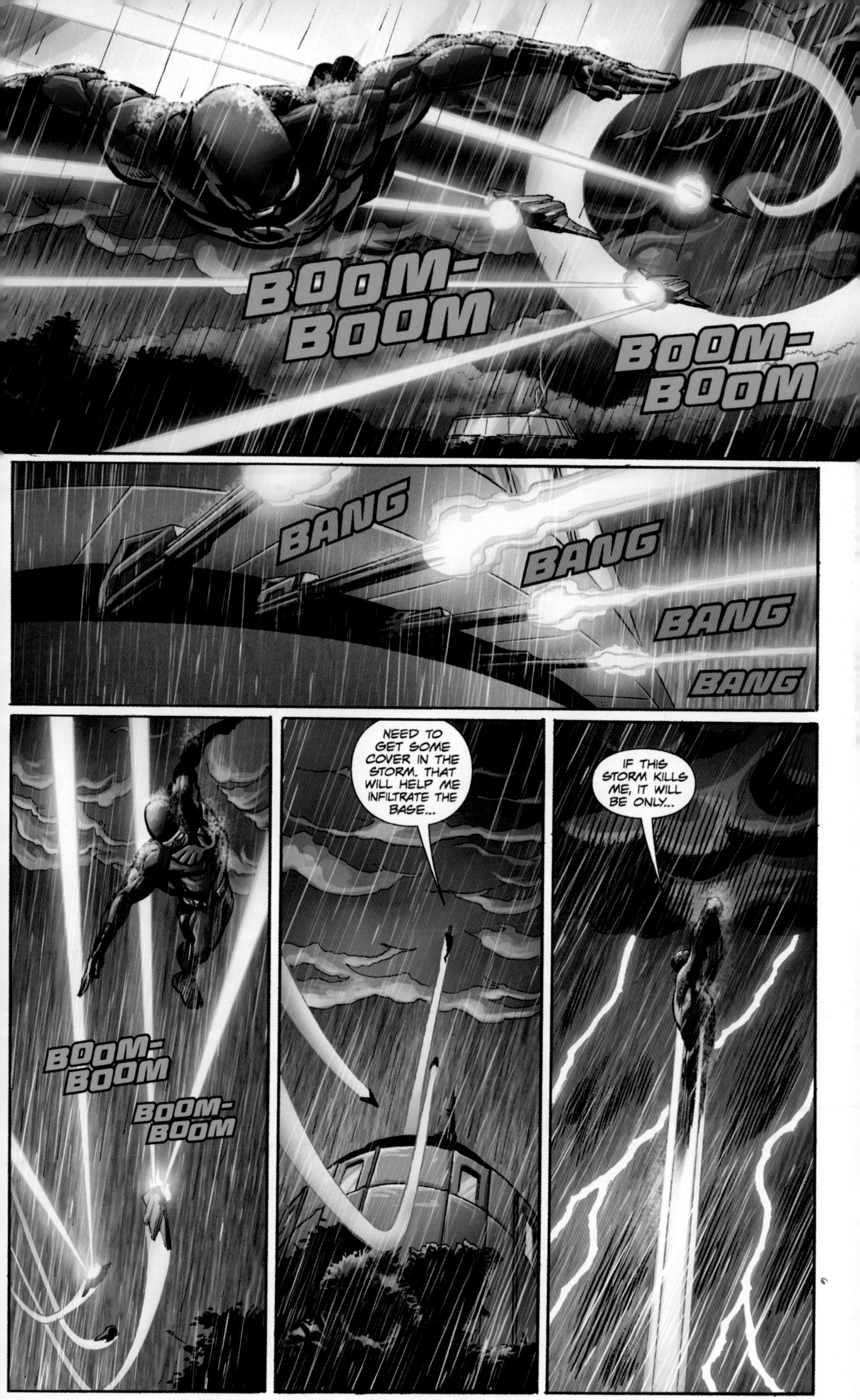
BOOM-BOOM
BOOM-BOOM
BANG
BANG
BANG
BANG
BOOM-BOOM
BOOM-BOOM
NEED TO GET SOME COVER IN THE STORM. THAT WILL HELP ME INFILTRATE THE BASE...
IF THIS STORM KILLS ME, IT WILL BE ONLY...

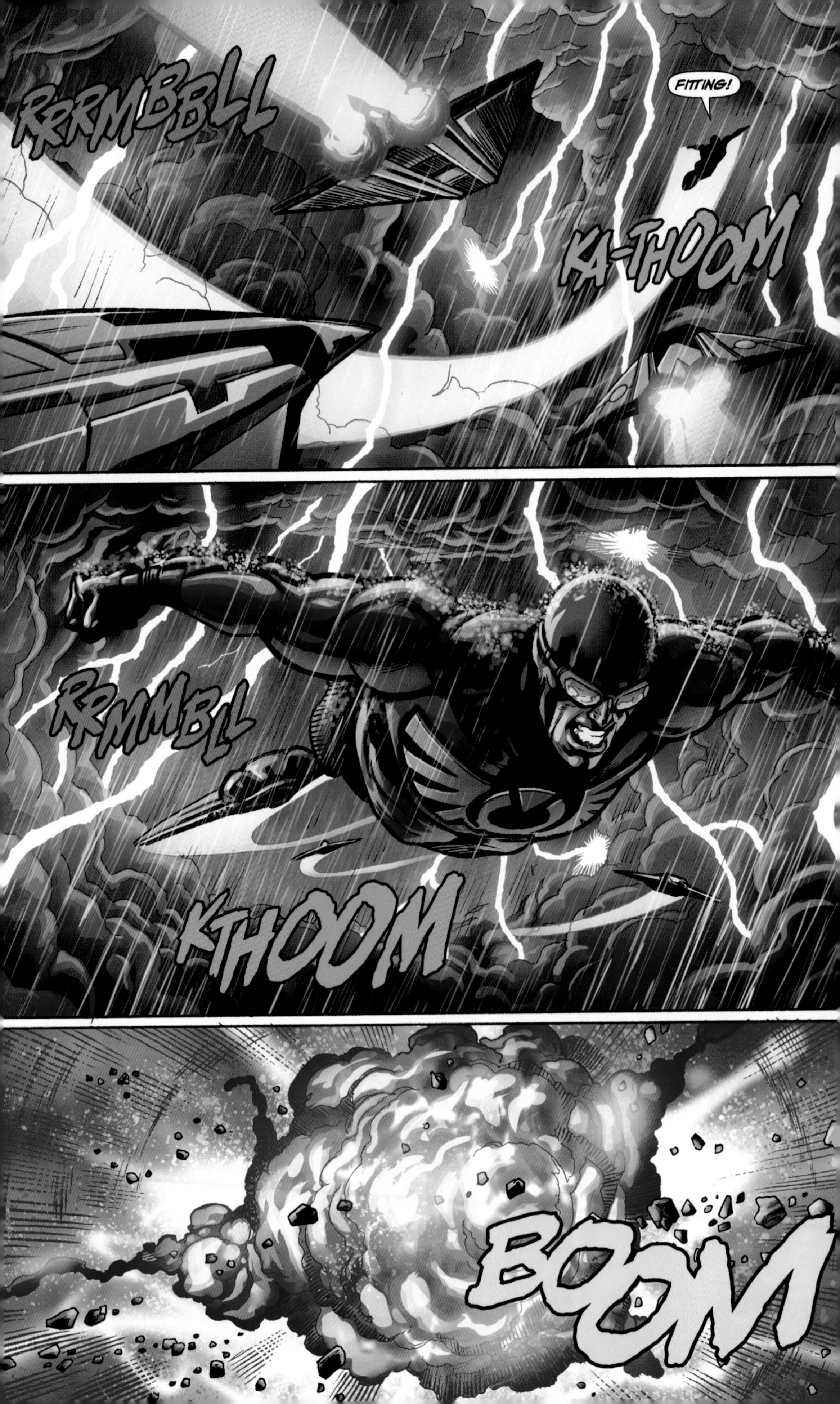
RRRMBBLL
FITTING!
KA-THOOM
RRMMBLL
KTHOOM
BOOM

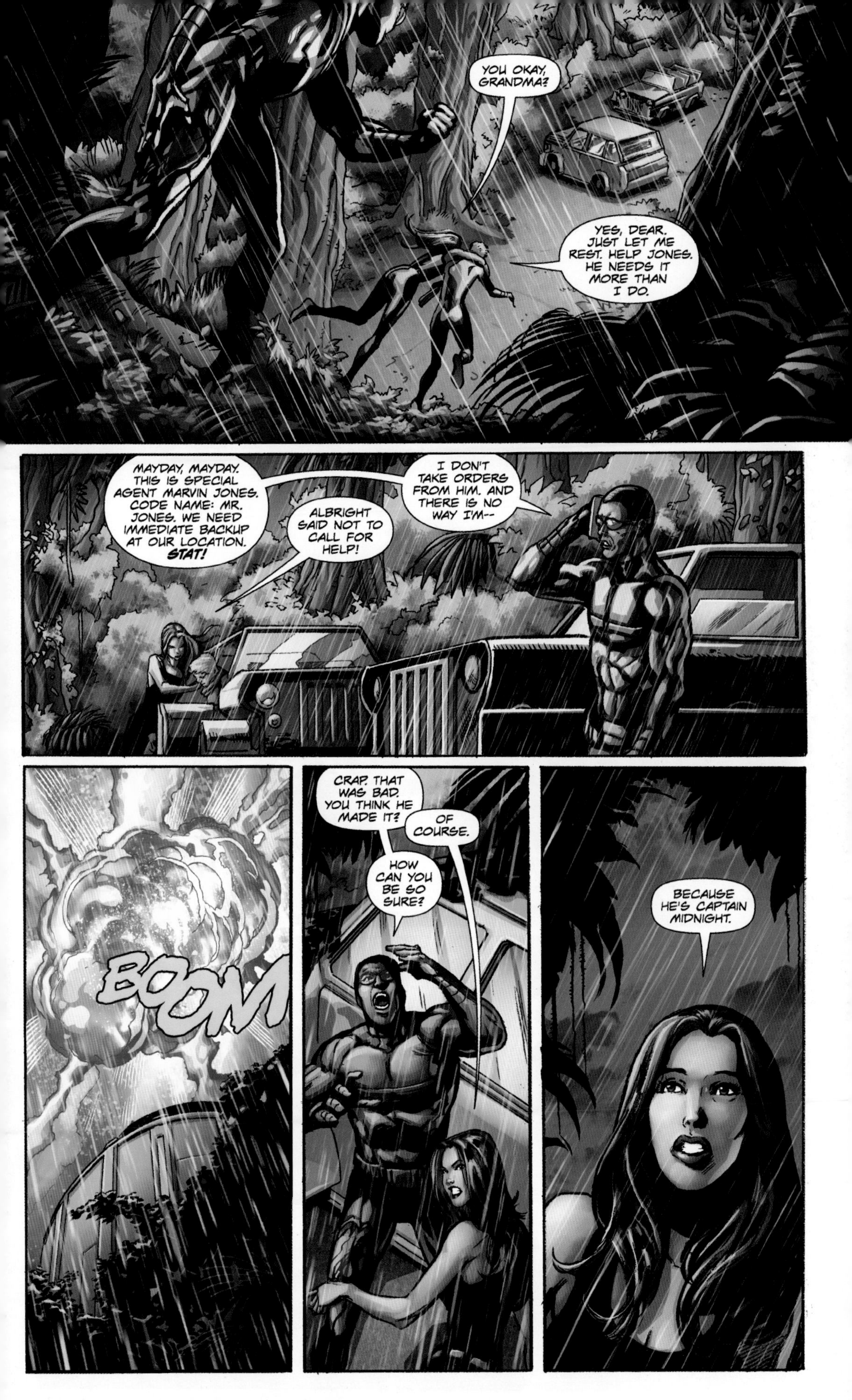

YOU OKAY, GRANDMA?
YES, DEAR. JUST LET ME REST. HELP JONES. HE NEEDS IT MORE THAN I DO.
MAYDAY, MAYDAY. THIS IS SPECIAL AGENT MARVIN JONES. CODE NAME: MR. JONES. WE NEED IMMEDIATE BACKUP AT OUR LOCATION. STAT!
ALBRIGHT SAID NOT TO CALL FOR HELP!
I DON'T TAKE ORDERS FROM HIM. AND THERE IS NO WAY I'M--
BOOM
CRAP. THAT WAS BAD. YOU THINK HE MADE IT?
OF COURSE.
HOW CAN YOU BE SO SURE?
BECAUSE HE'S CAPTAIN MIDNIGHT.

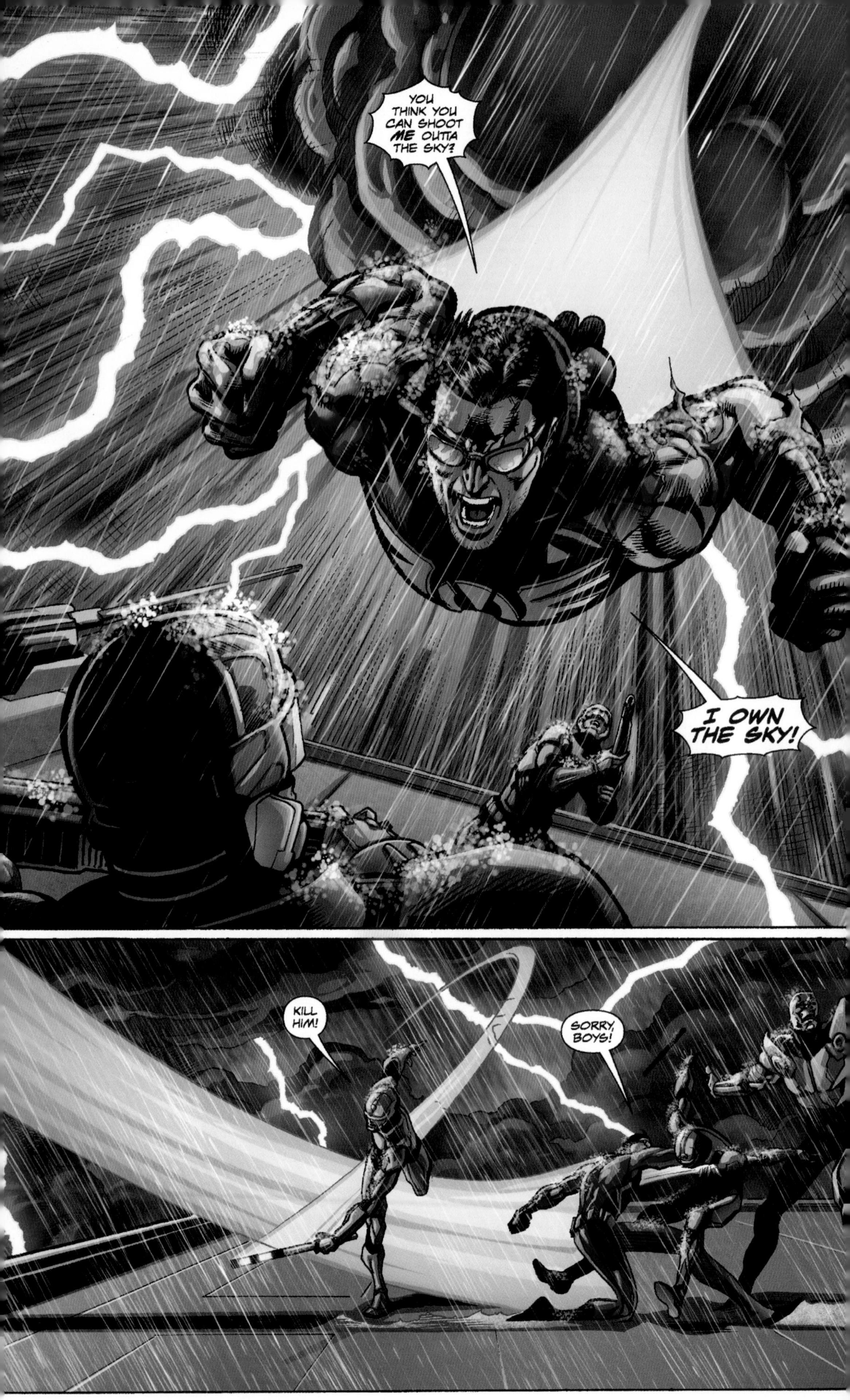
YOU THINK YOU CAN SHOOT ME OUTTA THE SKY?
I OWN THE SKY!
KILL HIM!
SORRY, BOYS!

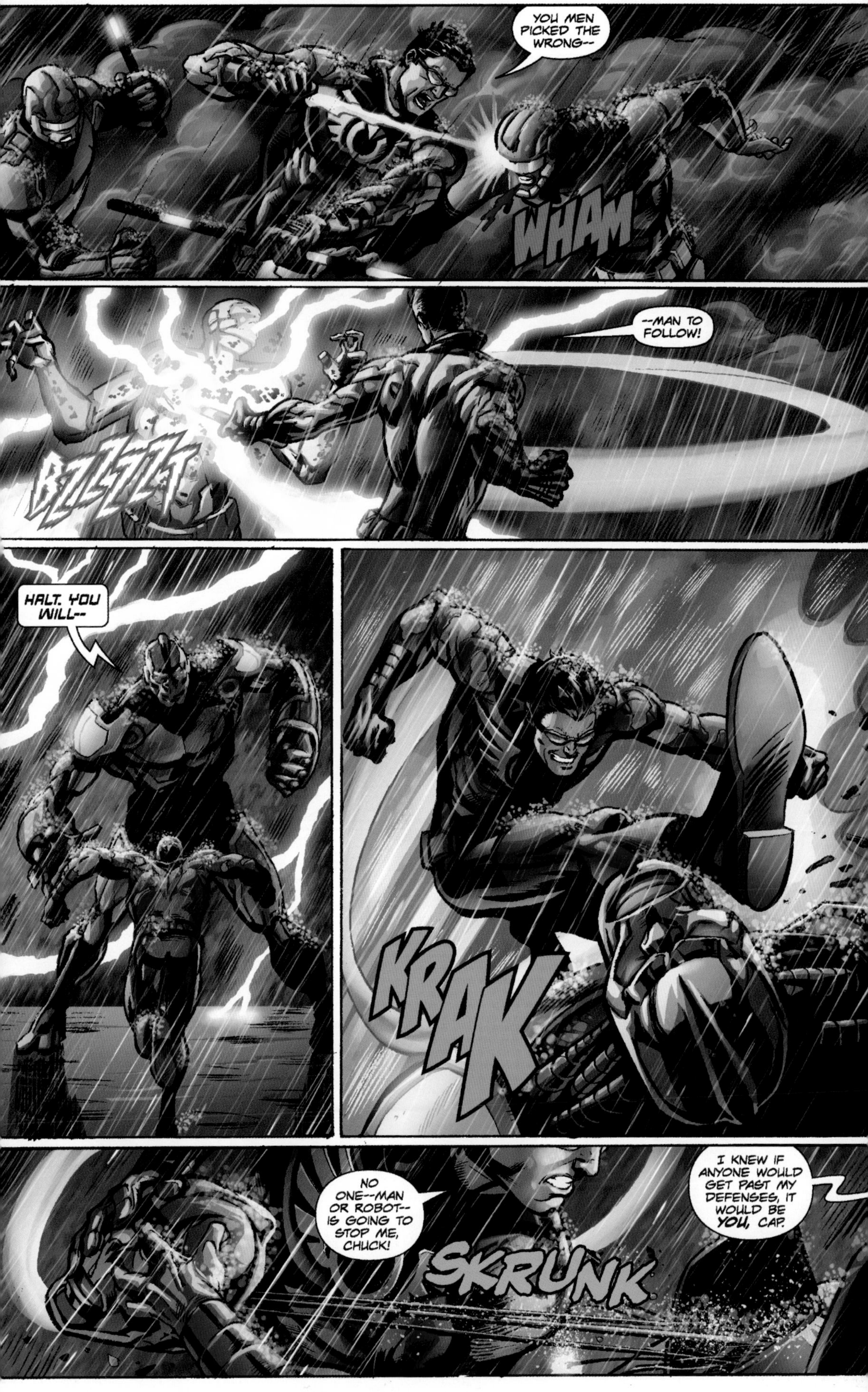
YOU MEN PICKED THE WRONG--
WHAM
--MAN TO FOLLOW!
BZZZZT
HALT. YOU WILL--
KRAK
NO ONE--MAN OR ROBOT--IS GOING TO STOP ME, CHUCK!
I KNEW IF ANYONE WOULD GET PAST MY DEFENSES, IT WOULD BE YOU, CAP.
SKRUNK

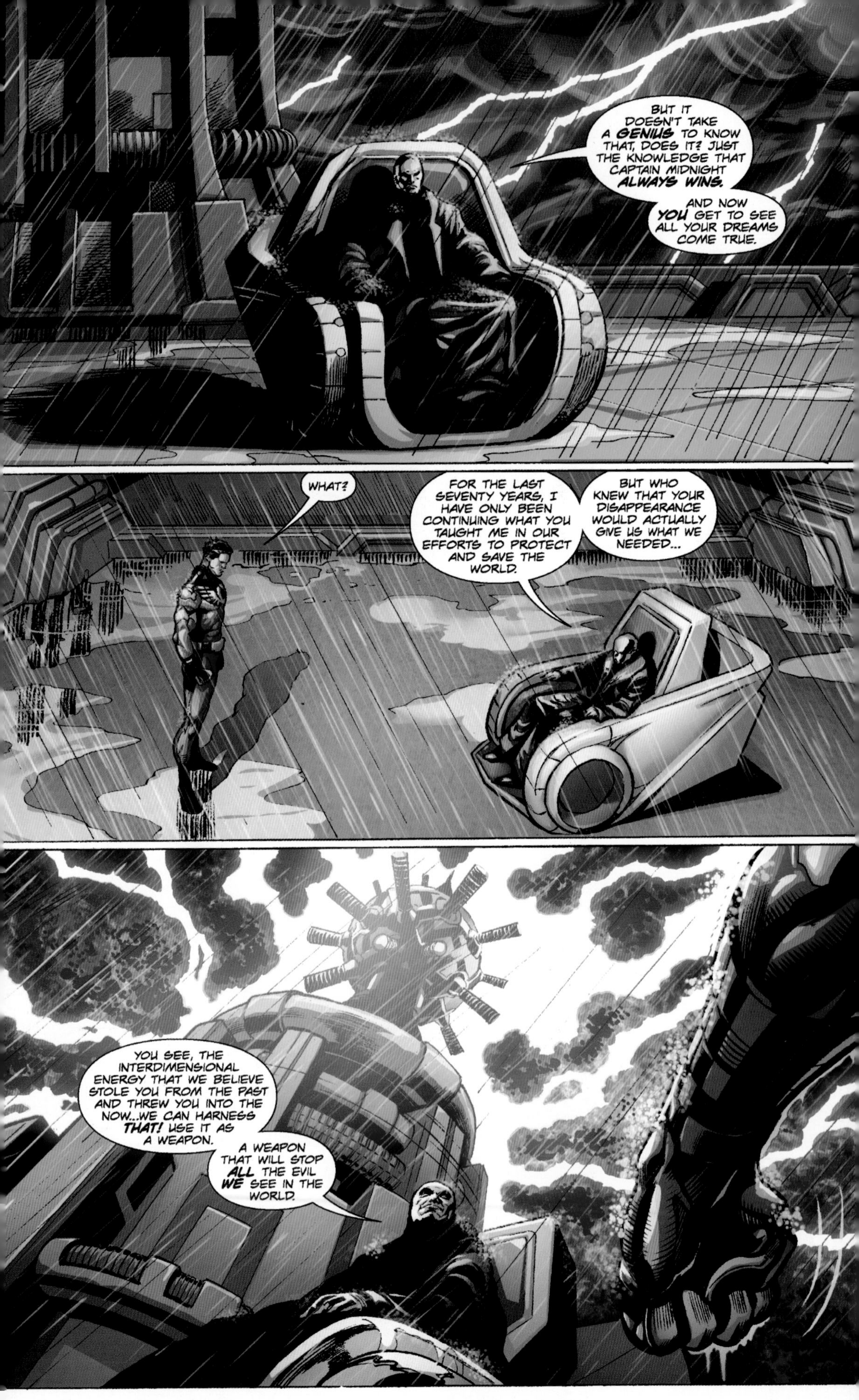
BUT IT DOESN'T TAKE A GENIUS TO KNOW THAT, DOES IT? JUST THE KNOWLEDGE THAT CAPTAIN MIDNIGHT ALWAYS WINS.
AND NOW YOU GET TO SEE ALL YOUR DREAMS COME TRUE.
WHAT?
FOR THE LAST SEVENTY YEARS, I HAVE ONLY BEEN CONTINUING WHAT YOU TAUGHT ME IN OUR EFFORTS TO PROTECT AND SAVE THE WORLD.
BUT WHO KNEW THAT YOUR DISAPPEARANCE WOULD ACTUALLY GIVE US WHAT WE NEEDED...
YOU SEE, THE INTERDIMENSIONAL ENERGY THAT WE BELIEVE STOLE YOU FROM THE PAST AND THREW YOU INTO THE NOW...WE CAN HARNESS THAT! USE IT AS A WEAPON.
A WEAPON THAT WILL STOP ALL THE EVIL WE SEE IN THE WORLD.

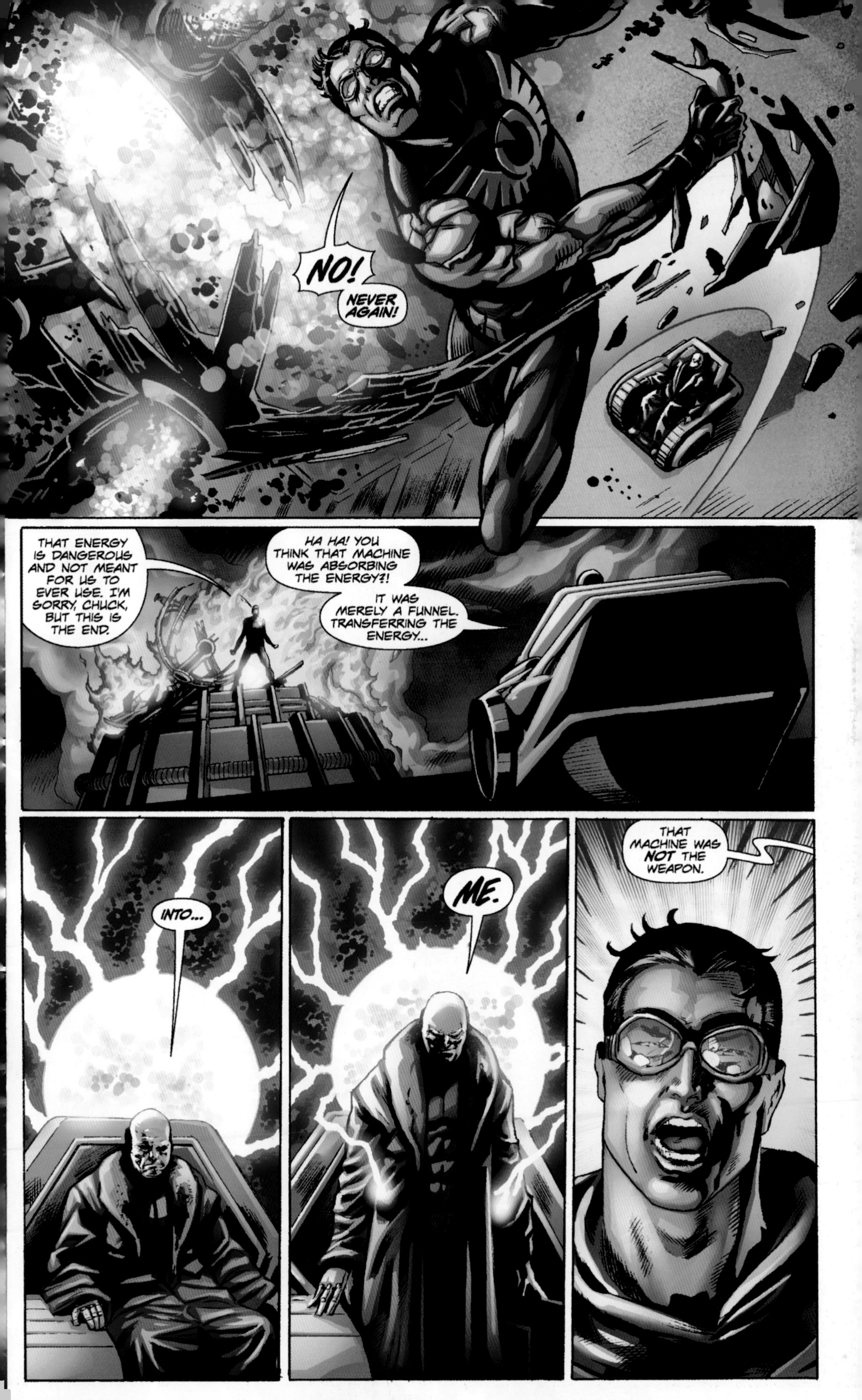
NO!
NEVER AGAIN!
THAT ENERGY IS DANGEROUS AND NOT MEANT FOR US TO EVER USE. I'M SORRY, CHUCK, BUT THIS IS THE END.
HA HA! YOU THINK THAT MACHINE WAS ABSORBING THE ENERGY?!
IT WAS MERELY A FUNNEL. TRANSFERRING THE ENERGY...
INTO...
ME.
THAT MACHINE WAS NOT THE WEAPON.

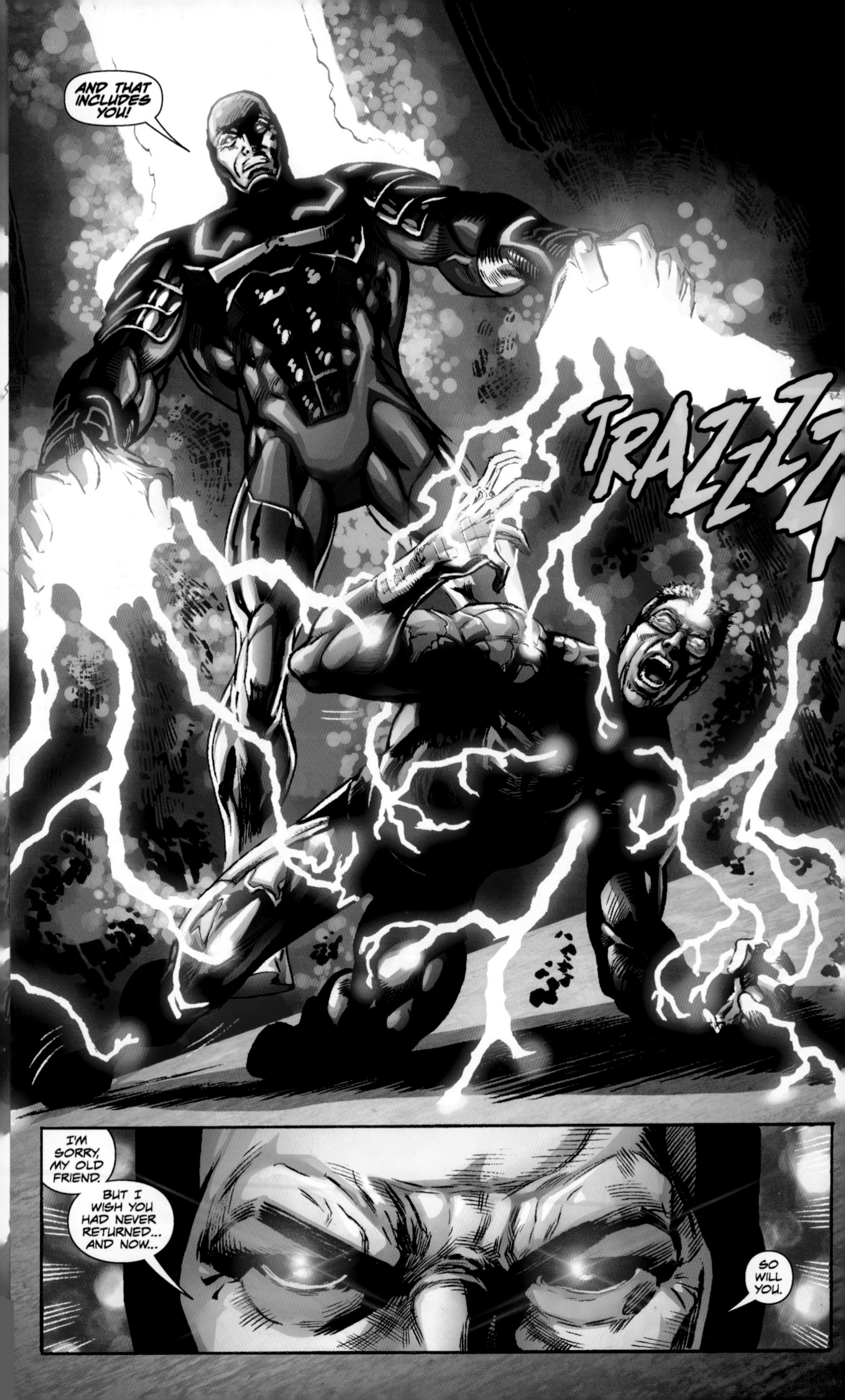
AND THAT INCLUDES YOU!
TRAZZZZ
I'M SORRY, MY OLD FRIEND.
BUT I WISH YOU HAD NEVER RETURNED... AND NOW...
SO WILL YOU.

CHAPTER 4

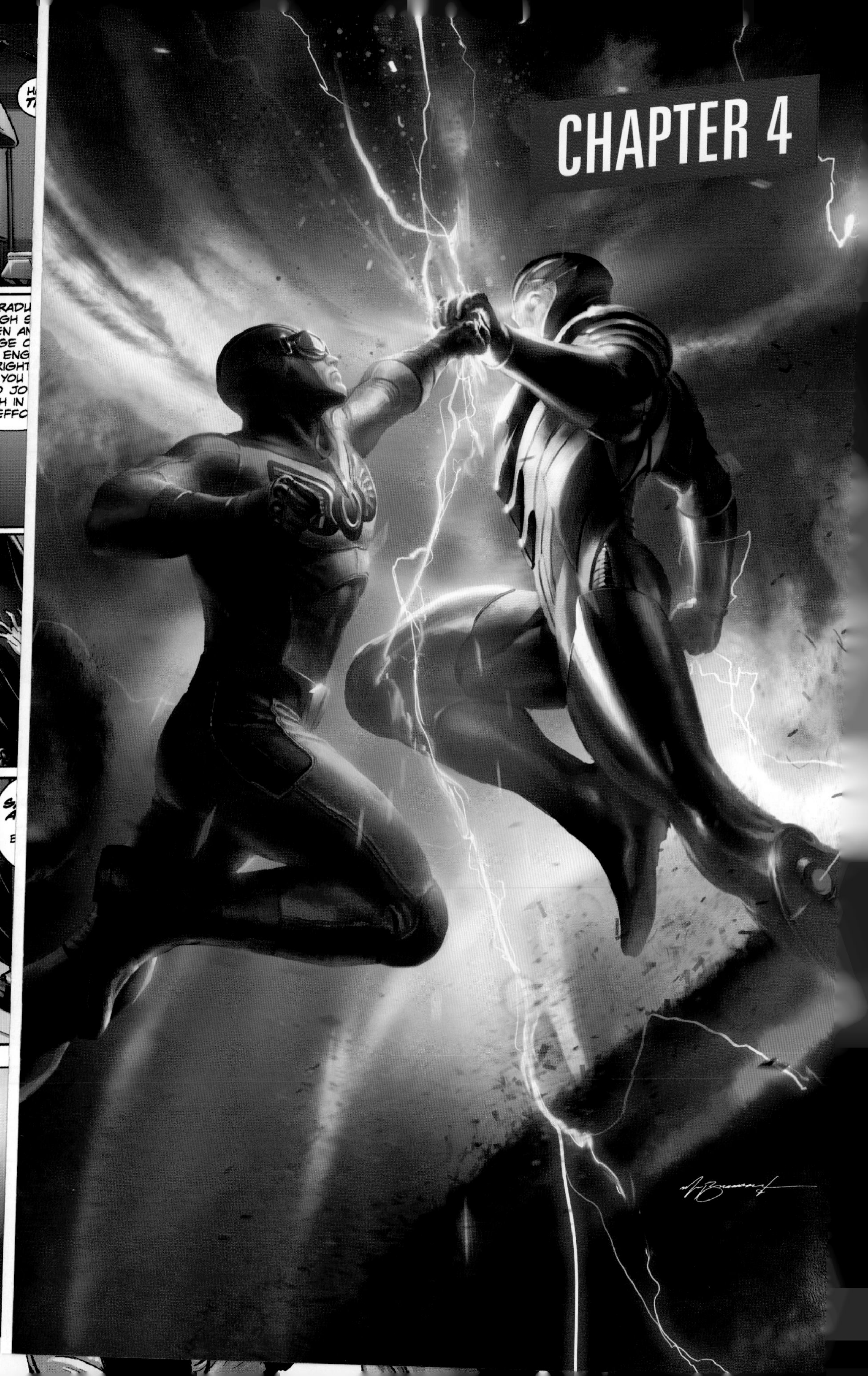

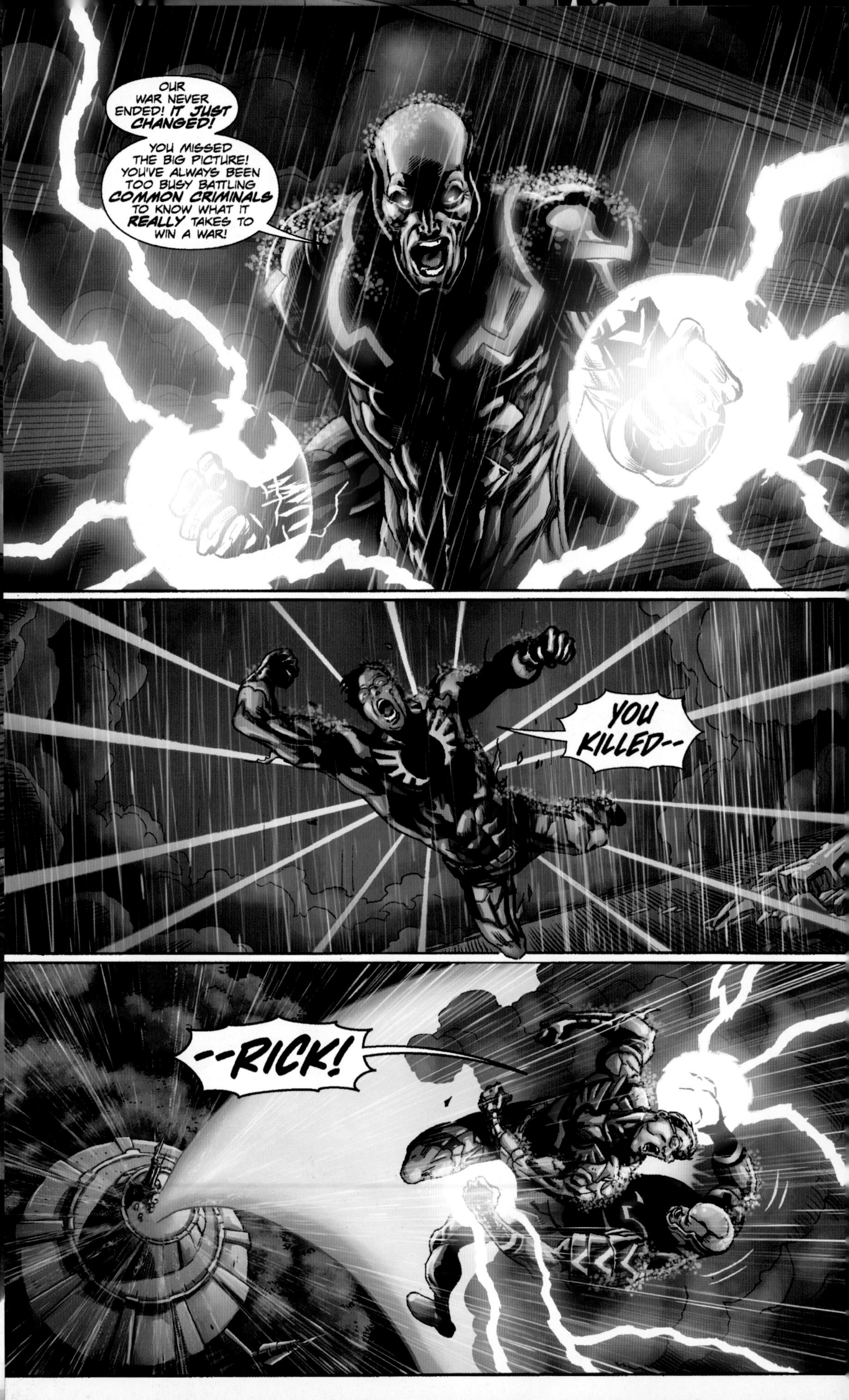
OUR WAR NEVER ENDED! IT JUST CHANGED!
YOU MISSED THE BIG PICTURE! YOU'VE ALWAYS BEEN TOO BUSY BATTLING COMMON CRIMINALS TO KNOW WHAT IT REALLY TAKES TO WIN A WAR!
YOU KILLED--
--RICK!

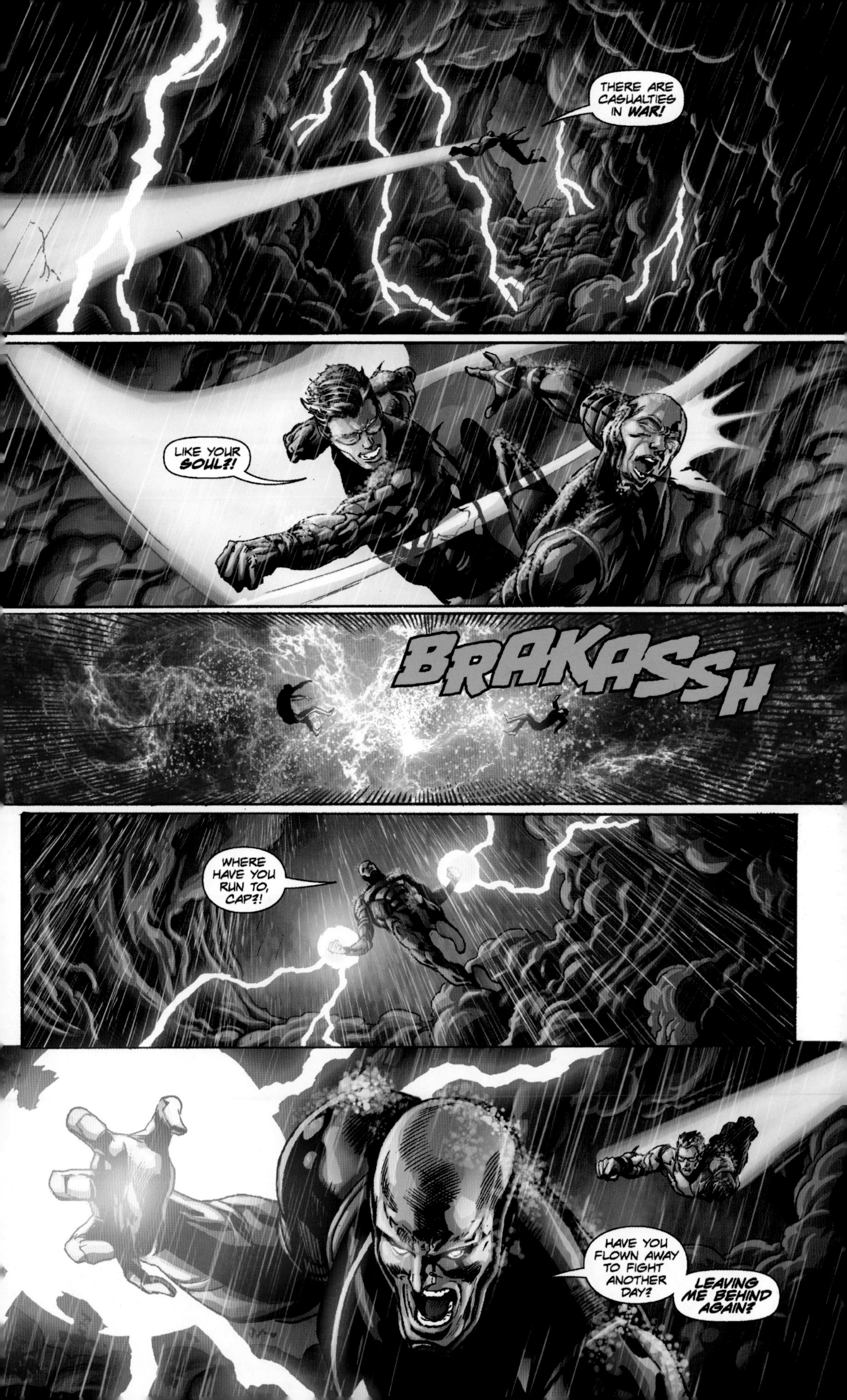
THERE ARE CASUALTIES IN WAR!
LIKE YOUR SOUL?!
BRAKASSH
WHERE HAVE YOU RUN TO, CAP?!
HAVE YOU FLOWN AWAY TO FIGHT ANOTHER DAY?
LEAVING ME BEHIND AGAIN?

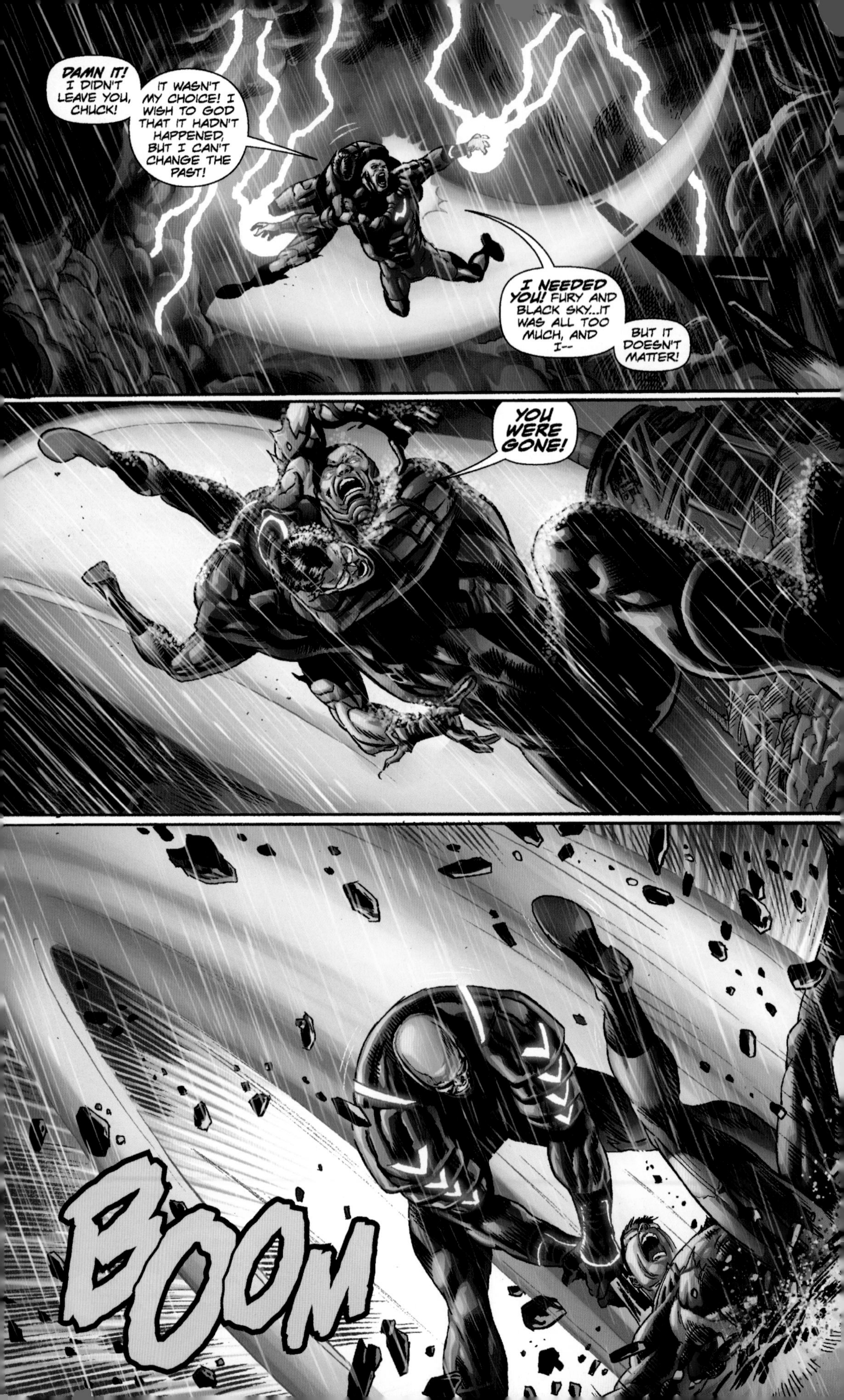

DAMN IT! I DIDN'T LEAVE YOU, CHUCK!
IT WASN'T MY CHOICE! I WISH TO GOD THAT IT HADN'T HAPPENED, BUT I CAN'T CHANGE THE PAST!
I NEEDED YOU! FURY AND BLACK SKY...IT WAS ALL TOO MUCH, AND I--
BUT IT DOESN'T MATTER!
YOU WERE GONE!
BOOM

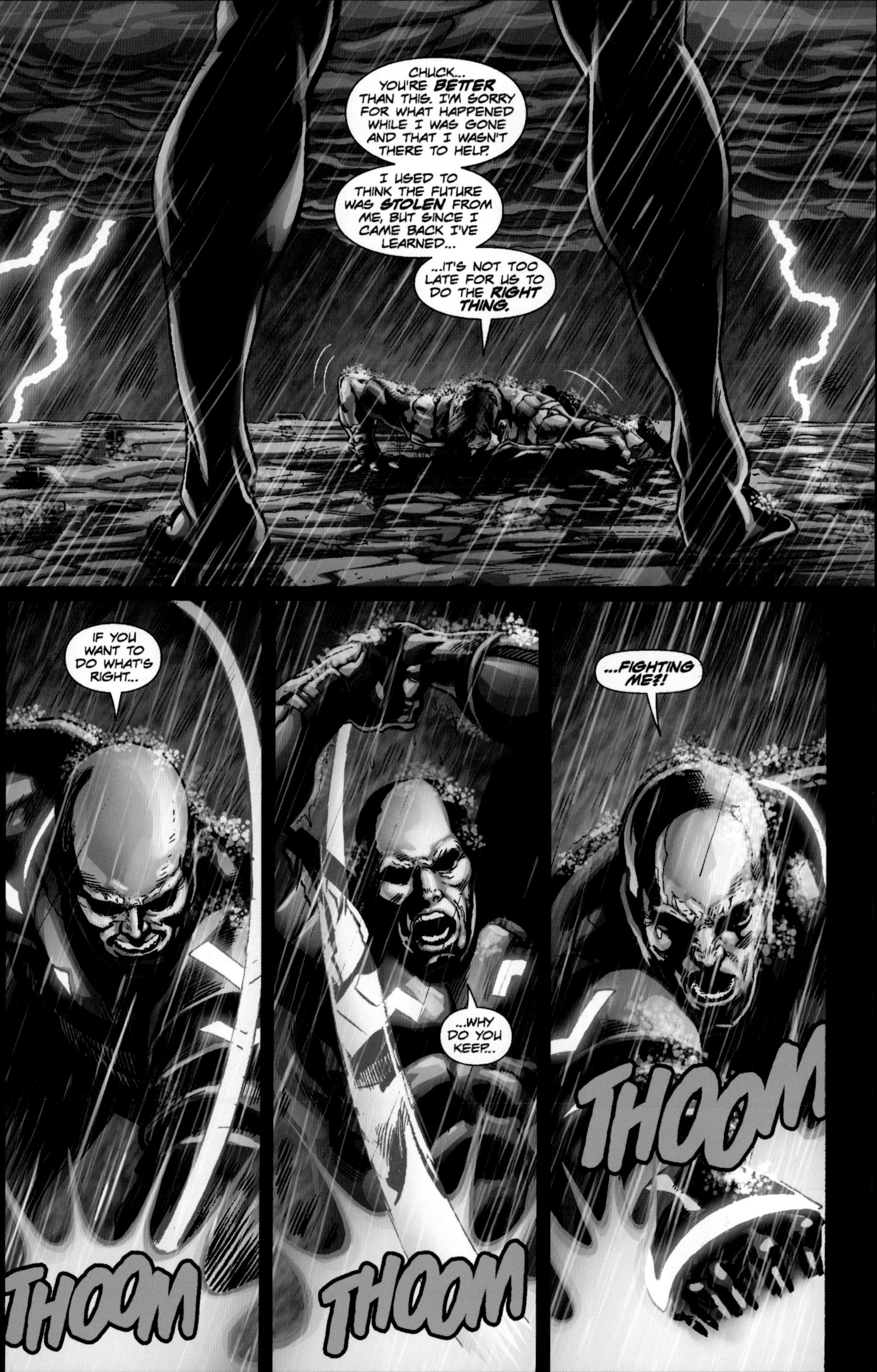
CHUCK... YOU'RE **BETTER** THAN THIS. I'M SORRY FOR WHAT HAPPENED WHILE I WAS GONE AND THAT I WASN'T THERE TO HELP.
I USED TO THINK THE FUTURE WAS **STOLEN** FROM ME, BUT SINCE I CAME BACK I'VE LEARNED...
...IT'S NOT TOO LATE FOR US TO DO THE **RIGHT THING.**
IF YOU WANT TO DO WHAT'S RIGHT...
THOOM
...WHY DO YOU KEEP...
THOOM
...FIGHTING ME?!
THOOM

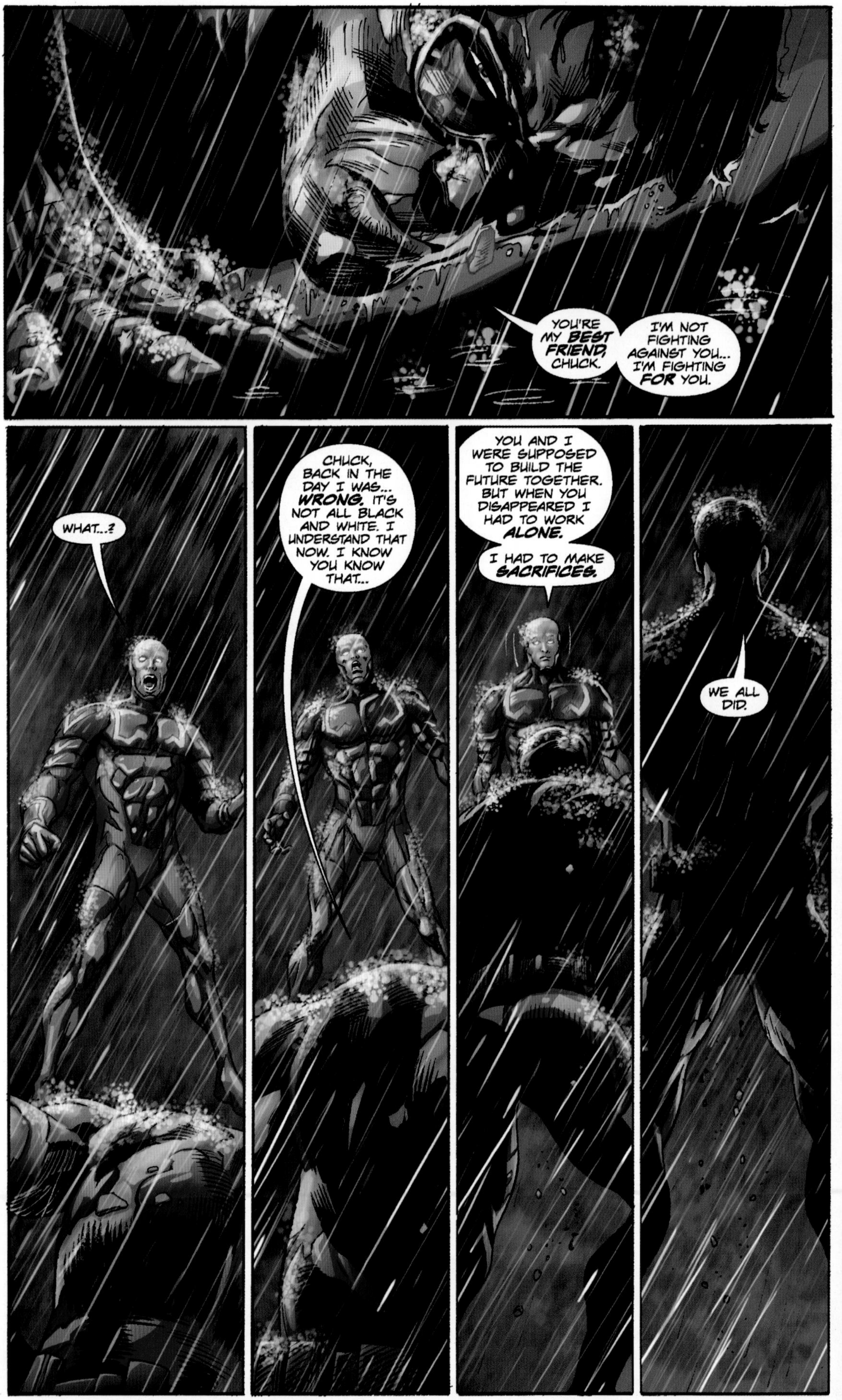
YOU'RE MY BEST FRIEND, CHUCK.
I'M NOT FIGHTING AGAINST YOU... I'M FIGHTING FOR YOU.
WHAT...?
CHUCK, BACK IN THE DAY I WAS... WRONG. IT'S NOT ALL BLACK AND WHITE. I UNDERSTAND THAT NOW. I KNOW YOU KNOW THAT...
YOU AND I WERE SUPPOSED TO BUILD THE FUTURE TOGETHER. BUT WHEN YOU DISAPPEARED I HAD TO WORK ALONE.
I HAD TO MAKE SACRIFICES.
WE ALL DID.

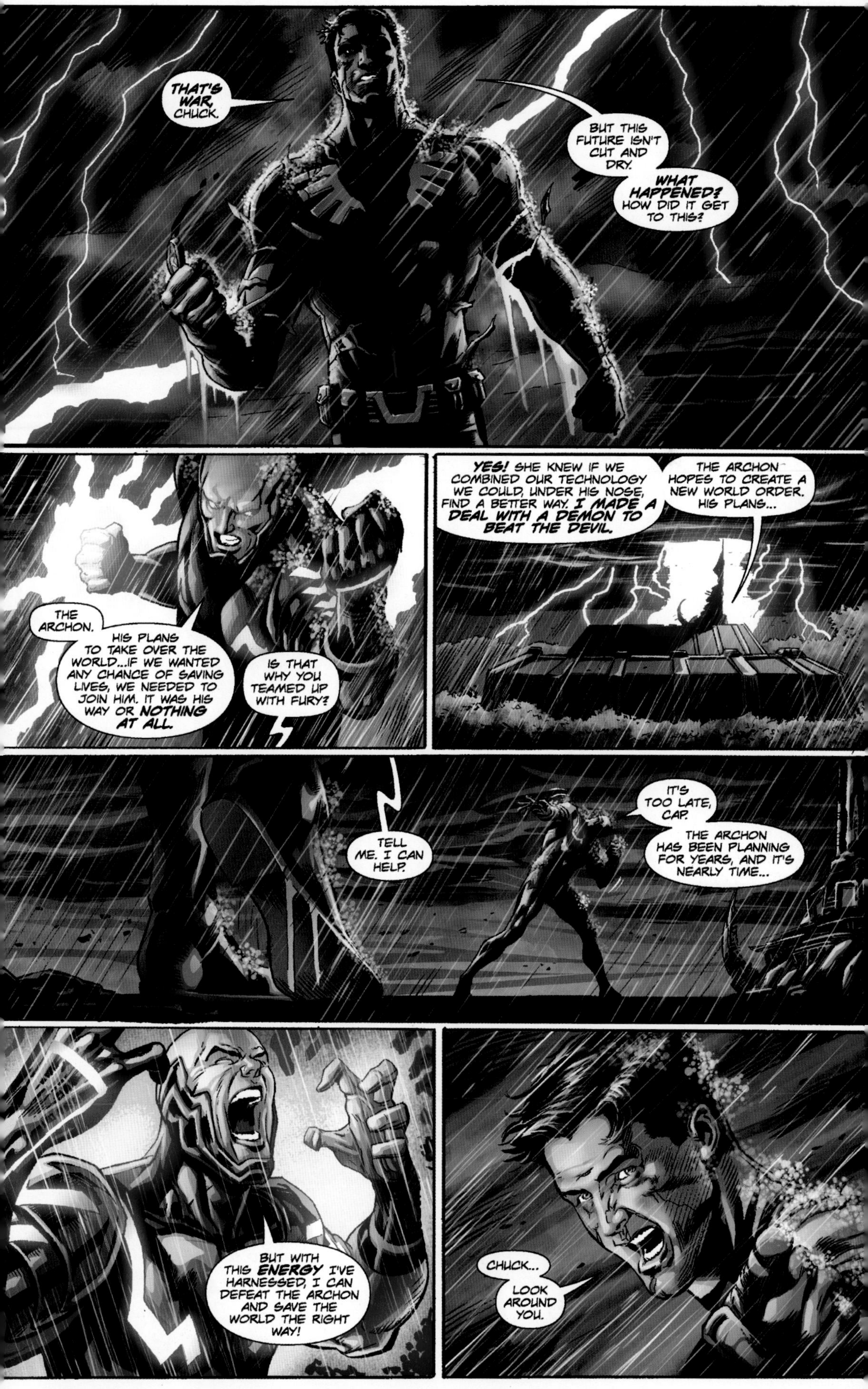
THAT'S WAR, CHUCK.
BUT THIS FUTURE ISN'T CUT AND DRY.
WHAT HAPPENED? HOW DID IT GET TO THIS?
THE ARCHON.
HIS PLANS TO TAKE OVER THE WORLD...IF WE WANTED ANY CHANCE OF SAVING LIVES, WE NEEDED TO JOIN HIM. IT WAS HIS WAY OR NOTHING AT ALL.
IS THAT WHY YOU TEAMED UP WITH FURY?
YES! SHE KNEW IF WE COMBINED OUR TECHNOLOGY WE COULD, UNDER HIS NOSE, FIND A BETTER WAY. I MADE A DEAL WITH A DEMON TO BEAT THE DEVIL.
THE ARCHON HOPES TO CREATE A NEW WORLD ORDER. HIS PLANS...
TELL ME. I CAN HELP.
IT'S TOO LATE, CAP.
THE ARCHON HAS BEEN PLANNING FOR YEARS, AND IT'S NEARLY TIME...
BUT WITH THIS ENERGY I'VE HARNESSED, I CAN DEFEAT THE ARCHON AND SAVE THE WORLD THE RIGHT WAY!
CHUCK...
LOOK AROUND YOU.

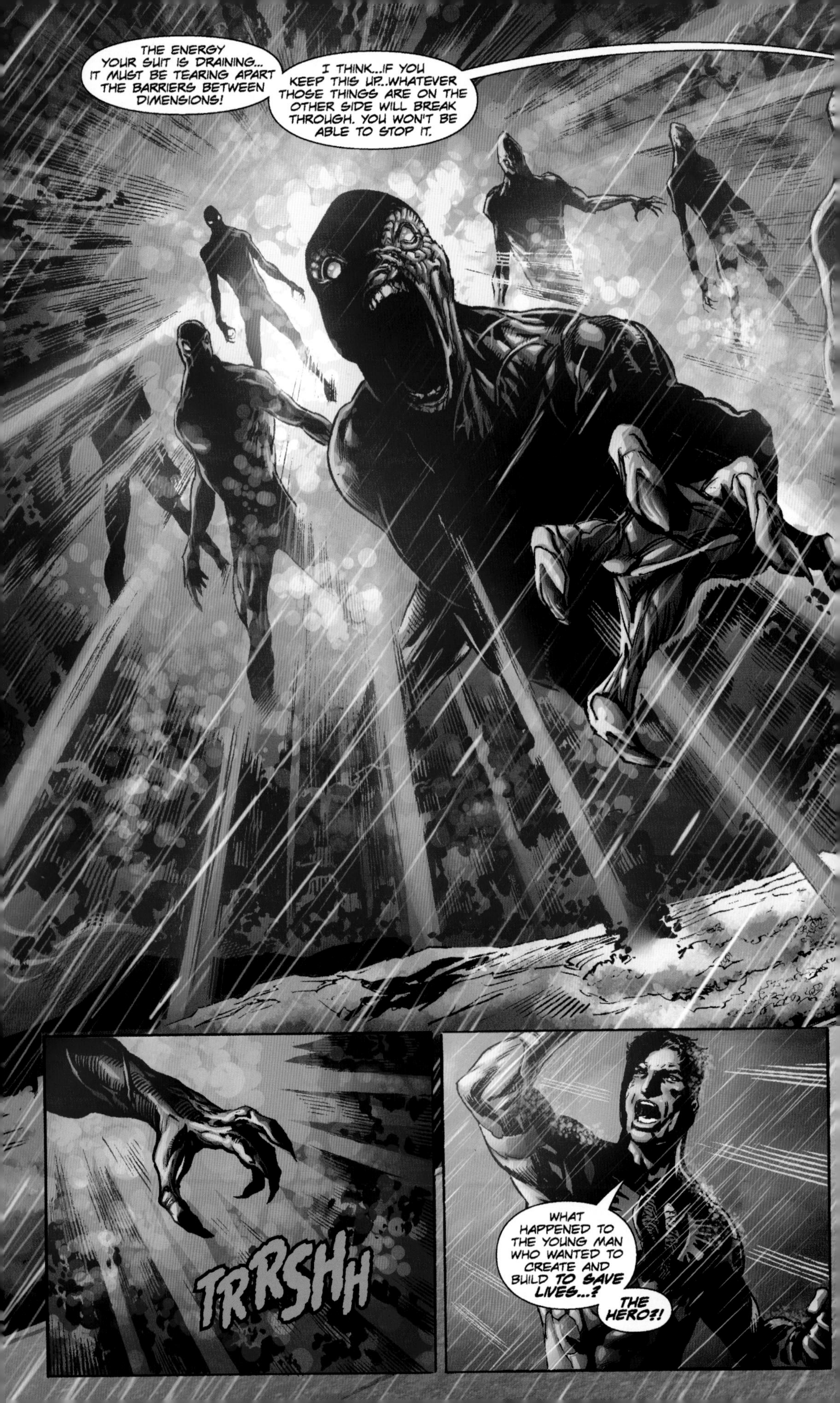
THE ENERGY YOUR SUIT IS DRAINING... IT MUST BE TEARING APART THE BARRIERS BETWEEN DIMENSIONS!
I THINK...IF YOU KEEP THIS UP..WHATEVER THOSE THINGS ARE ON THE OTHER SIDE WILL BREAK THROUGH. YOU WON'T BE ABLE TO STOP IT.
TRRSHH
WHAT HAPPENED TO THE YOUNG MAN WHO WANTED TO CREATE AND BUILD TO SAVE LIVES...?
THE HERO?!

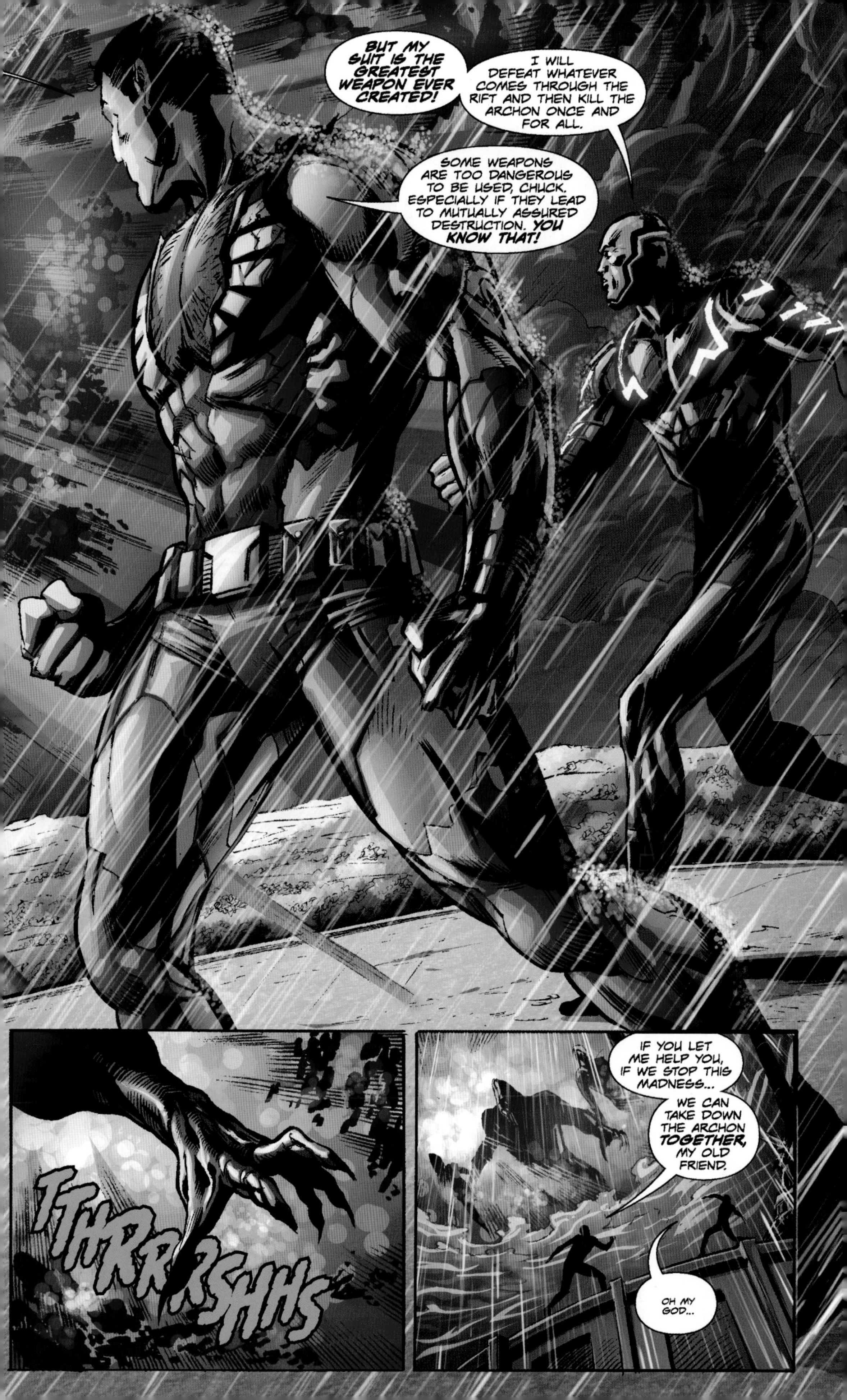
BUT MY SUIT IS THE GREATEST WEAPON EVER CREATED!
I WILL DEFEAT WHATEVER COMES THROUGH THE RIFT AND THEN KILL THE ARCHON ONCE AND FOR ALL.
SOME WEAPONS ARE TOO DANGEROUS TO BE USED, CHUCK. ESPECIALLY IF THEY LEAD TO MUTUALLY ASSURED DESTRUCTION. YOU KNOW THAT!
TTHRRSHHS
IF YOU LET ME HELP YOU, IF WE STOP THIS MADNESS...
WE CAN TAKE DOWN THE ARCHON TOGETHER, MY OLD FRIEND.
OH MY GOD...

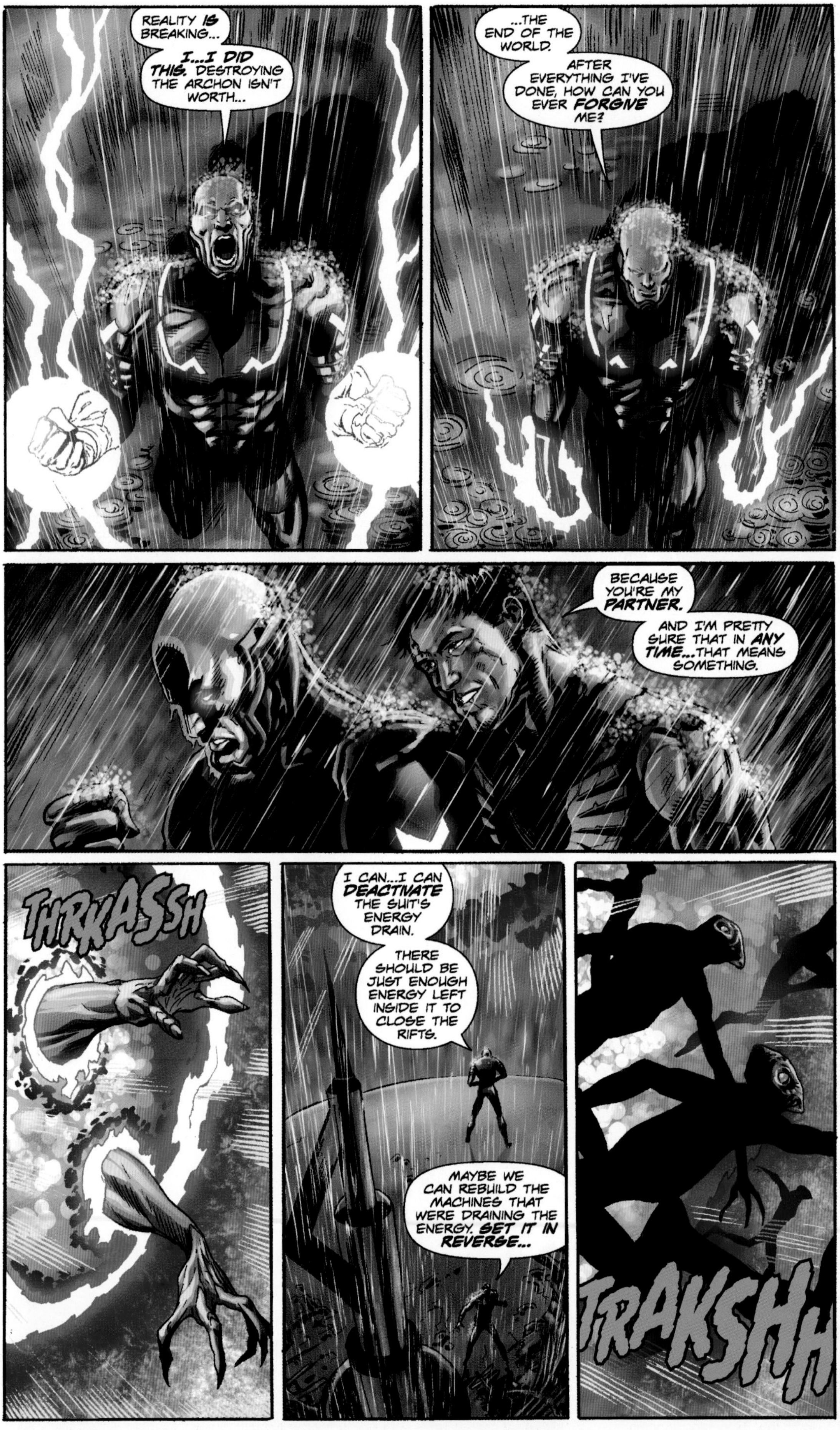
REALITY IS BREAKING...
I...I DID THIS. DESTROYING THE ARCHON ISN'T WORTH...
...THE END OF THE WORLD.
AFTER EVERYTHING I'VE DONE, HOW CAN YOU EVER FORGIVE ME?
BECAUSE YOU'RE MY PARTNER.
AND I'M PRETTY SURE THAT IN ANY TIME...THAT MEANS SOMETHING.
THRKASSH
I CAN...I CAN DEACTIVATE THE SUIT'S ENERGY DRAIN.
THERE SHOULD BE JUST ENOUGH ENERGY LEFT INSIDE IT TO CLOSE THE RIFTS.
MAYBE WE CAN REBUILD THE MACHINES THAT WERE DRAINING THE ENERGY. SET IT IN REVERSE...
TRAKSHH

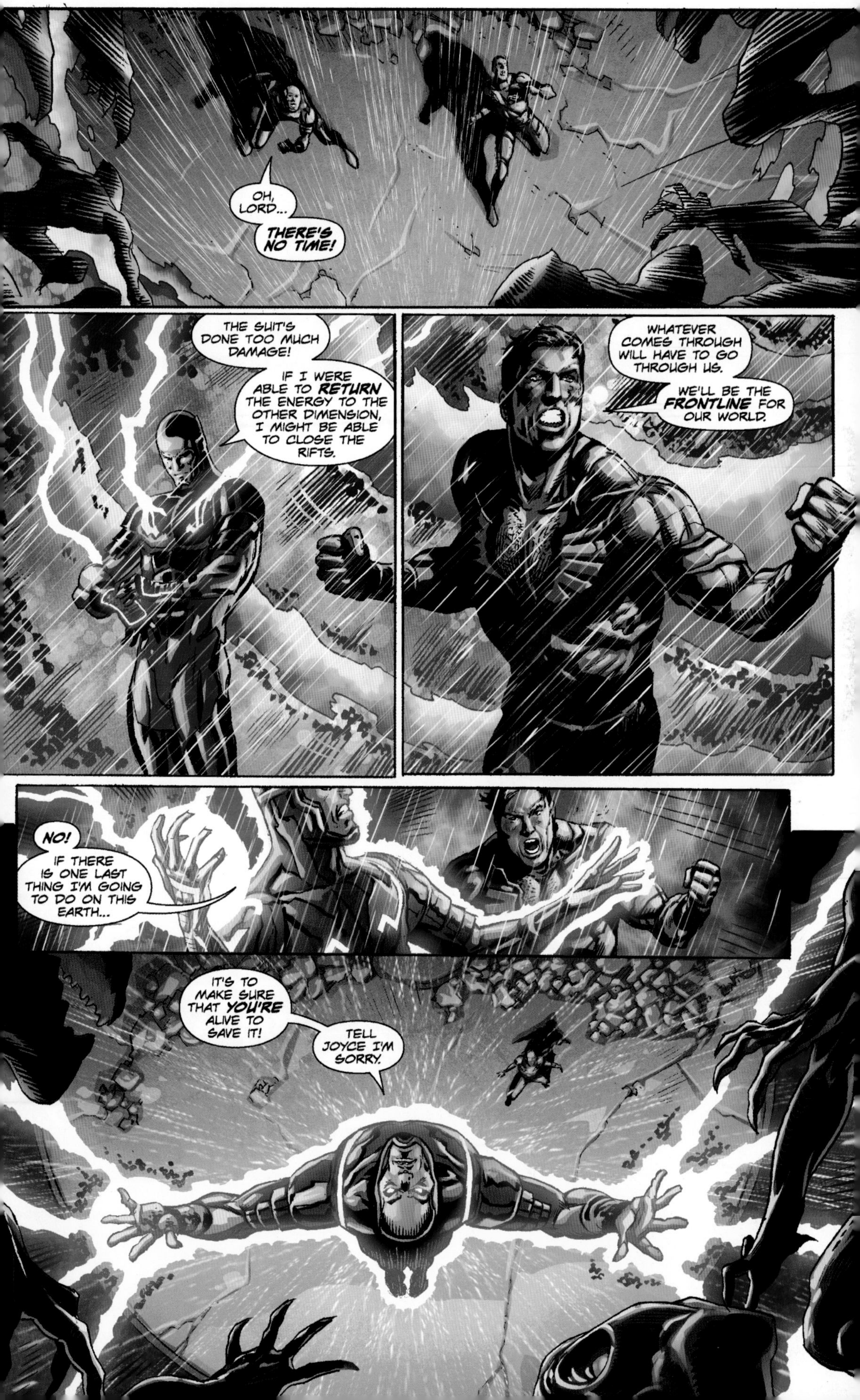
OH, LORD... THERE'S NO TIME!
THE SUIT'S DONE TOO MUCH DAMAGE!
IF I WERE ABLE TO RETURN THE ENERGY TO THE OTHER DIMENSION, I MIGHT BE ABLE TO CLOSE THE RIFTS.
WHATEVER COMES THROUGH WILL HAVE TO GO THROUGH US.
WE'LL BE THE FRONTLINE FOR OUR WORLD.
NO!
IF THERE IS ONE LAST THING I'M GOING TO DO ON THIS EARTH...
IT'S TO MAKE SURE THAT YOU'RE ALIVE TO SAVE IT!
TELL JOYCE I'M SORRY.

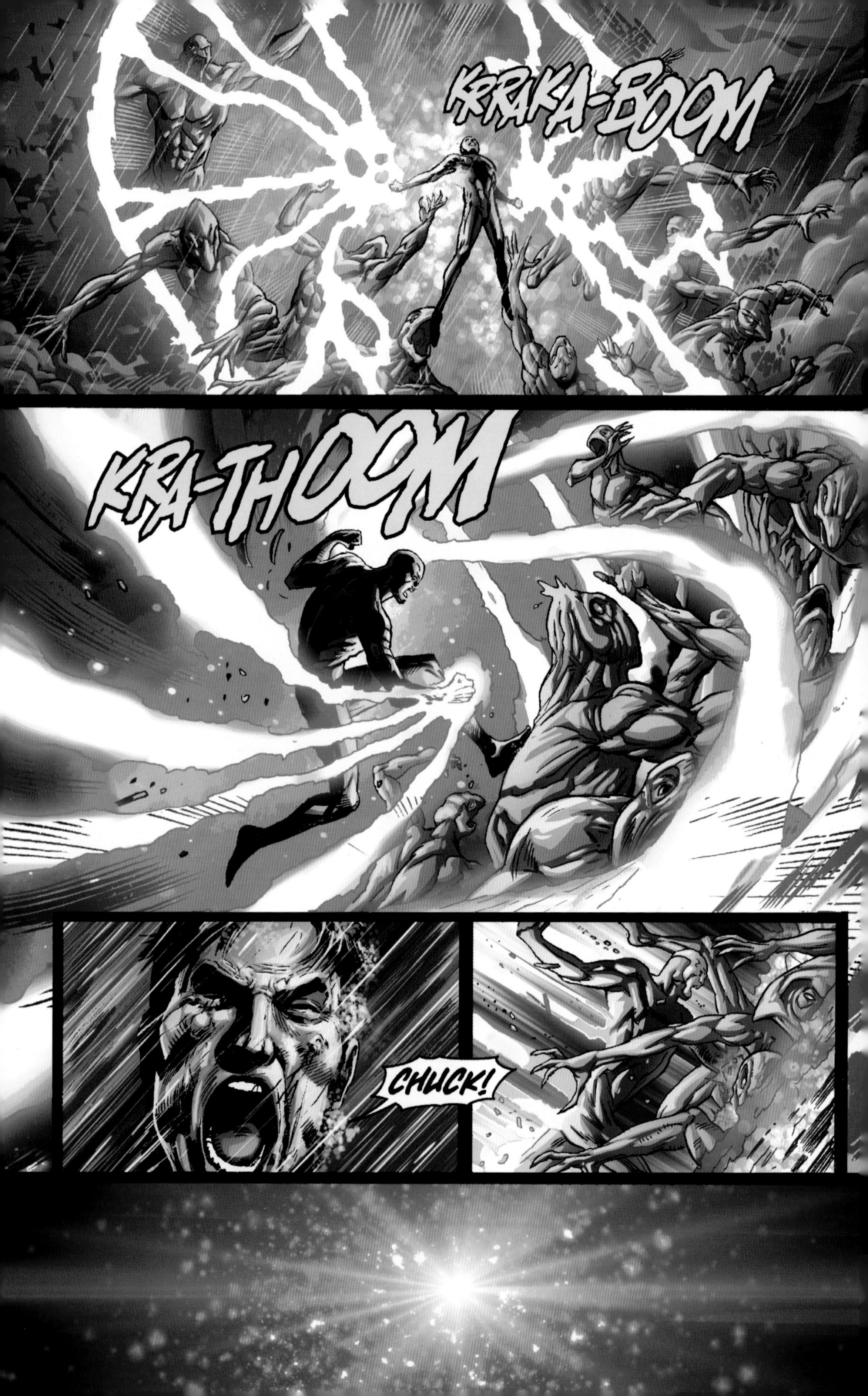
KRRAKA-BOOM
KRA-THOOM
CHUCK!

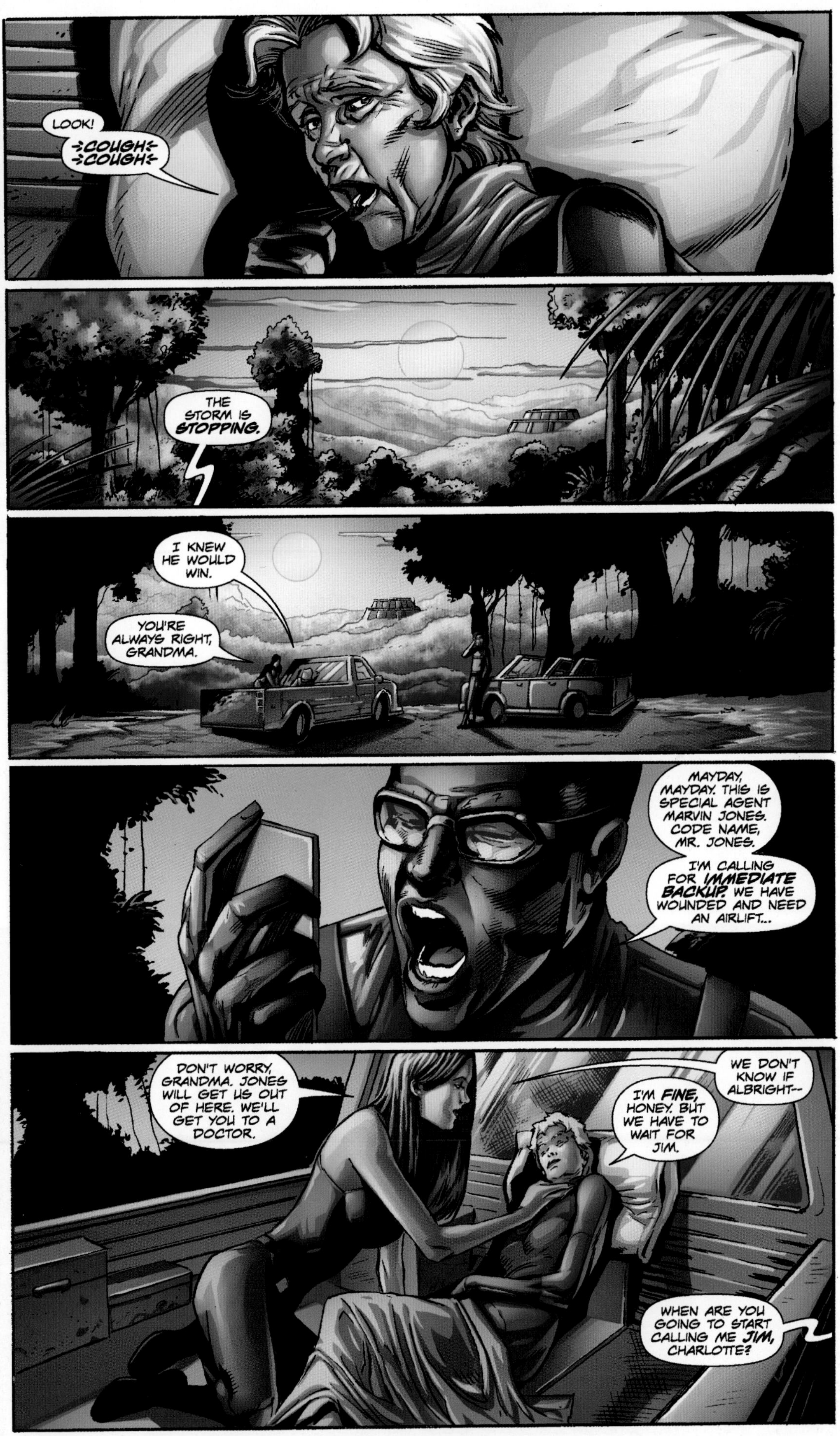
LOOK!
COUGH COUGH
THE STORM IS STOPPING.
I KNEW HE WOULD WIN.
YOU'RE ALWAYS RIGHT, GRANDMA.
MAYDAY, MAYDAY. THIS IS SPECIAL AGENT MARVIN JONES. CODE NAME, MR. JONES.
I'M CALLING FOR IMMEDIATE BACKUP. WE HAVE WOUNDED AND NEED AN AIRLIFT...
DON'T WORRY, GRANDMA. JONES WILL GET US OUT OF HERE. WE'LL GET YOU TO A DOCTOR.
WE DON'T KNOW IF ALBRIGHT--
I'M FINE, HONEY. BUT WE HAVE TO WAIT FOR JIM.
WHEN ARE YOU GOING TO START CALLING ME JIM, CHARLOTTE?

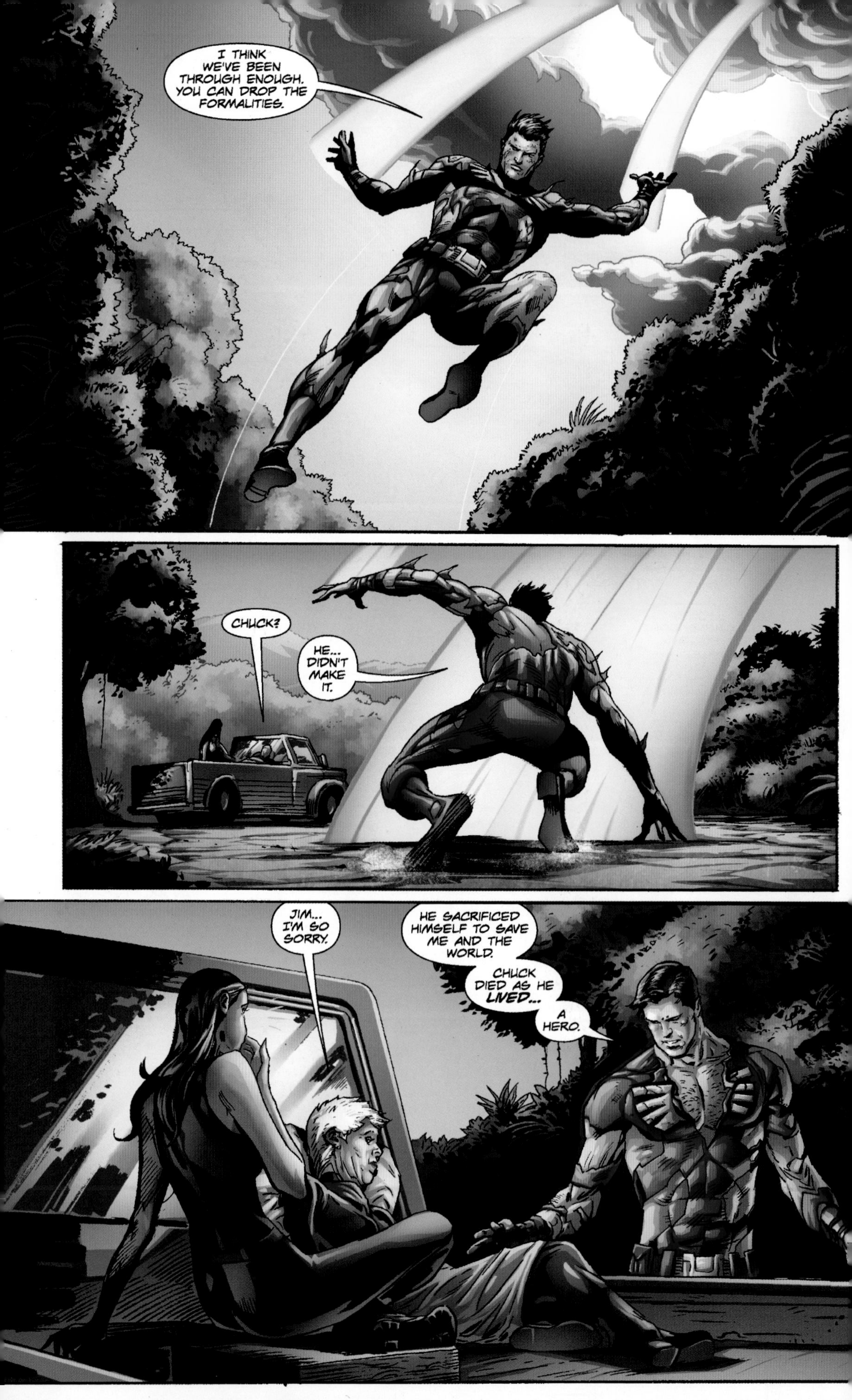
I THINK WE'VE BEEN THROUGH ENOUGH. YOU CAN DROP THE FORMALITIES.
CHUCK?
HE... DIDN'T MAKE IT.
JIM... I'M SO SORRY.
HE SACRIFICED HIMSELF TO SAVE ME AND THE WORLD.
CHUCK DIED AS HE LIVED...
A HERO.

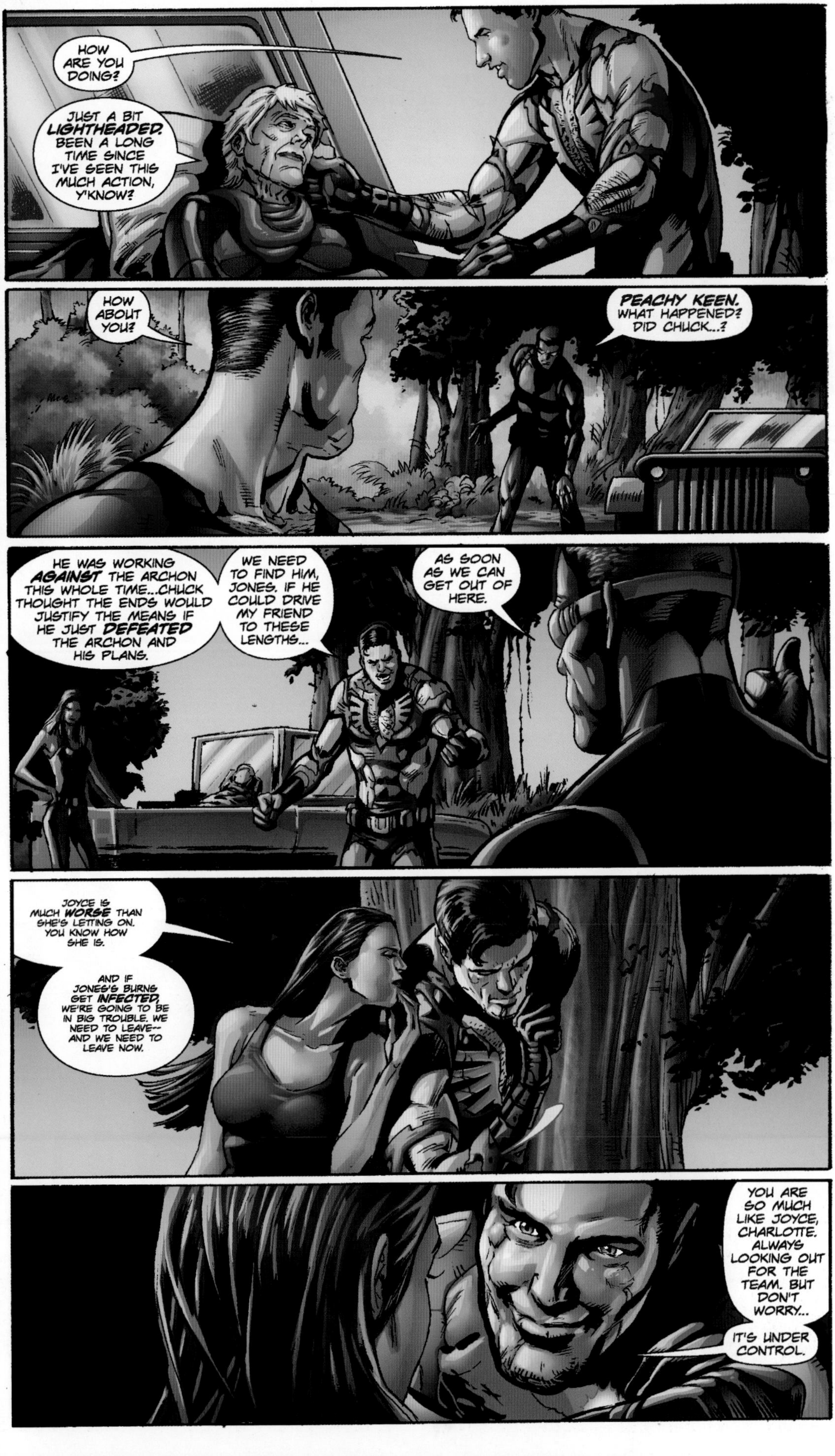
HOW ARE YOU DOING?
JUST A BIT LIGHTHEADED. BEEN A LONG TIME SINCE I'VE SEEN THIS MUCH ACTION, Y'KNOW?
HOW ABOUT YOU?
PEACHY KEEN. WHAT HAPPENED? DID CHUCK...?
HE WAS WORKING AGAINST THE ARCHON THIS WHOLE TIME...CHUCK THOUGHT THE ENDS WOULD JUSTIFY THE MEANS IF HE JUST DEFEATED THE ARCHON AND HIS PLANS.
WE NEED TO FIND HIM, JONES. IF HE COULD DRIVE MY FRIEND TO THESE LENGTHS...
AS SOON AS WE CAN GET OUT OF HERE.
JOYCE IS MUCH WORSE THAN SHE'S LETTING ON. YOU KNOW HOW SHE IS.
AND IF JONES'S BURNS GET INFECTED, WE'RE GOING TO BE IN BIG TROUBLE. WE NEED TO LEAVE-- AND WE NEED TO LEAVE NOW.
YOU ARE SO MUCH LIKE JOYCE, CHARLOTTE. ALWAYS LOOKING OUT FOR THE TEAM. BUT DON'T WORRY...
IT'S UNDER CONTROL.

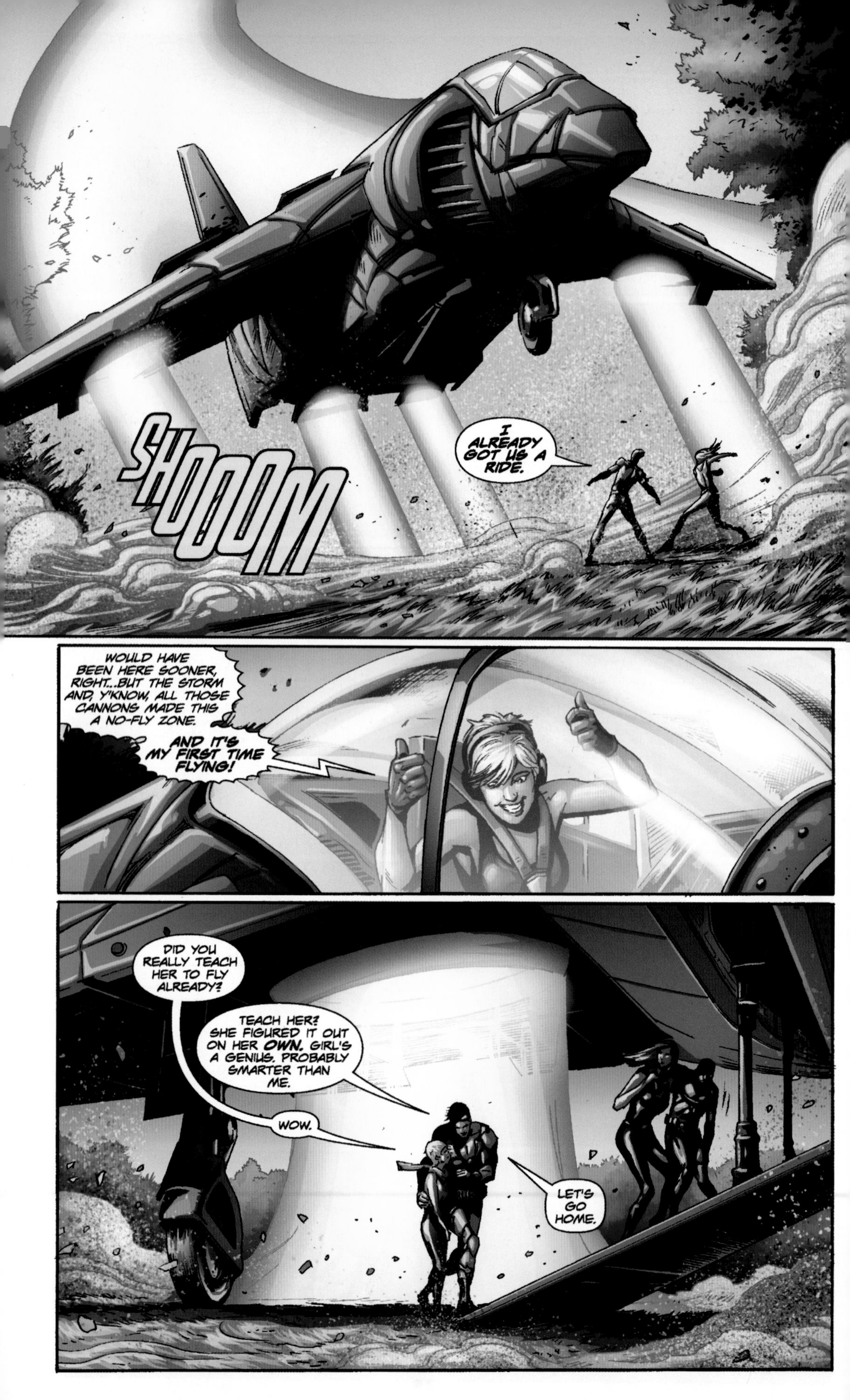
SHOOOM
I ALREADY GOT US A RIDE.
WOULD HAVE BEEN HERE SOONER, RIGHT...BUT THE STORM AND, Y'KNOW, ALL THOSE CANNONS MADE THIS A NO-FLY ZONE.
AND IT'S MY FIRST TIME FLYING!
DID YOU REALLY TEACH HER TO FLY ALREADY?
TEACH HER? SHE FIGURED IT OUT ON HER OWN. GIRL'S A GENIUS. PROBABLY SMARTER THAN ME.
WOW.
LET'S GO HOME.

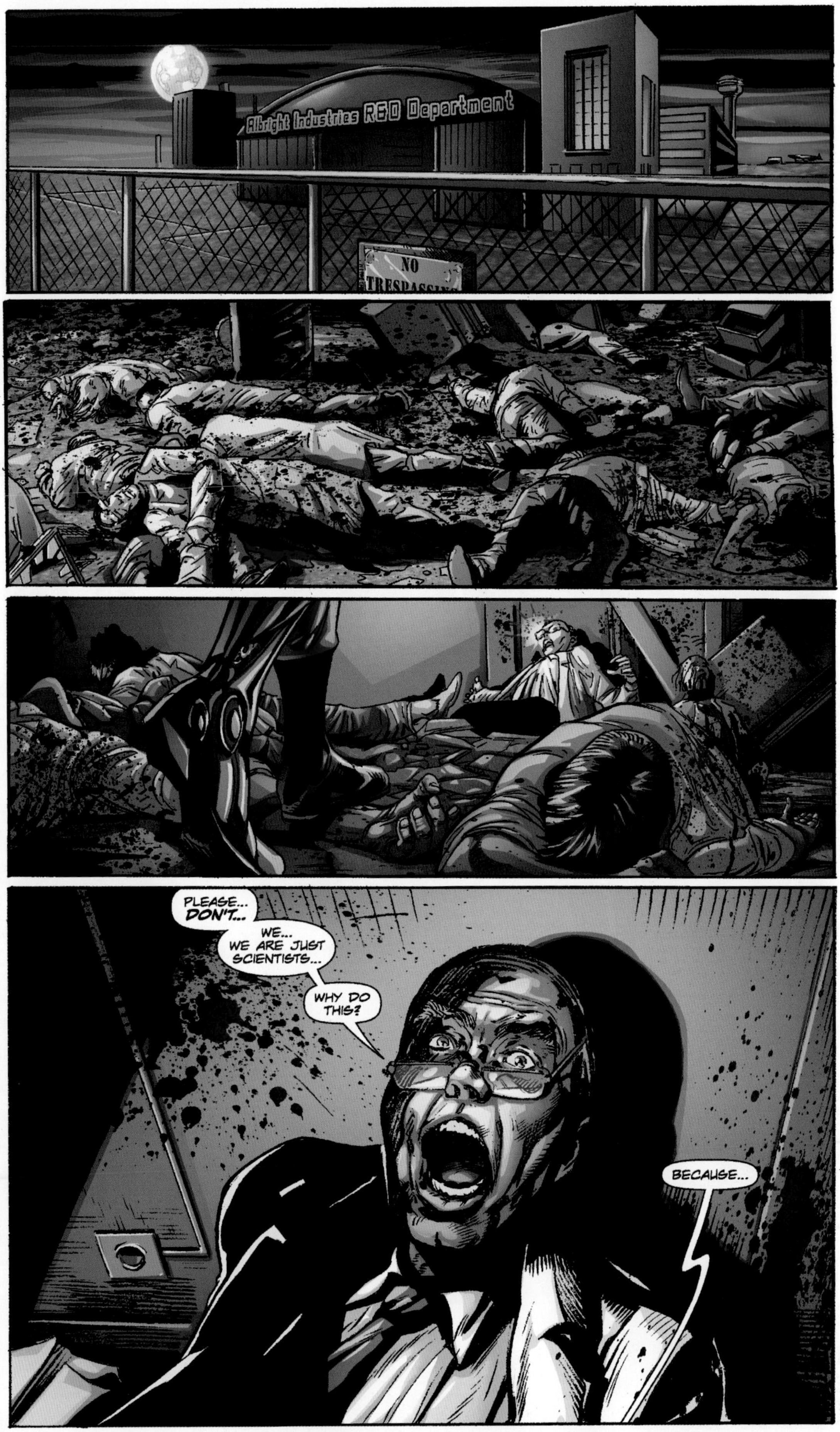
Albright Industries R&D Department
NO TRESPASSING
PLEASE... DON'T...
WE... WE ARE JUST SCIENTISTS...
WHY DO THIS?
BECAUSE...

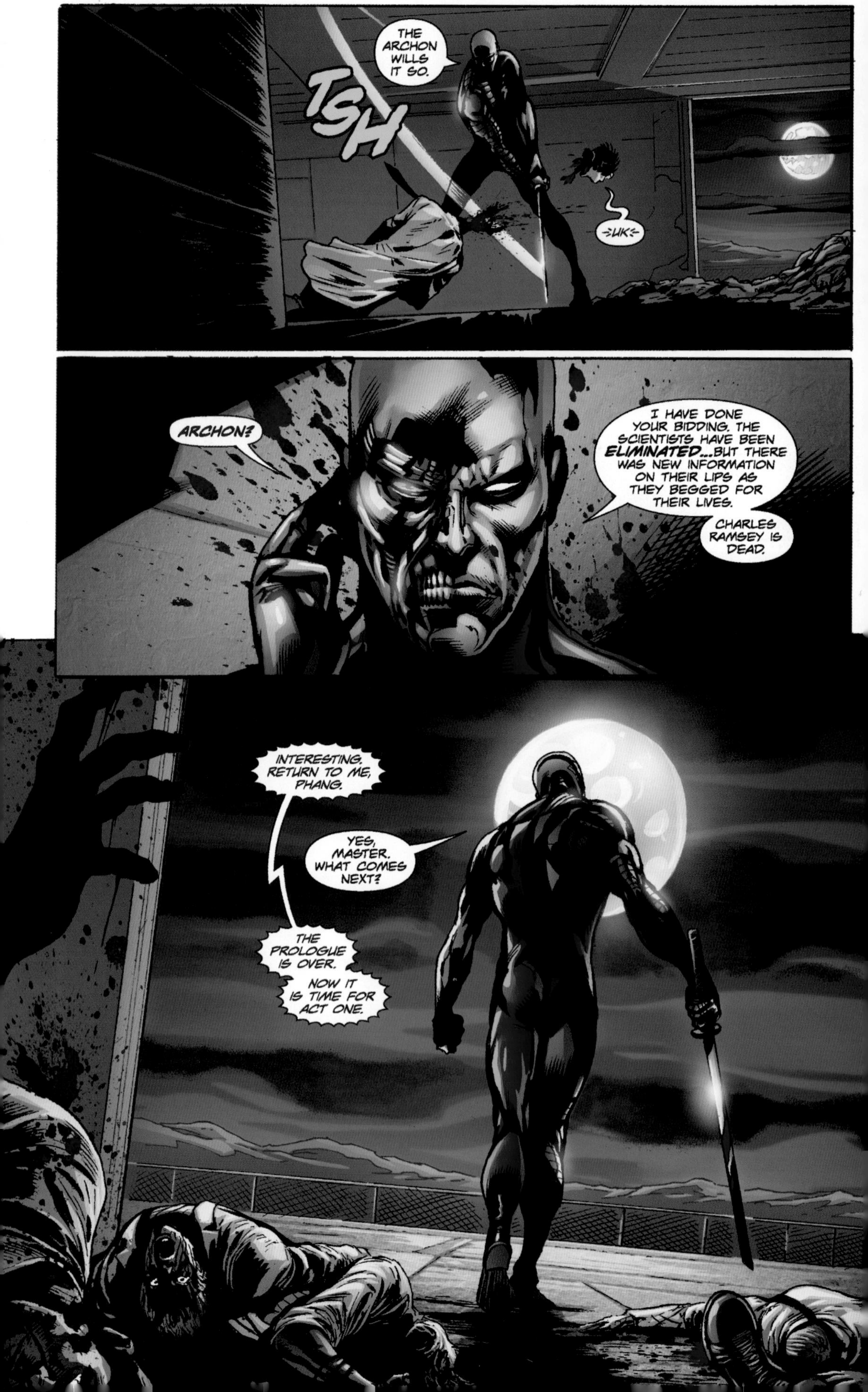
THE ARCHON WILLS IT SO.
TSH
UK
ARCHON?
I HAVE DONE YOUR BIDDING. THE SCIENTISTS HAVE BEEN ELIMINATED...BUT THERE WAS NEW INFORMATION ON THEIR LIPS AS THEY BEGGED FOR THEIR LIVES.
CHARLES RAMSEY IS DEAD.
INTERESTING. RETURN TO ME, PHANG.
YES, MASTER. WHAT COMES NEXT?
THE PROLOGUE IS OVER.
NOW IT IS TIME FOR ACT ONE.

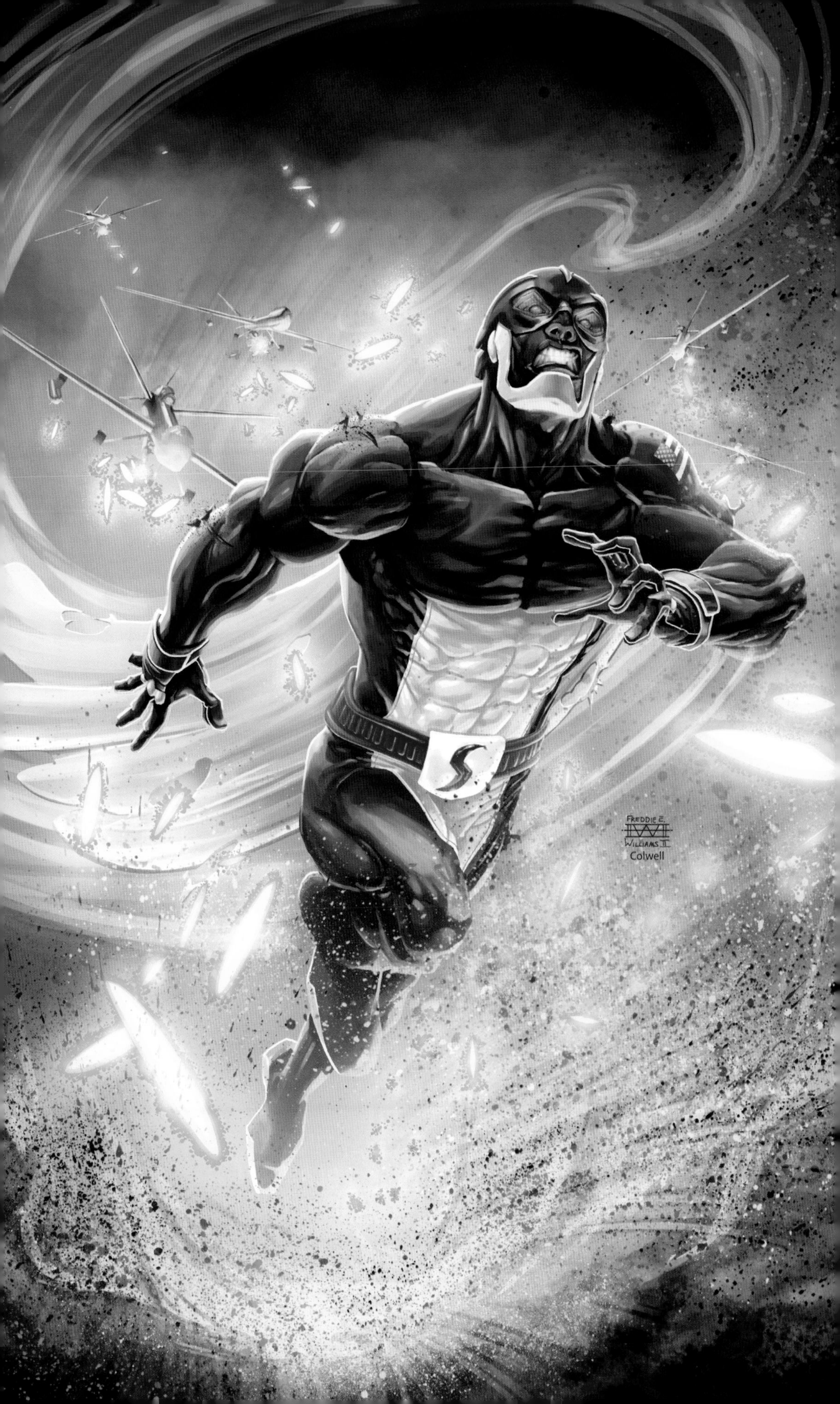
FREDDIE E. WILLIAMS II
Colwell

SKYMAN ™

Sergeant Eric Reid was injured in Afghanistan, but due to an experimental military program, he gained the ability to fly, aided by a powerful belt that utilizes technology similar to that which powers Captain Midnight's glider wings. However, the Skyman Program was not all it seemed, and, with the help of Captain Midnight, Sergeant Reid survived the program's assassins and exposed its corruption. Now, he's free to pursue heroism on his own as **Skyman**.

Project Black Sky is a covert government agency established to protect Earth from the potential of extraterrestrial threats. The first on the scene of any reported UFO crash or sighting, these brave men and women shoot first and ask questions later when it comes to protecting the planet.

FIRST CONTACT

STORY BY **SPENCER CUSHING**

PENCILS BY **MANUEL GARCIA**

INKS BY **BIT**

COLORS BY **MARTA MARTÍNEZ**

LETTERING BY **NATE PIEKOS** OF **BLAMBOT**®

CHAPTER BREAK ART BY **FREDDIE WILLIAMS II** AND **JEREMY COLWELL**

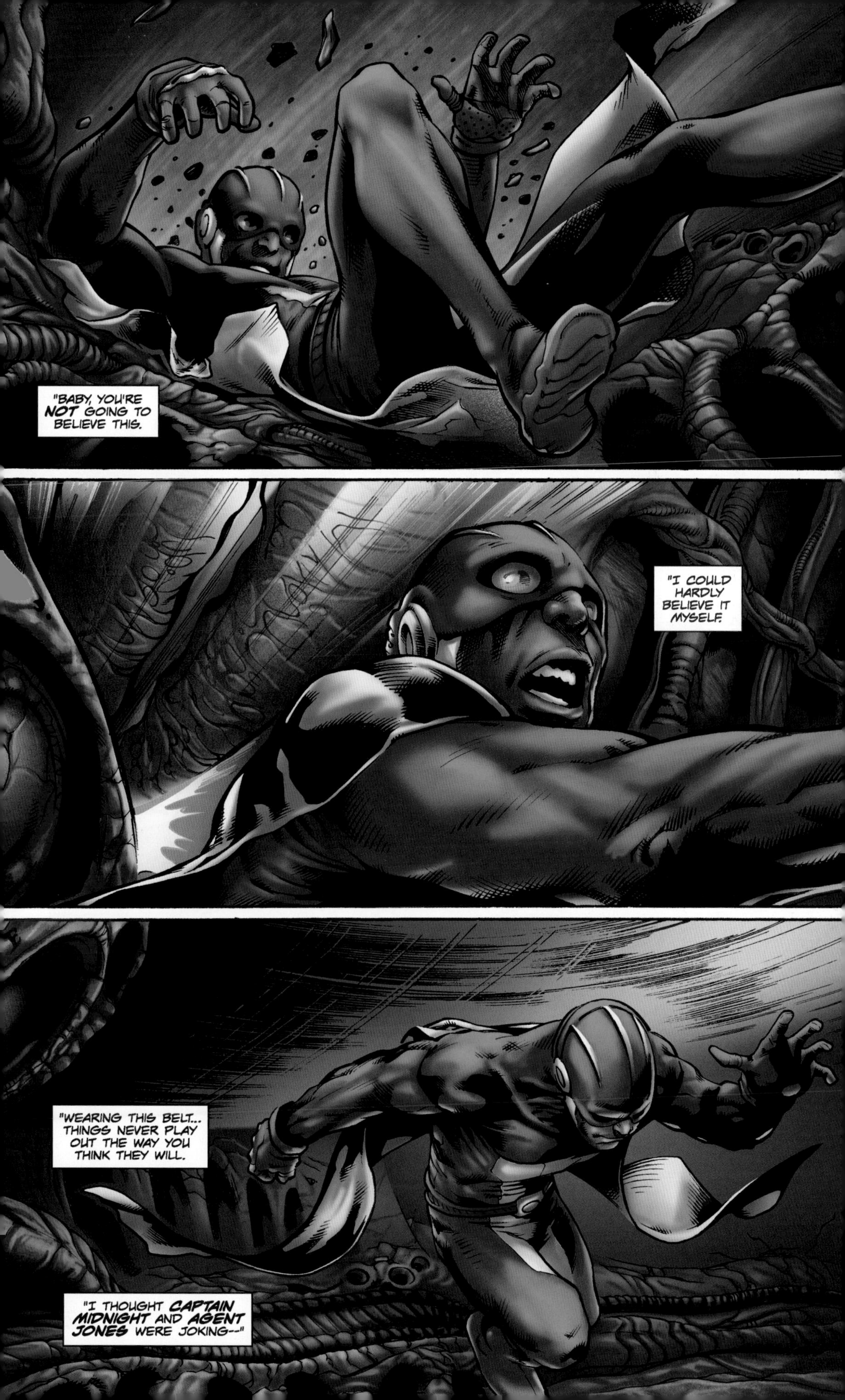
"BABY, YOU'RE **NOT** GOING TO BELIEVE THIS.
"I COULD HARDLY BELIEVE IT MYSELF.
"WEARING THIS BELT... THINGS NEVER PLAY OUT THE WAY YOU THINK THEY WILL.
"I THOUGHT **CAPTAIN MIDNIGHT** AND **AGENT JONES** WERE JOKING--"

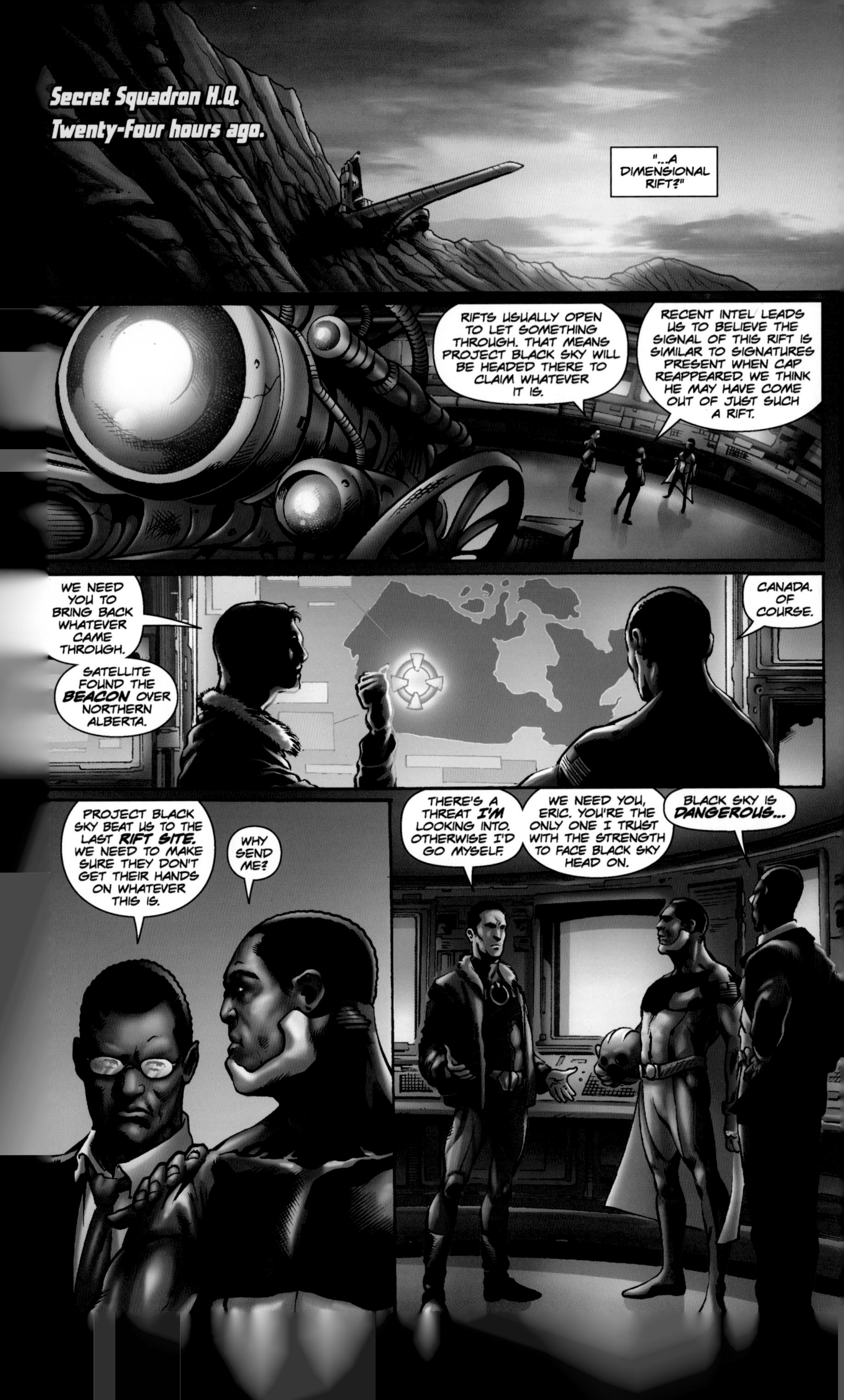
Secret Squadron H.Q.
Twenty-Four hours ago.
"...A DIMENSIONAL RIFT?"
RIFTS USUALLY OPEN TO LET SOMETHING THROUGH. THAT MEANS PROJECT BLACK SKY WILL BE HEADED THERE TO CLAIM WHATEVER IT IS.
RECENT INTEL LEADS US TO BELIEVE THE SIGNAL OF THIS RIFT IS SIMILAR TO SIGNATURES PRESENT WHEN CAP REAPPEARED. WE THINK HE MAY HAVE COME OUT OF JUST SUCH A RIFT.
WE NEED YOU TO BRING BACK WHATEVER CAME THROUGH.
SATELLITE FOUND THE BEACON OVER NORTHERN ALBERTA.
CANADA. OF COURSE.
PROJECT BLACK SKY BEAT US TO THE LAST RIFT SITE. WE NEED TO MAKE SURE THEY DON'T GET THEIR HANDS ON WHATEVER THIS IS.
WHY SEND ME?
THERE'S A THREAT I'M LOOKING INTO. OTHERWISE I'D GO MYSELF.
WE NEED YOU, ERIC. YOU'RE THE ONLY ONE I TRUST WITH THE STRENGTH TO FACE BLACK SKY HEAD ON.
BLACK SKY IS DANGEROUS...

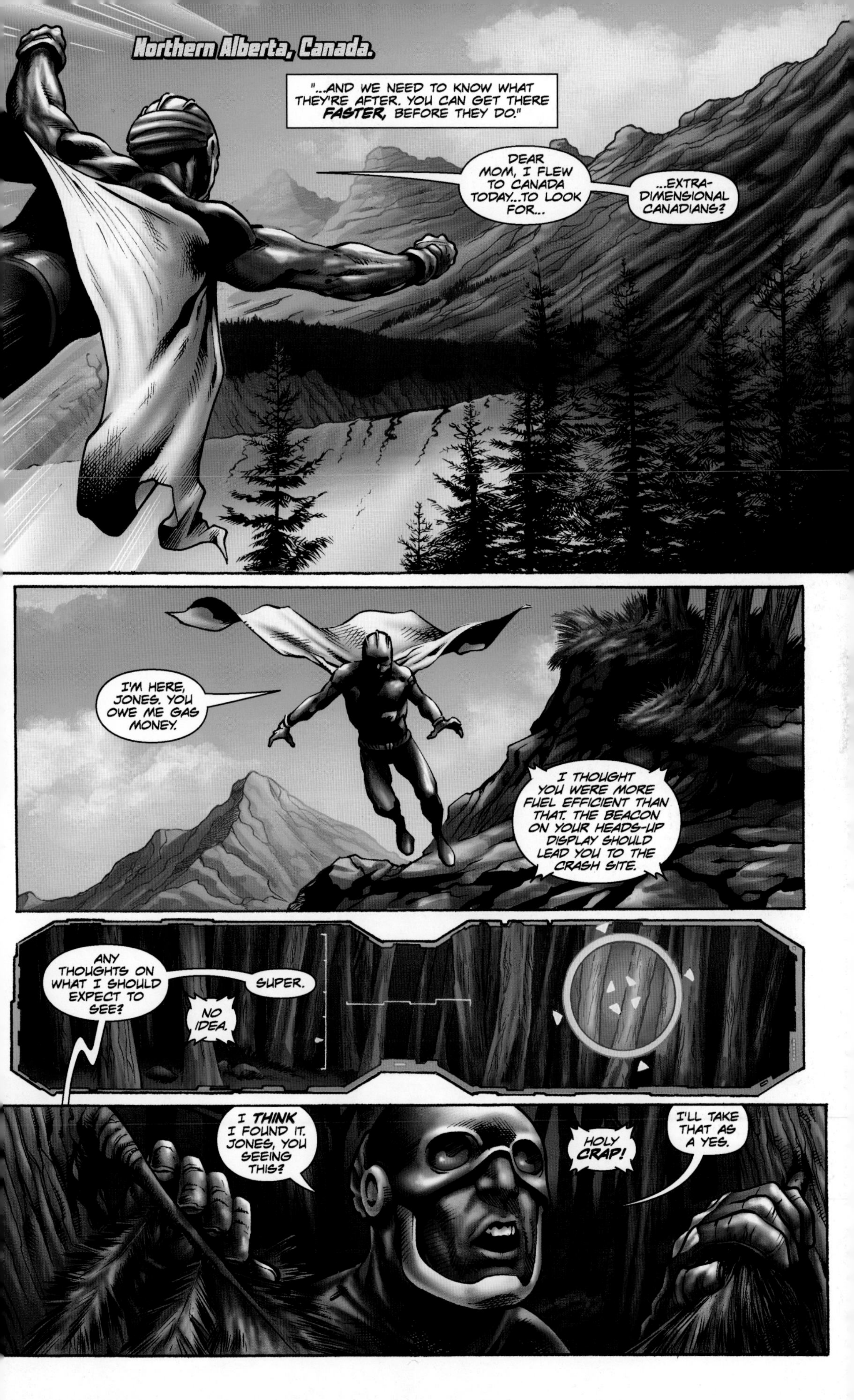
Northern Alberta, Canada.
"...AND WE NEED TO KNOW WHAT THEY'RE AFTER. YOU CAN GET THERE FASTER, BEFORE THEY DO."
DEAR MOM, I FLEW TO CANADA TODAY...TO LOOK FOR...
...EXTRA-DIMENSIONAL CANADIANS?
I'M HERE, JONES. YOU OWE ME GAS MONEY.
I THOUGHT YOU WERE MORE FUEL EFFICIENT THAN THAT. THE BEACON ON YOUR HEADS-UP DISPLAY SHOULD LEAD YOU TO THE CRASH SITE.
ANY THOUGHTS ON WHAT I SHOULD EXPECT TO SEE?
NO IDEA.
SUPER.
I THINK I FOUND IT. JONES, YOU SEEING THIS?
HOLY CRAP!
I'LL TAKE THAT AS A YES.

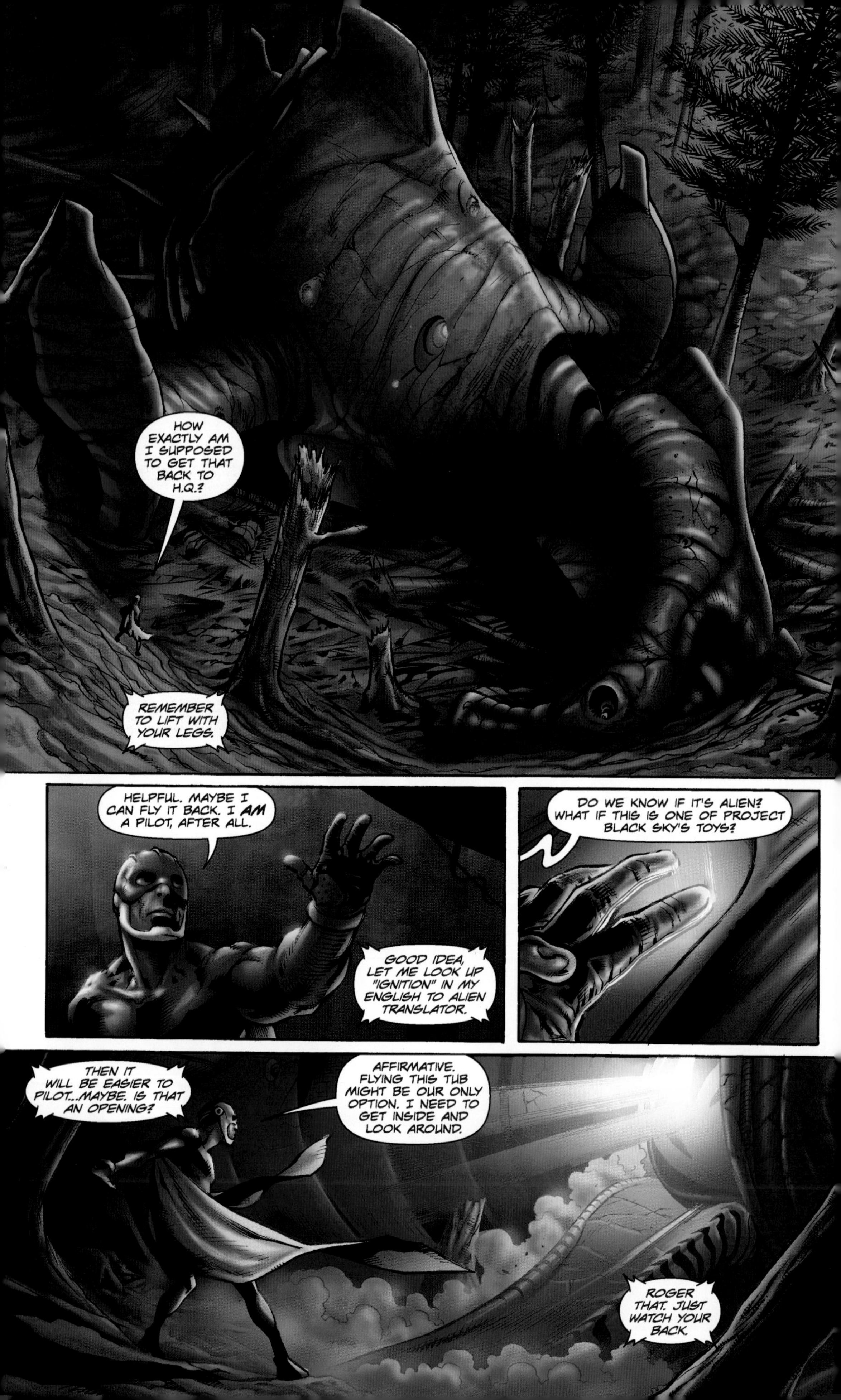
HOW EXACTLY AM I SUPPOSED TO GET THAT BACK TO H.Q.?
REMEMBER TO LIFT WITH YOUR LEGS.
HELPFUL. MAYBE I CAN FLY IT BACK. I **AM** A PILOT, AFTER ALL.
GOOD IDEA, LET ME LOOK UP "IGNITION" IN MY ENGLISH TO ALIEN TRANSLATOR.
DO WE KNOW IF IT'S ALIEN? WHAT IF THIS IS ONE OF PROJECT BLACK SKY'S TOYS?
THEN IT WILL BE EASIER TO PILOT...MAYBE. IS THAT AN OPENING?
AFFIRMATIVE. FLYING THIS TUB MIGHT BE OUR ONLY OPTION. I NEED TO GET INSIDE AND LOOK AROUND.
ROGER THAT. JUST WATCH YOUR BACK.

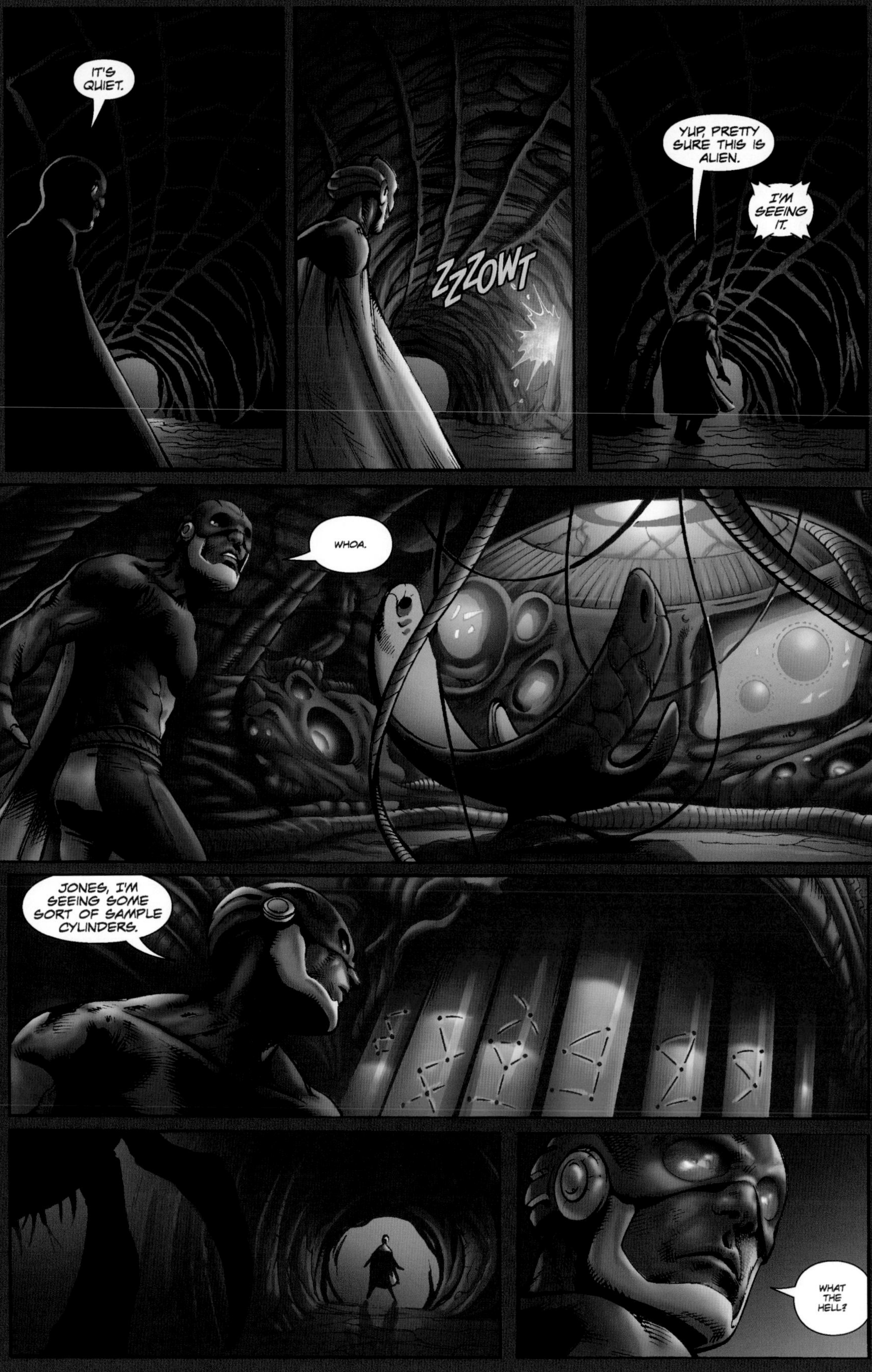
IT'S QUIET.
ZZZOWT
YUP, PRETTY SURE THIS IS ALIEN.
I'M SEEING IT.
WHOA.
JONES, I'M SEEING SOME SORT OF SAMPLE CYLINDERS.
WHAT THE HELL?

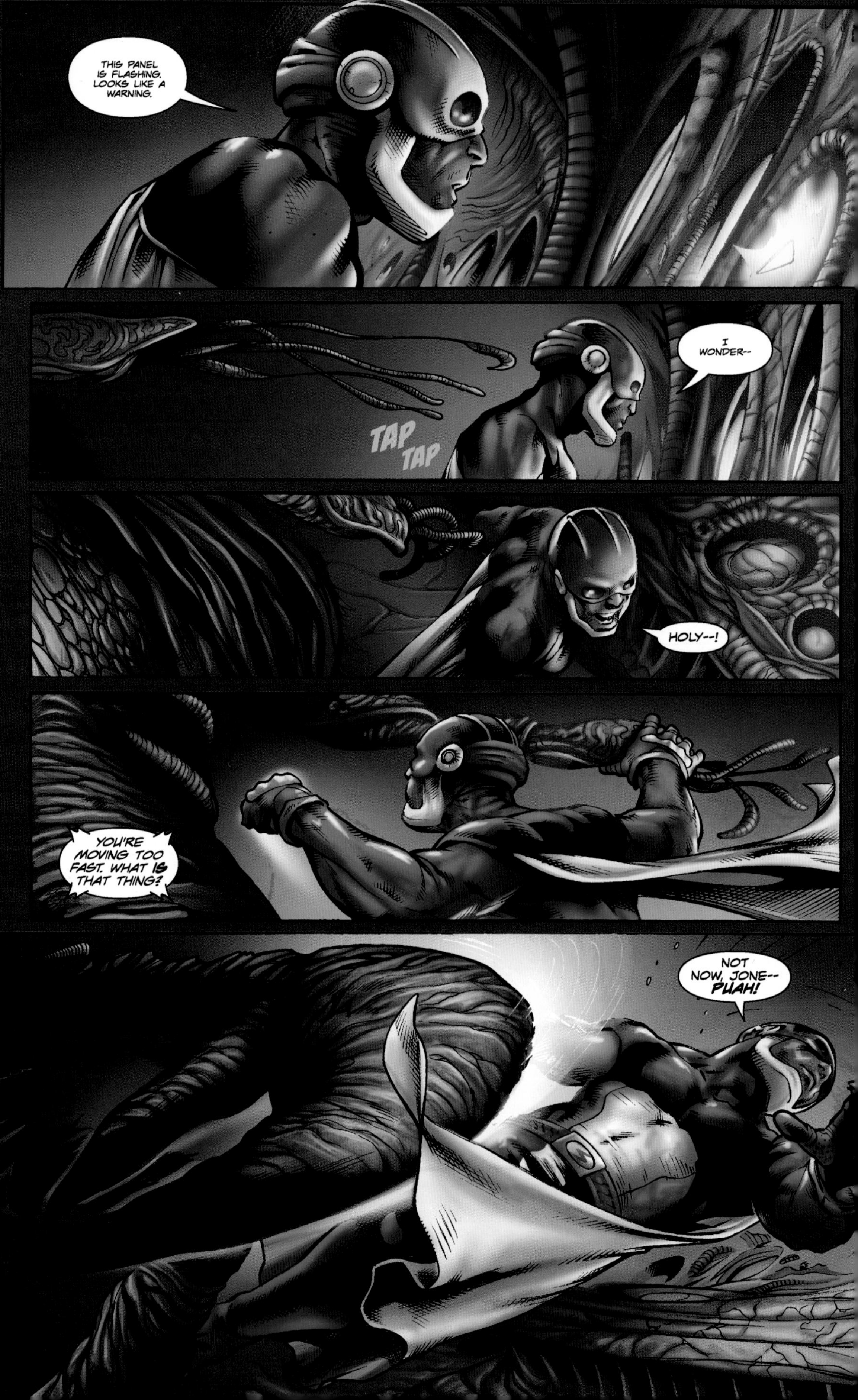
THIS PANEL IS FLASHING. LOOKS LIKE A WARNING.
I WONDER--
TAP TAP
HOLY--!
YOU'RE MOVING TOO FAST. WHAT IS THAT THING?
NOT NOW, JONE-- PUAH!

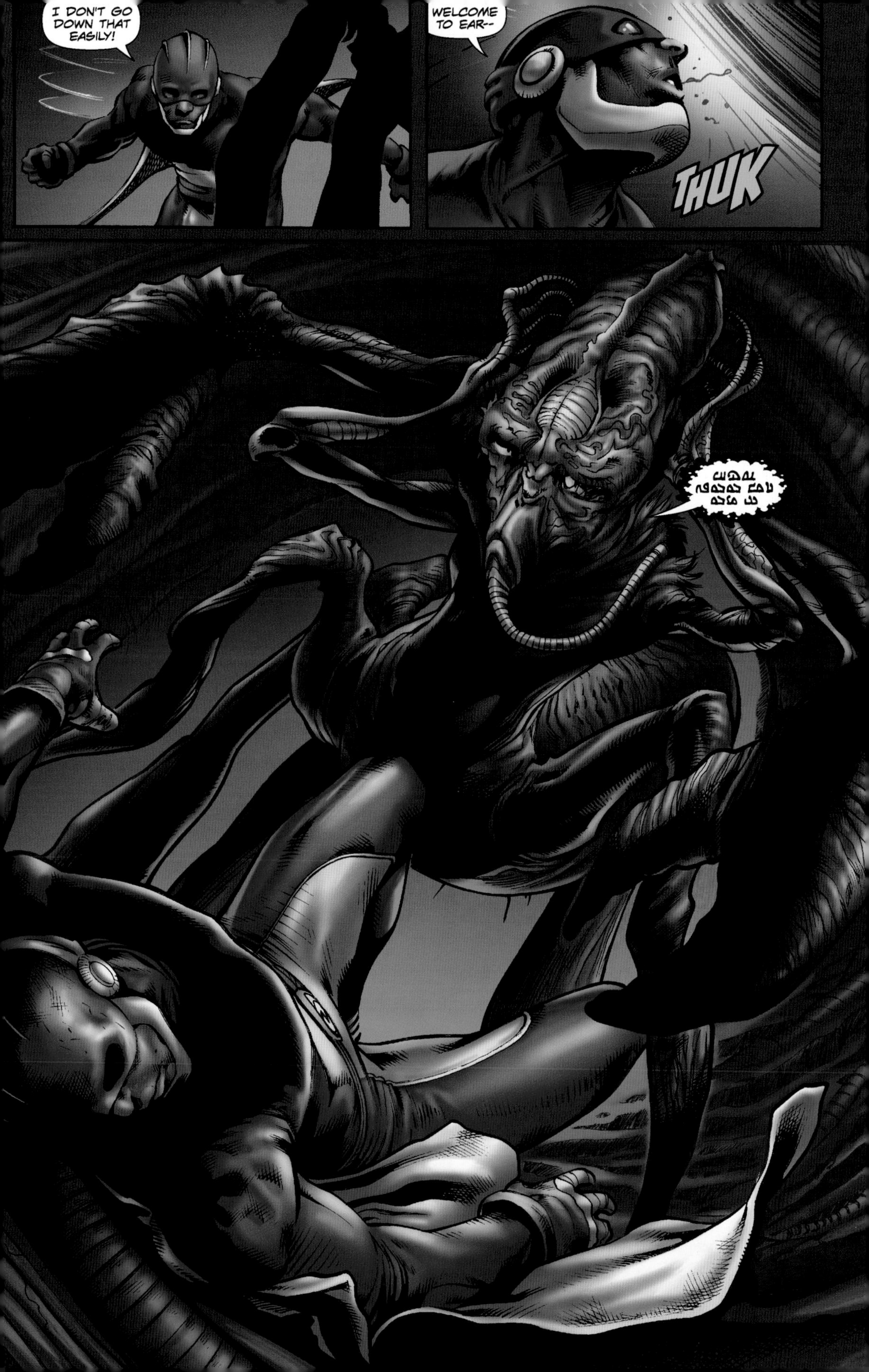
I DON'T GO DOWN THAT EASILY!
WELCOME TO EAR--
THUK

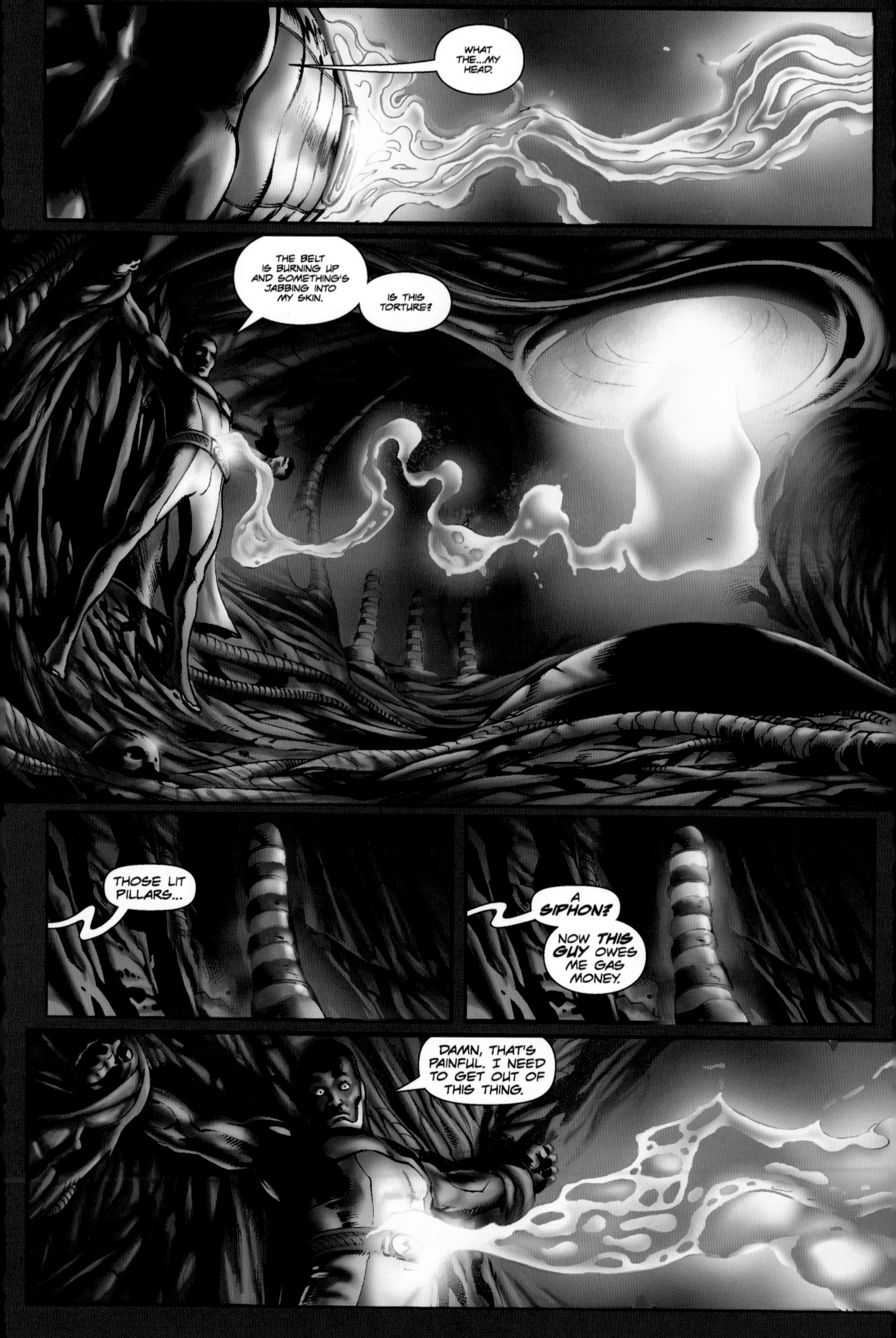
WHAT THE...MY HEAD.
THE BELT IS BURNING UP AND SOMETHING'S JABBING INTO MY SKIN.
IS THIS TORTURE?
THOSE LIT PILLARS...
A SIPHON?
NOW THIS GUY OWES ME GAS MONEY.
DAMN, THAT'S PAINFUL. I NEED TO GET OUT OF THIS THING.

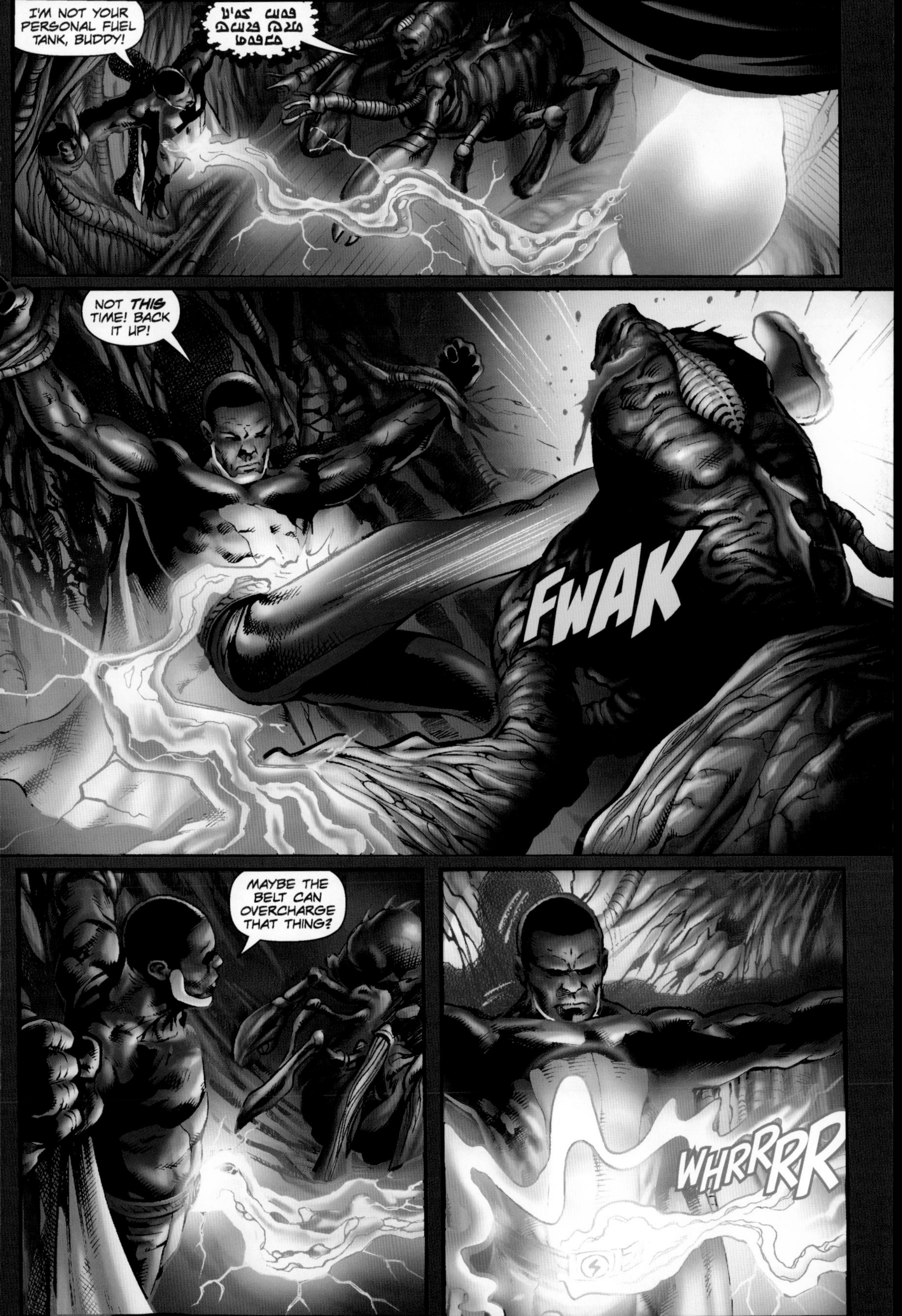
I'M NOT YOUR PERSONAL FUEL TANK, BUDDY!
NOT THIS TIME! BACK IT UP!
FWAK
MAYBE THE BELT CAN OVERCHARGE THAT THING?
WHRRRR

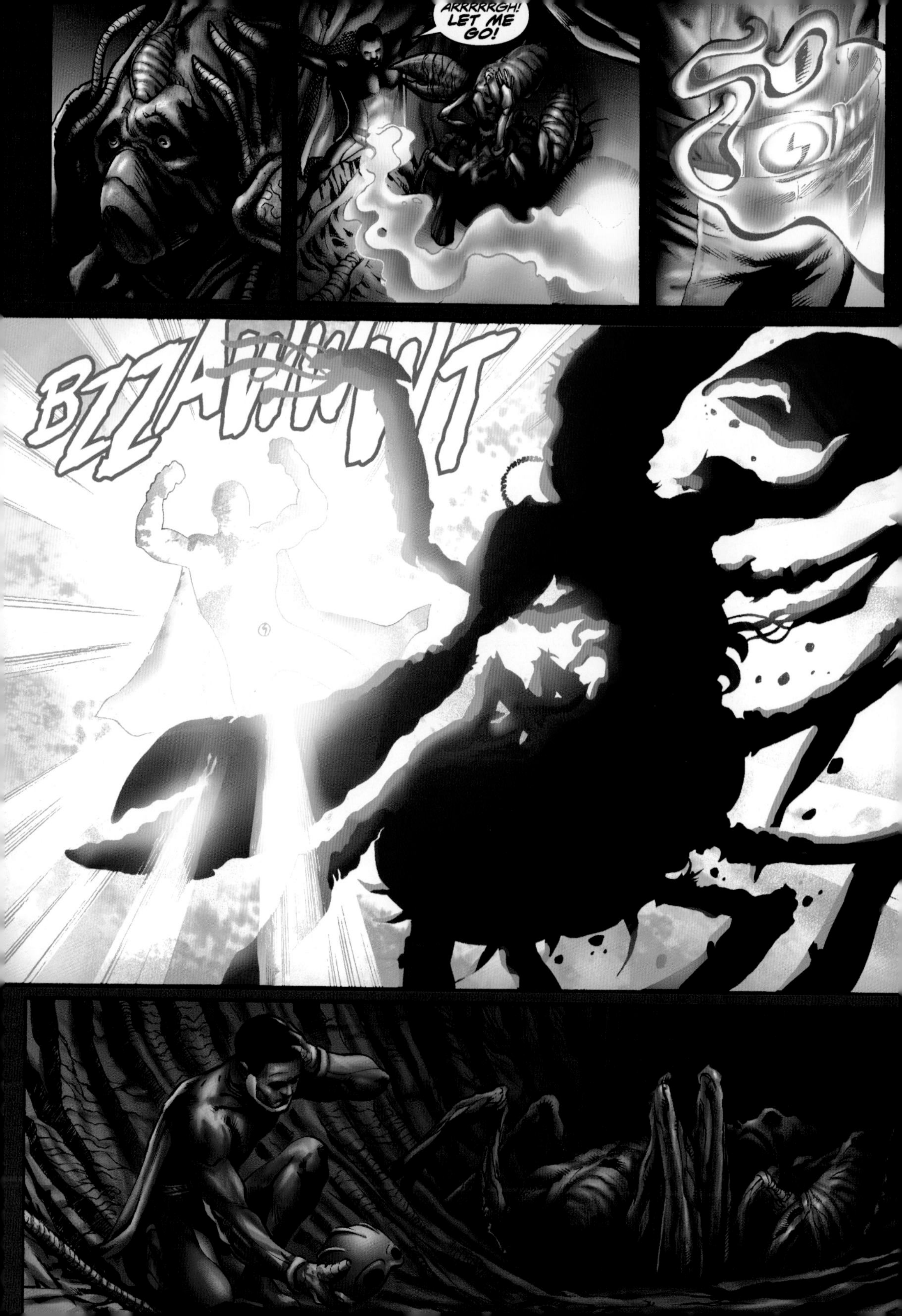
ARRRRRGH! LET ME GO!
BZZAAAAAT

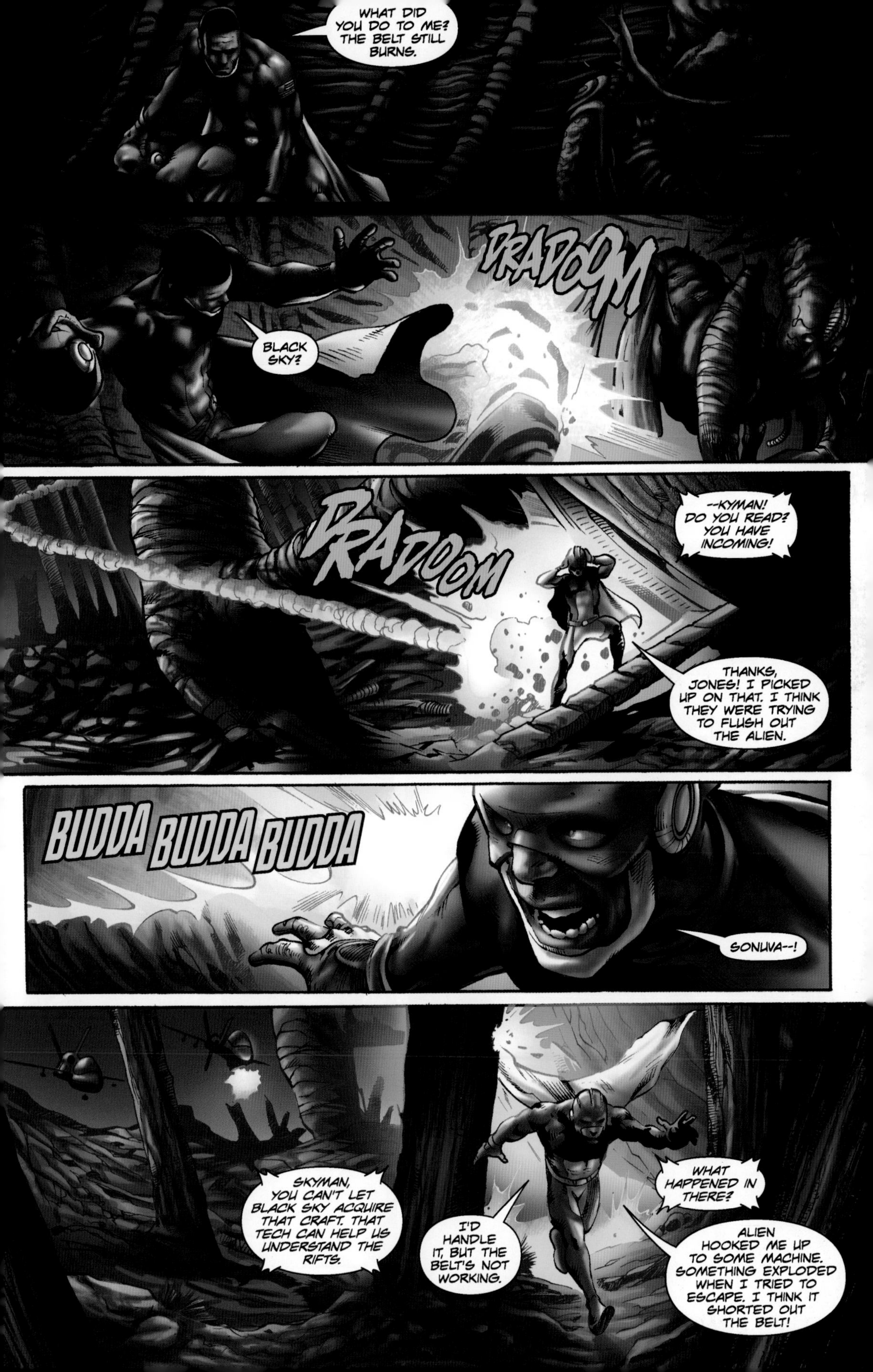
WHAT DID YOU DO TO ME? THE BELT STILL BURNS.
DRADOOM
BLACK SKY?
DRADOOM
--KYMAN! DO YOU READ? YOU HAVE INCOMING!
THANKS, JONES! I PICKED UP ON THAT. I THINK THEY WERE TRYING TO FLUSH OUT THE ALIEN.
BUDDA BUDDA BUDDA
SONUVA--!
WHAT HAPPENED IN THERE?
ALIEN HOOKED ME UP TO SOME MACHINE. SOMETHING EXPLODED WHEN I TRIED TO ESCAPE. I THINK IT SHORTED OUT THE BELT!
SKYMAN, YOU CAN'T LET BLACK SKY ACQUIRE THAT CRAFT. THAT TECH CAN HELP US UNDERSTAND THE RIFTS.
I'D HANDLE IT, BUT THE BELT'S NOT WORKING.

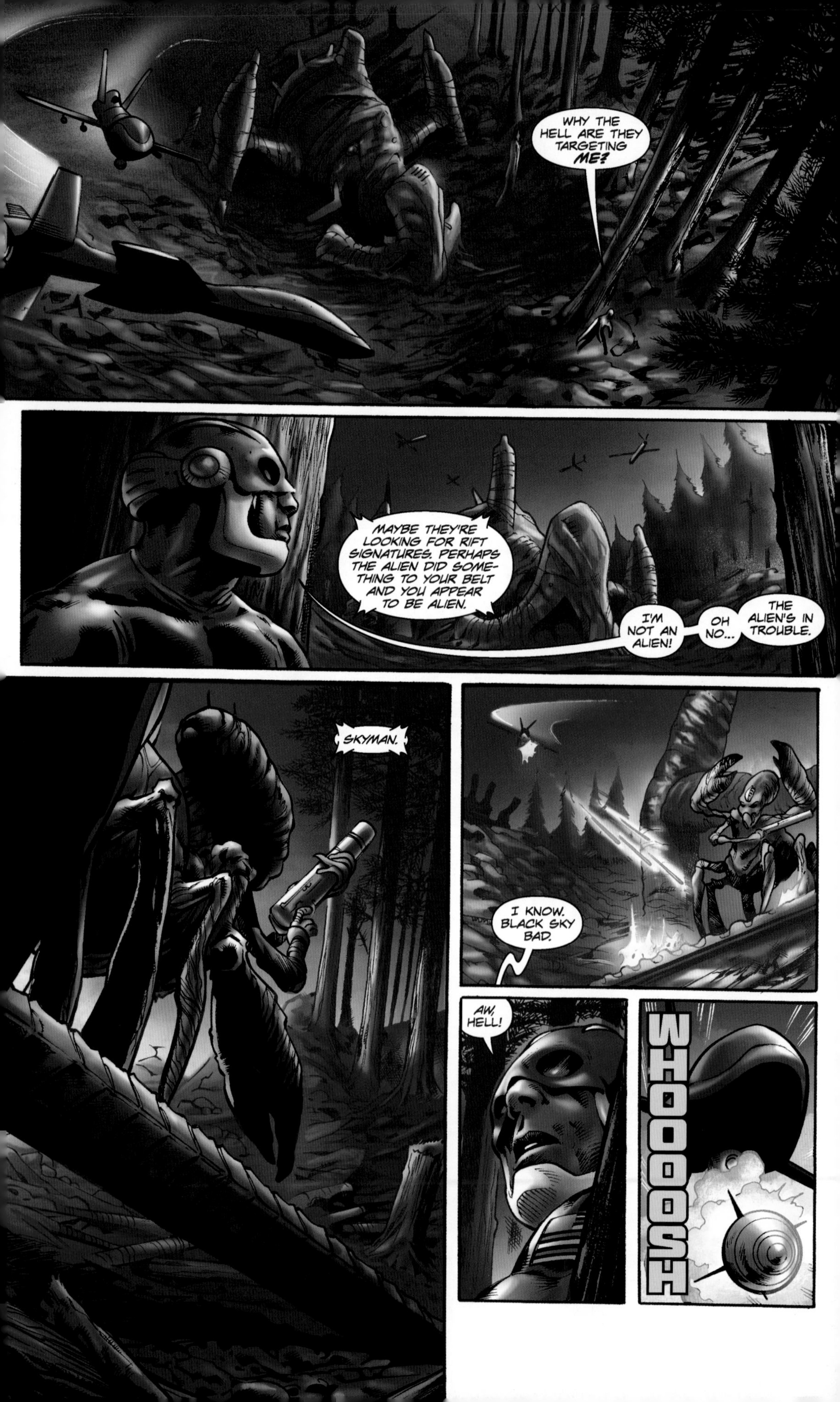
WHY THE HELL ARE THEY TARGETING ME?
MAYBE THEY'RE LOOKING FOR RIFT SIGNATURES. PERHAPS THE ALIEN DID SOMETHING TO YOUR BELT AND YOU APPEAR TO BE ALIEN.
I'M NOT AN ALIEN!
OH NO...
THE ALIEN'S IN TROUBLE.
SKYMAN.
I KNOW. BLACK SKY BAD.
AW, HELL!
WHOOOOSH

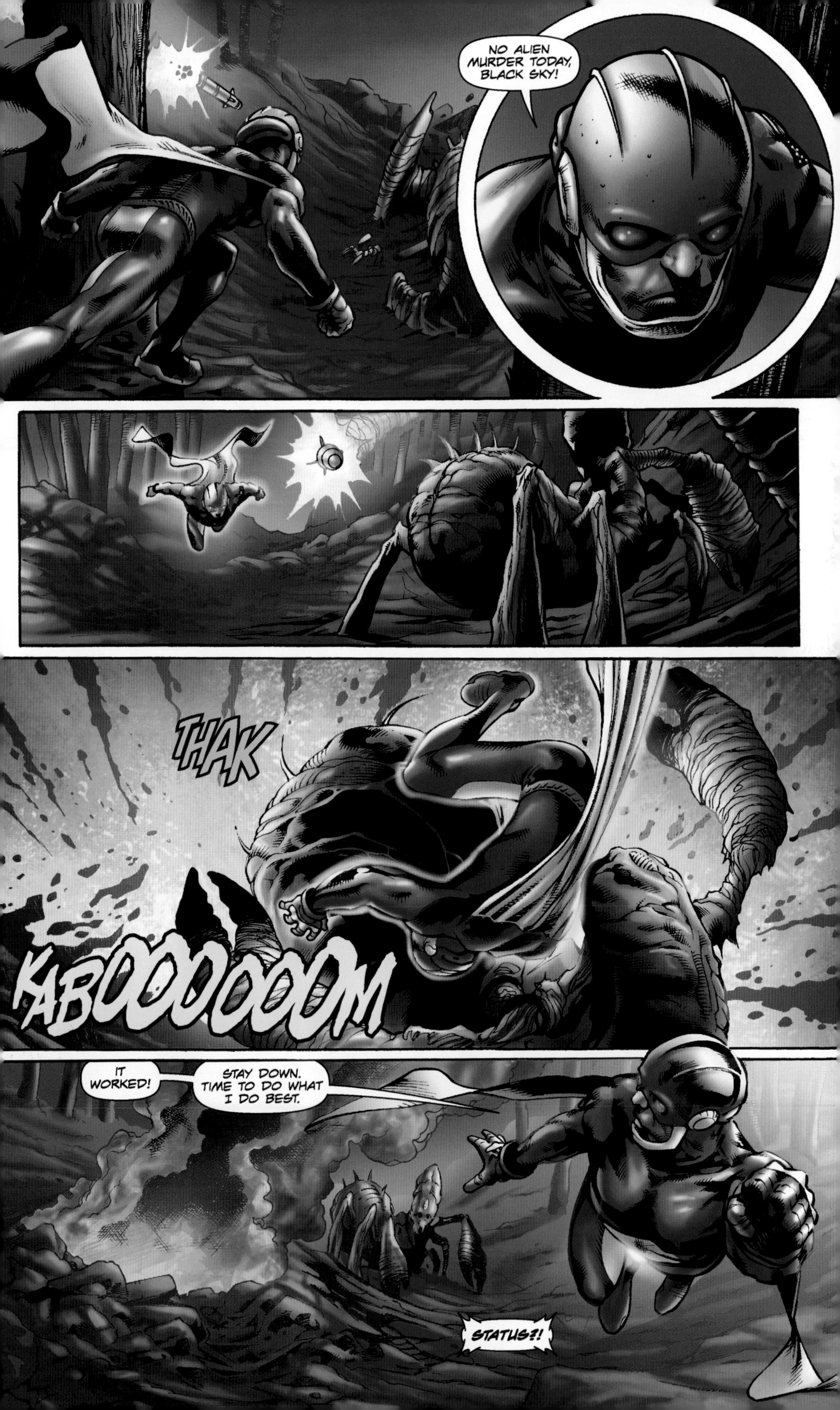
NO ALIEN MURDER TODAY, BLACK SKY!
THAK
KABOOOOOOM
IT WORKED!
STAY DOWN. TIME TO DO WHAT I DO BEST.
STATUS?!

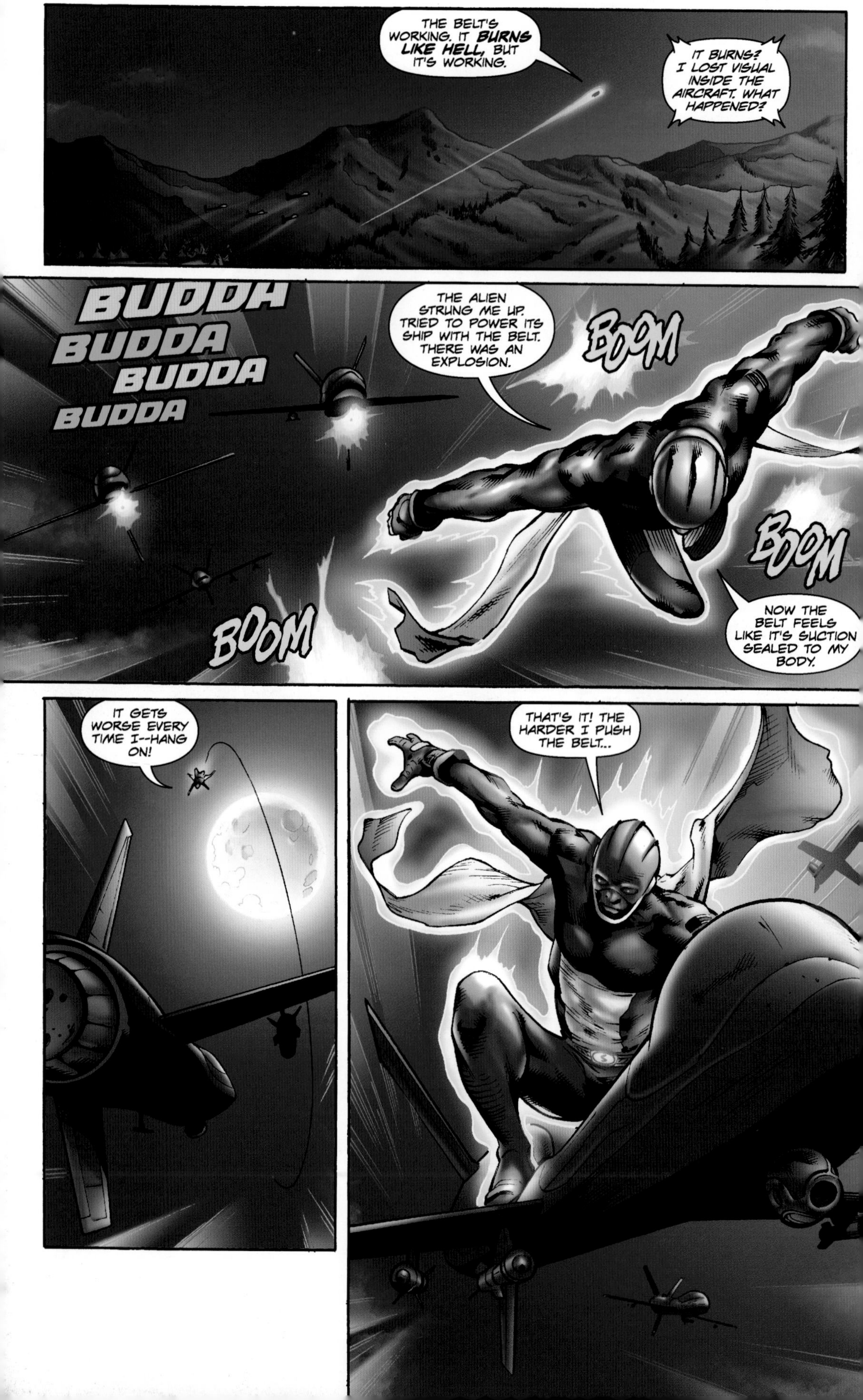
THE BELT'S WORKING. IT **BURNS LIKE HELL**, BUT IT'S WORKING.
IT BURNS? I LOST VISUAL INSIDE THE AIRCRAFT. WHAT HAPPENED?
BUDDA BUDDA BUDDA BUDDA
THE ALIEN STRUNG ME UP. TRIED TO POWER ITS SHIP WITH THE BELT. THERE WAS AN EXPLOSION.
BOOM
BOOM
BOOM
NOW THE BELT FEELS LIKE IT'S SUCTION SEALED TO MY BODY.
IT GETS WORSE EVERY TIME I--HANG ON!
THAT'S IT! THE HARDER I PUSH THE BELT...

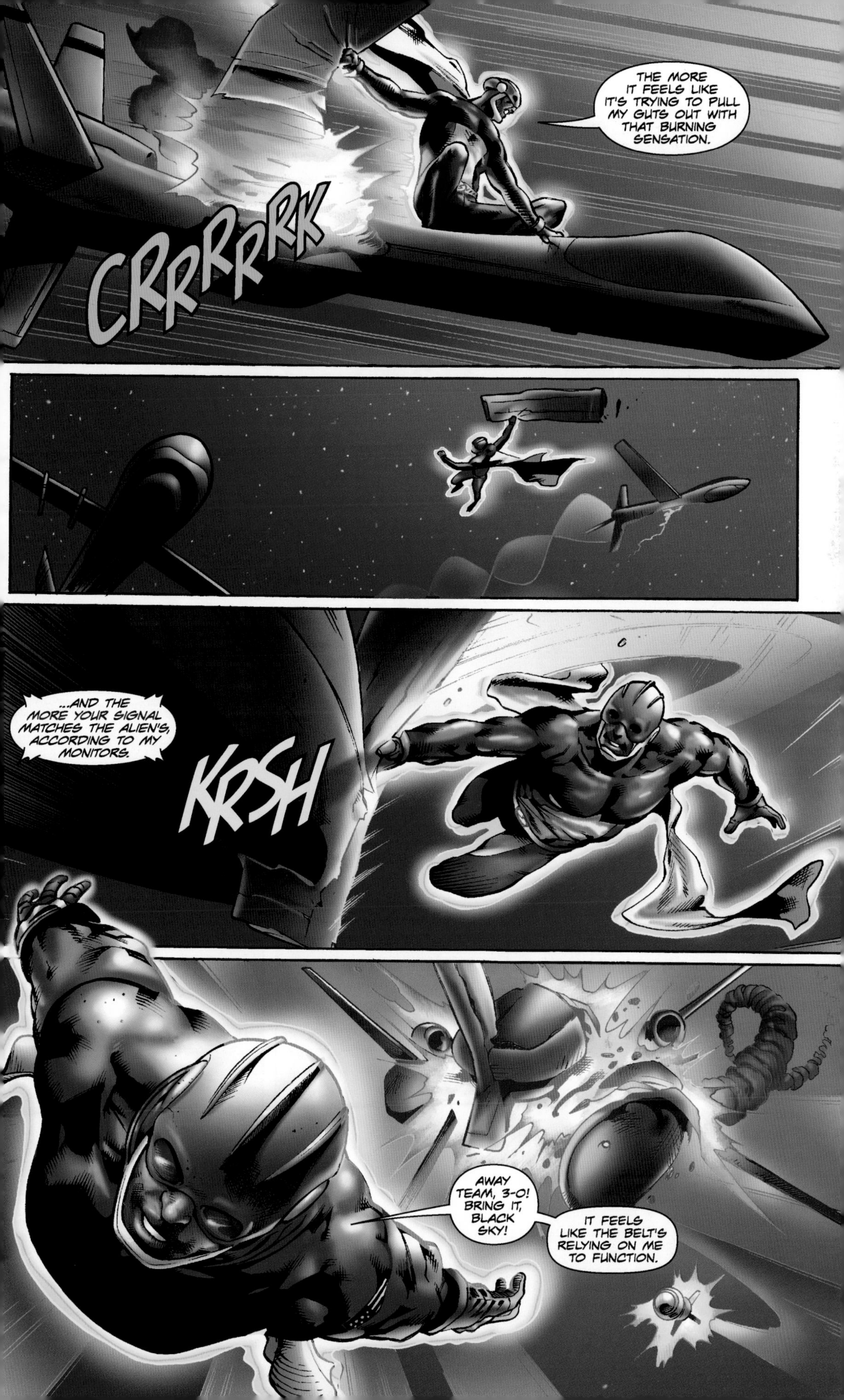
THE MORE IT FEELS LIKE IT'S TRYING TO PULL MY GUTS OUT WITH THAT BURNING SENSATION.
CRRRRRK
...AND THE MORE YOUR SIGNAL MATCHES THE ALIEN'S, ACCORDING TO MY MONITORS.
KRSH
AWAY TEAM, 3-0! BRING IT, BLACK SKY!
IT FEELS LIKE THE BELT'S RELYING ON ME TO FUNCTION.

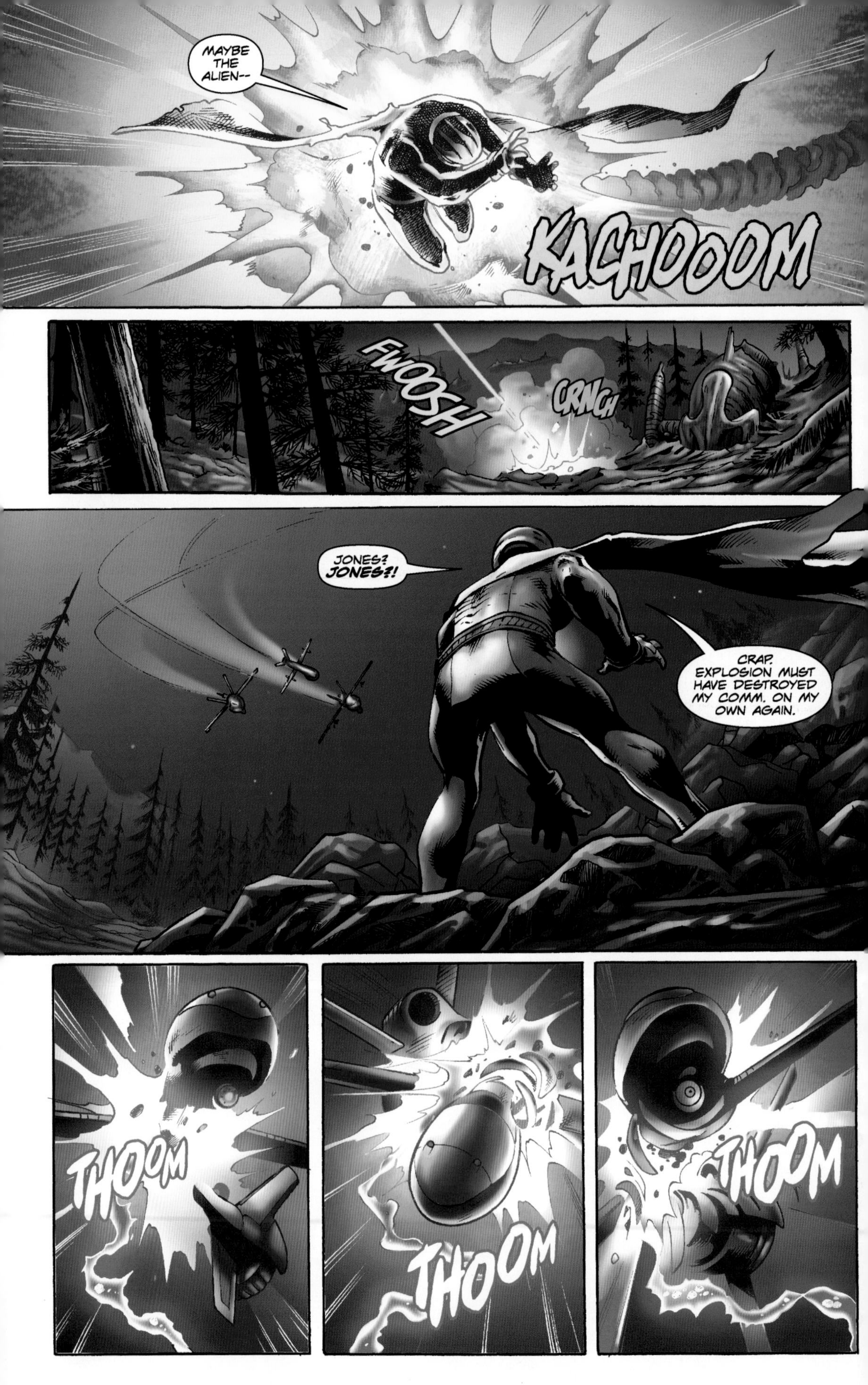
MAYBE THE ALIEN--
KACHOOOOM
FWOOSH
CRNCH
JONES? JONES?!
CRAP. EXPLOSION MUST HAVE DESTROYED MY COMM. ON MY OWN AGAIN.
THOOM
THOOM
THOOM

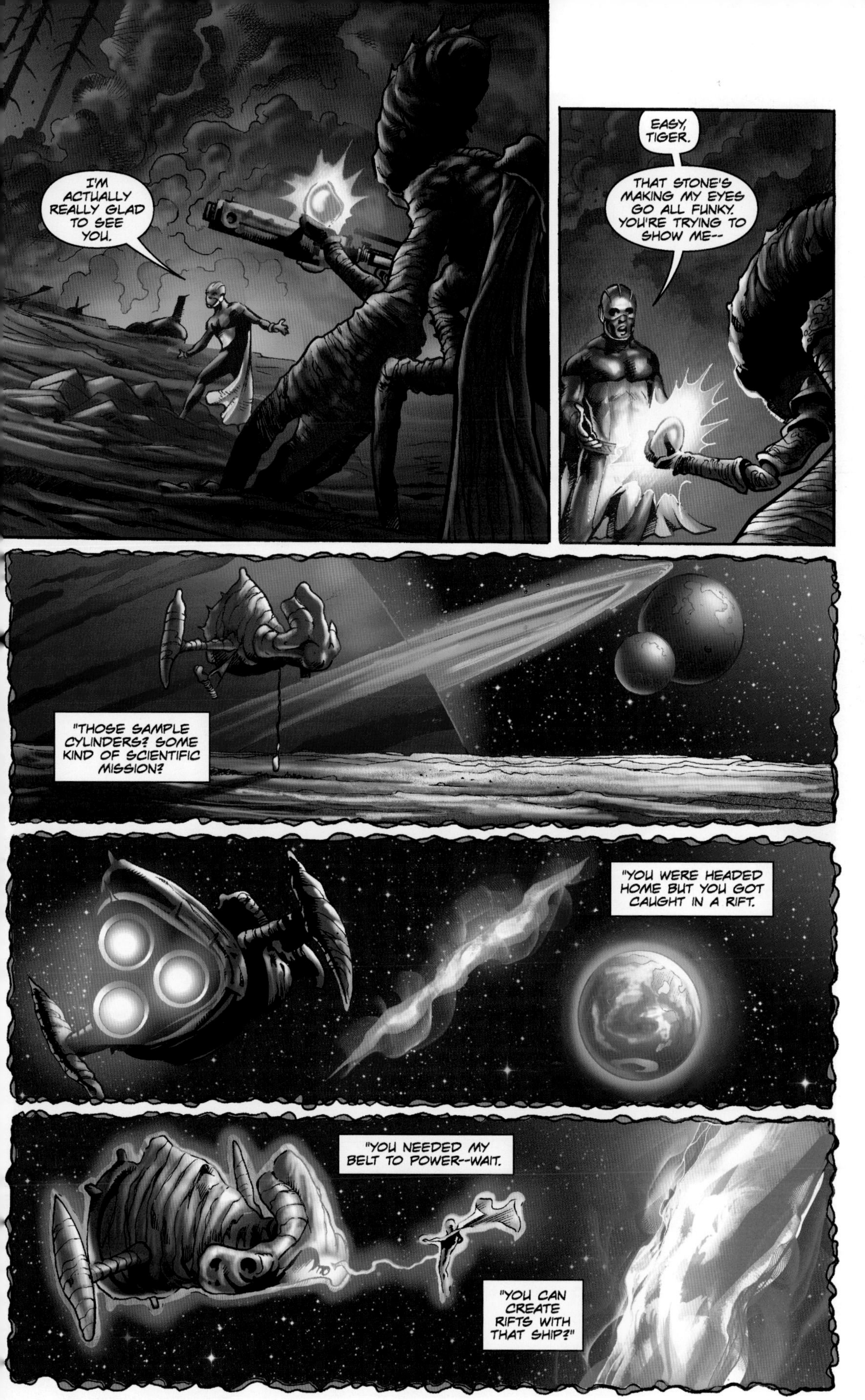
I'M ACTUALLY REALLY GLAD TO SEE YOU.
EASY, TIGER.
THAT STONE'S MAKING MY EYES GO ALL FUNKY. YOU'RE TRYING TO SHOW ME--
"THOSE SAMPLE CYLINDERS? SOME KIND OF SCIENTIFIC MISSION?
"YOU WERE HEADED HOME BUT YOU GOT CAUGHT IN A RIFT.
"YOU NEEDED MY BELT TO POWER--WAIT.
"YOU CAN CREATE RIFTS WITH THAT SHIP?"

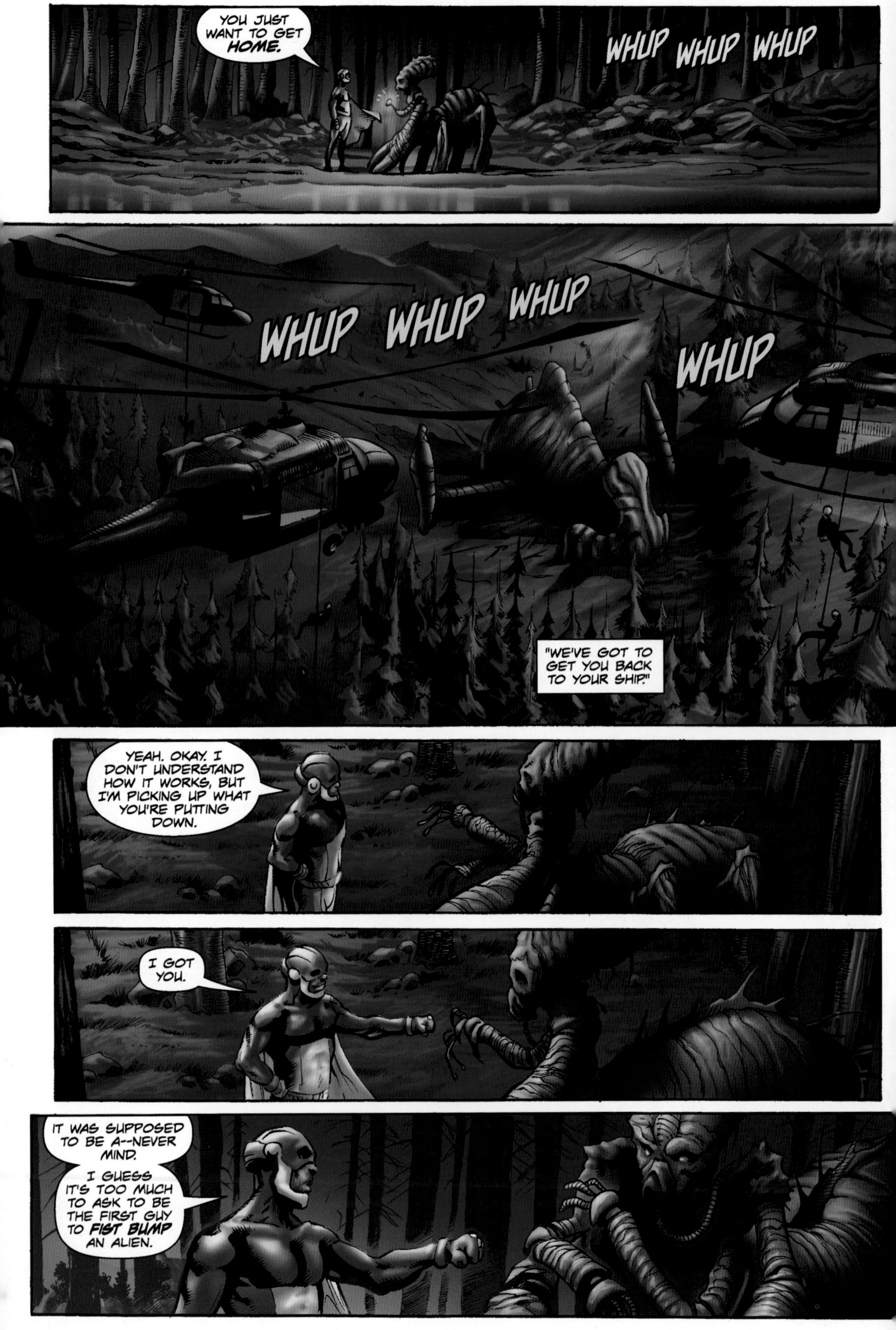
YOU JUST WANT TO GET HOME.
WHUP WHUP WHUP
WHUP WHUP WHUP
WHUP
"WE'VE GOT TO GET YOU BACK TO YOUR SHIP."
YEAH. OKAY. I DON'T UNDERSTAND HOW IT WORKS, BUT I'M PICKING UP WHAT YOU'RE PUTTING DOWN.
I GOT YOU.
IT WAS SUPPOSED TO BE A--NEVER MIND.
I GUESS IT'S TOO MUCH TO ASK TO BE THE FIRST GUY TO FIST BUMP AN ALIEN.

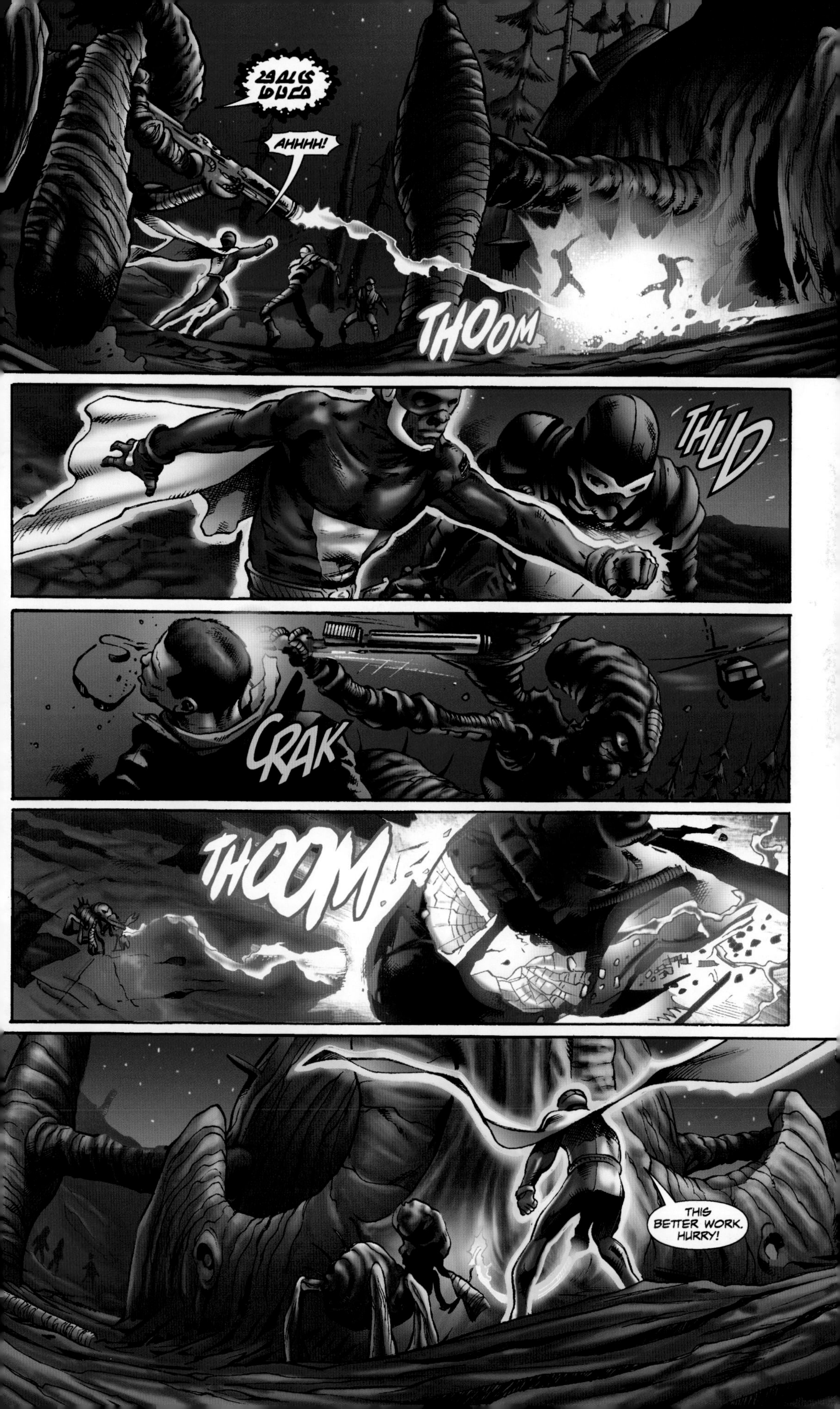
AHHHH!
THOOM
THUD
CRAK
THOOM
THIS BETTER WORK. HURRY!

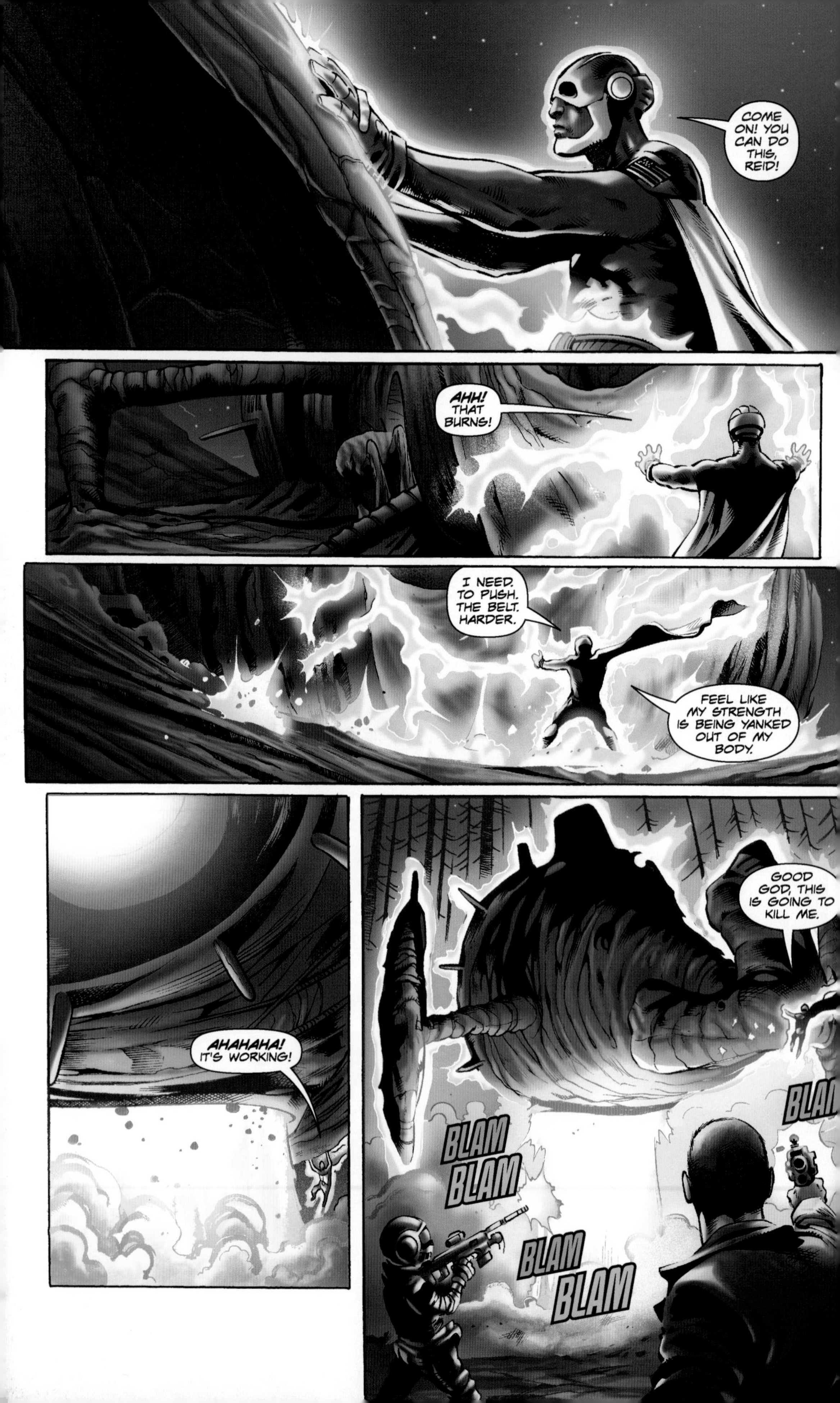
COME ON! YOU CAN DO THIS, REID!
AHH! THAT BURNS!
I NEED. TO PUSH. THE BELT. HARDER.
FEEL LIKE MY STRENGTH IS BEING YANKED OUT OF MY BODY.
AHAHAHA! IT'S WORKING!
GOOD GOD, THIS IS GOING TO KILL ME.
BLAM
BLAM
BLAM
BLAM
BLAM

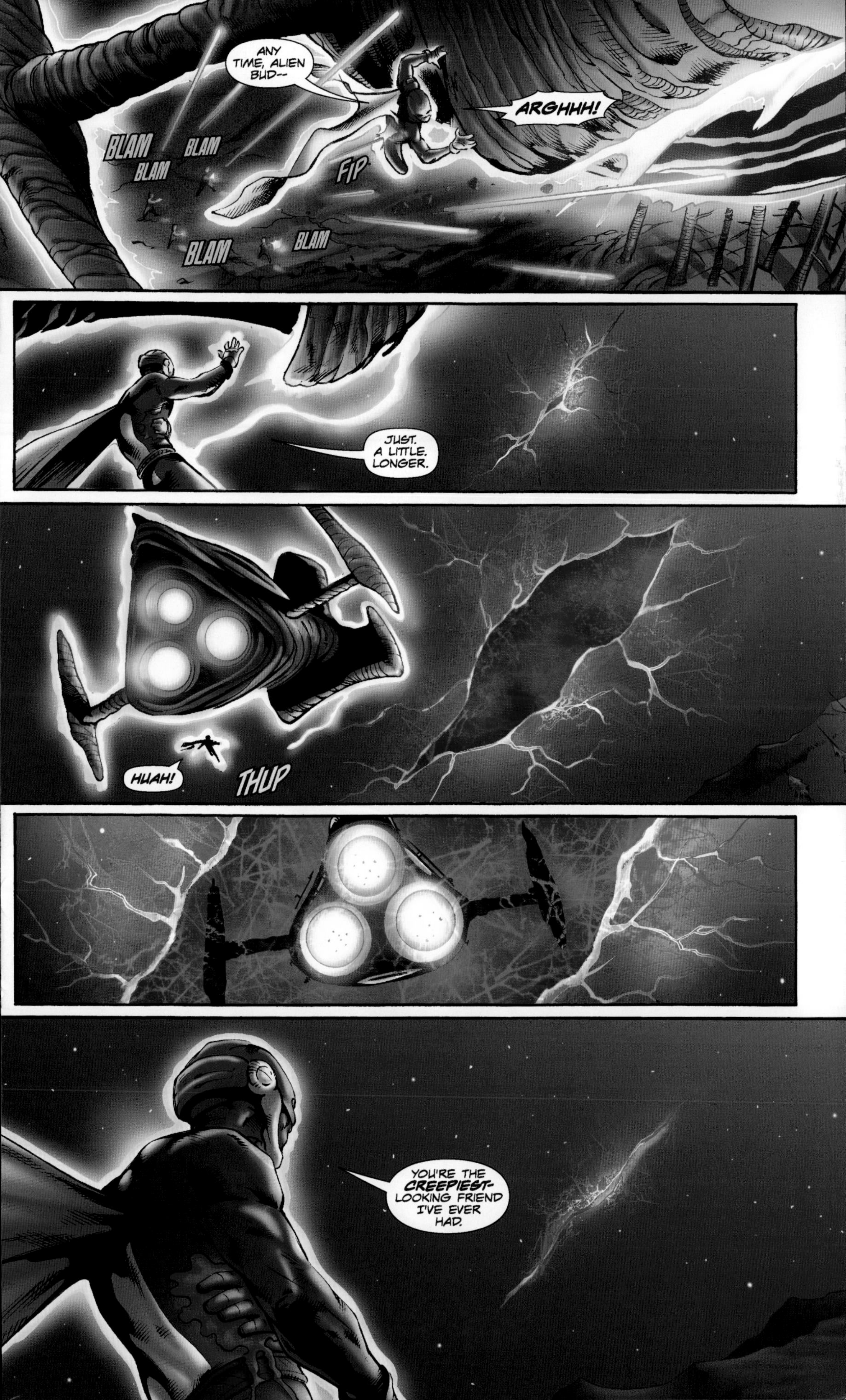
ANY TIME, ALIEN BUD--
ARGHHH!
BLAM
BLAM
BLAM
FIP
BLAM
BLAM
JUST. A LITTLE. LONGER.
HUAH!
THUP
YOU'RE THE CREEPIEST-LOOKING FRIEND I'VE EVER HAD.

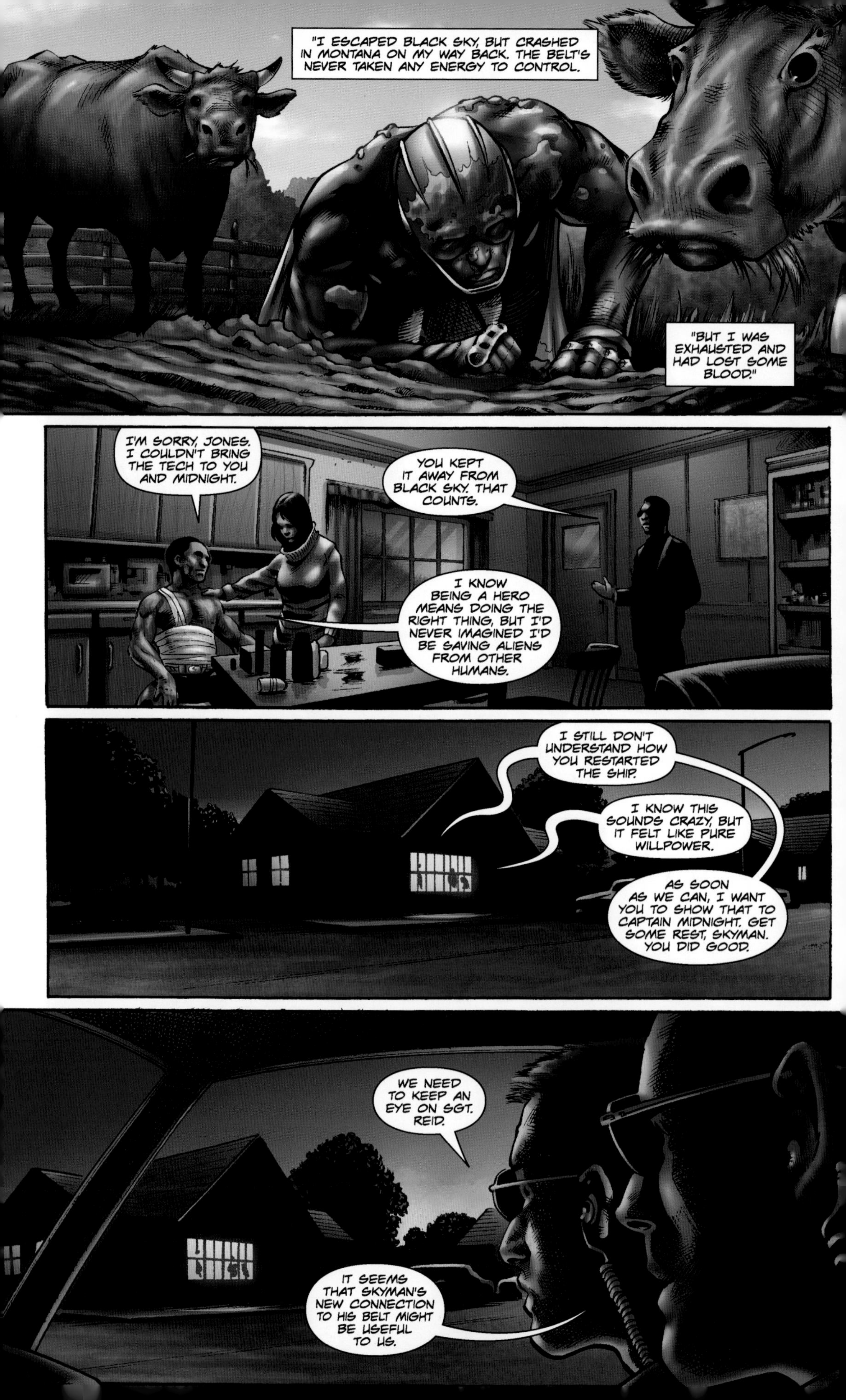

"I ESCAPED BLACK SKY, BUT CRASHED IN MONTANA ON MY WAY BACK. THE BELT'S NEVER TAKEN ANY ENERGY TO CONTROL.
"BUT I WAS EXHAUSTED AND HAD LOST SOME BLOOD."
I'M SORRY, JONES. I COULDN'T BRING THE TECH TO YOU AND MIDNIGHT.
YOU KEPT IT AWAY FROM BLACK SKY. THAT COUNTS.
I KNOW BEING A HERO MEANS DOING THE RIGHT THING, BUT I'D NEVER IMAGINED I'D BE SAVING ALIENS FROM OTHER HUMANS.
I STILL DON'T UNDERSTAND HOW YOU RESTARTED THE SHIP.
I KNOW THIS SOUNDS CRAZY, BUT IT FELT LIKE PURE WILLPOWER.
AS SOON AS WE CAN, I WANT YOU TO SHOW THAT TO CAPTAIN MIDNIGHT. GET SOME REST, SKYMAN. YOU DID GOOD.
WE NEED TO KEEP AN EYE ON SGT. REID.
IT SEEMS THAT SKYMAN'S NEW CONNECTION TO HIS BELT MIGHT BE USEFUL TO US.

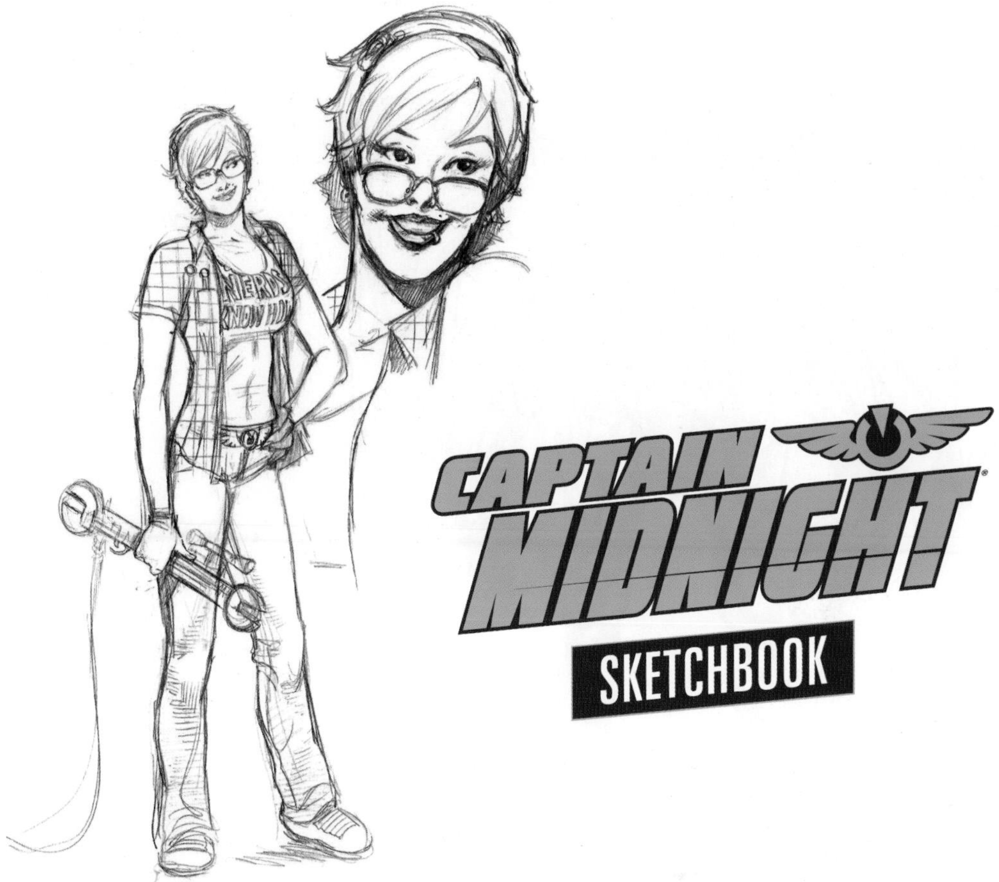

CAPTAIN MIDNIGHT SKETCHBOOK

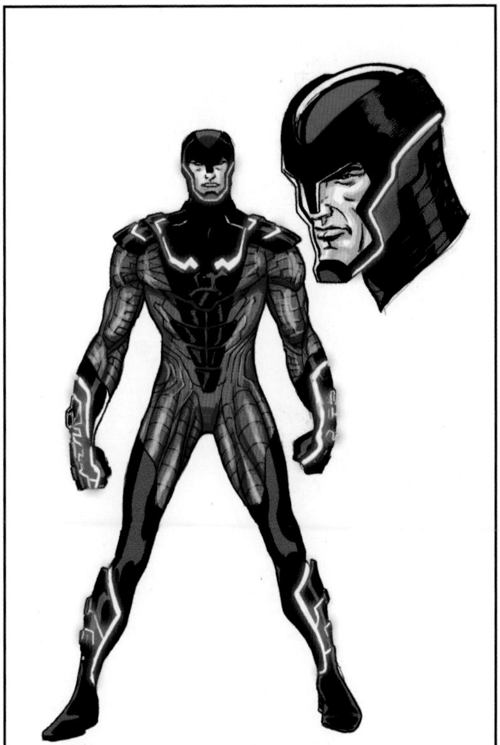

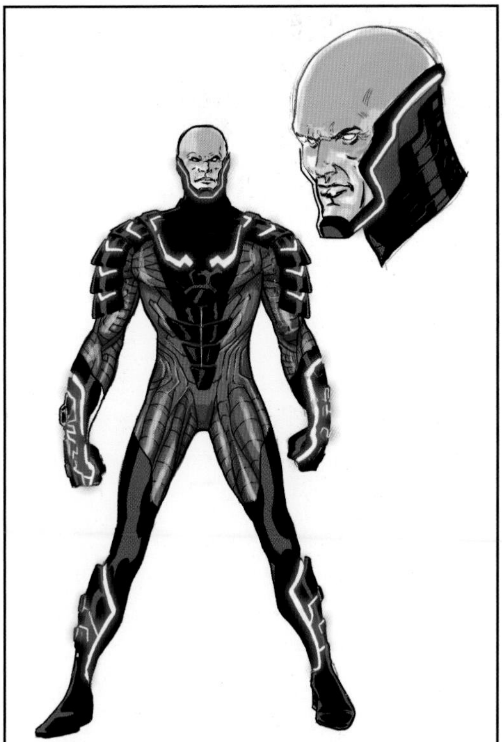

This arc of *Captain Midnight* featured the most new characters to be introduced in a while. Here are Fernando Dagnino's designs for both Goody and Chuck's reality-destroying supersuit. Chuck's suit was based on the costume of the Vortex Man from Dark Horse's Comics' Greatest World comics. A nod to the past and an Easter egg for eagle-eyed readers!

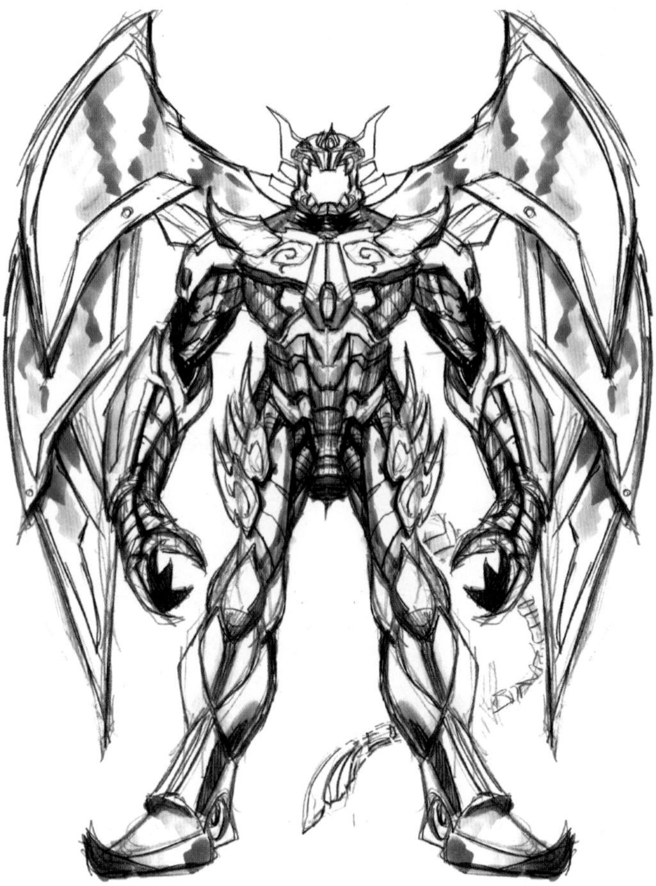

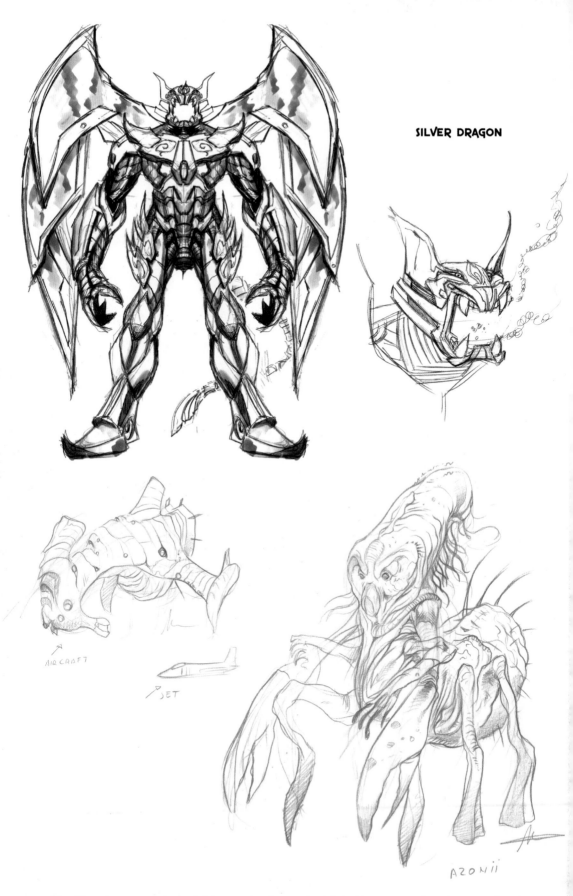

SILVER DRAGON

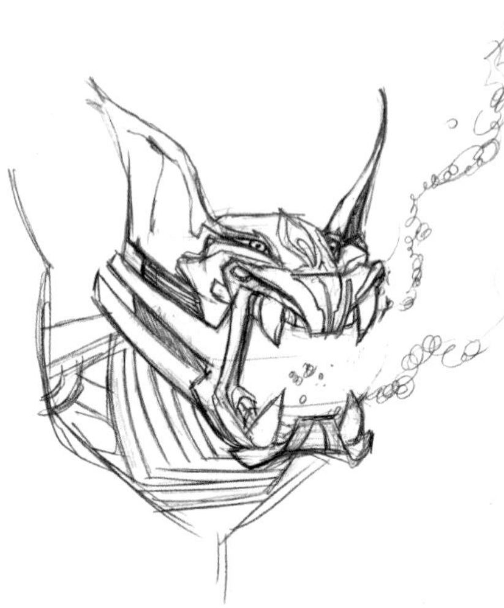

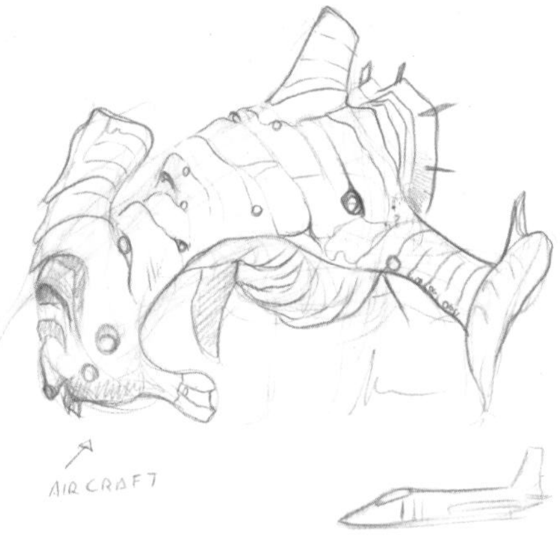
AIRCRAFT
JET

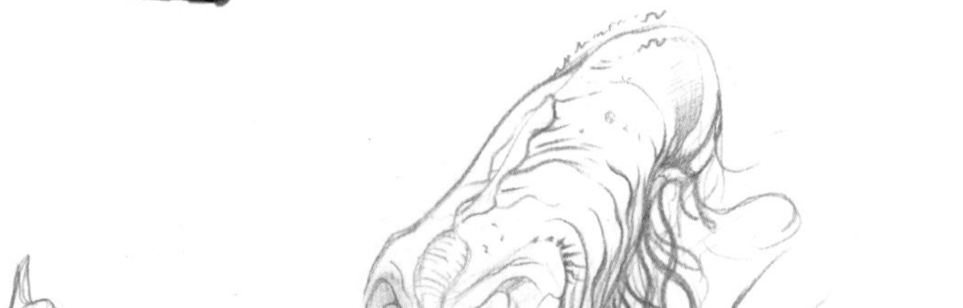
AZONii

The Silver Dragon only had a brief scene, but he got the full design treatment from Fernando Dagnino. Introducing a brand-new alien species also required some design. Manuel Garcia nailed the Azonii alien and his ship on the first take with some outlandish and awesome designs.

PROJECT BLACK SKY

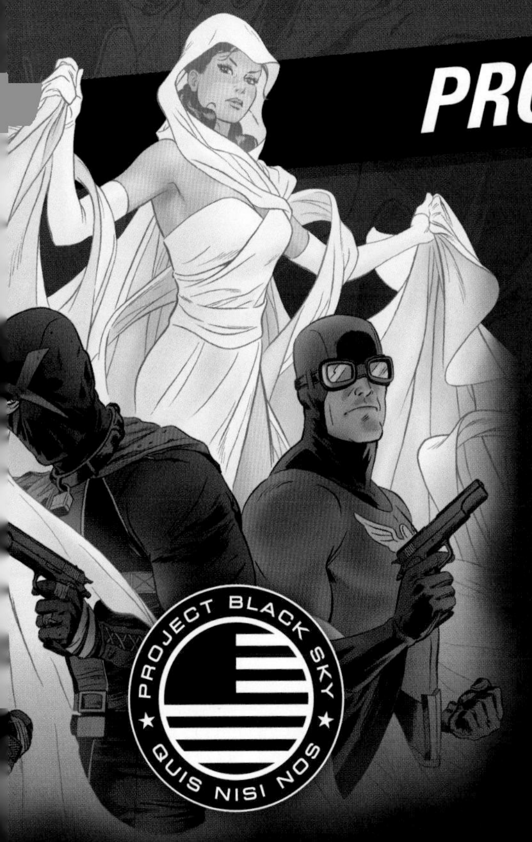
PROJECT BLACK SKY
QUIS NISI NOS

X

Duane Swierczynski and Eric Nguyen

A masked vigilante dispenses justice without mercy to the criminals of the decaying city of Arcadia. Nonstop, visceral action, with Dark Horse's most brutal and exciting character—X!

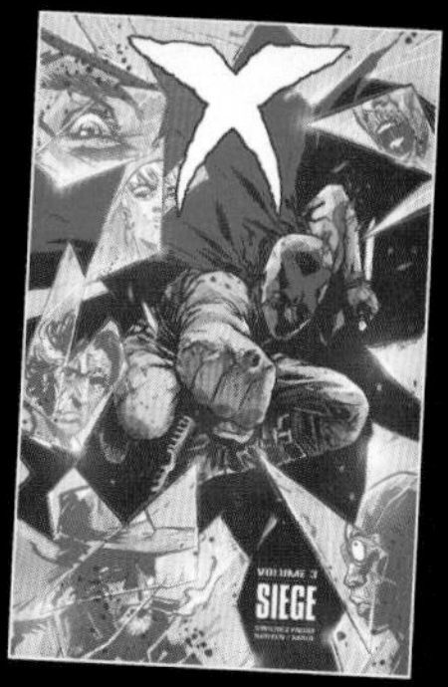
X
SIEGE

VOLUME 1: BIG BAD
978-1-61655-241-1 | $14.99

VOLUME 2: THE DOGS OF WAR
978-1-61655-327-2 | $14.99

VOLUME 3: SIEGE
978-1-61655-458-3 | $14.99

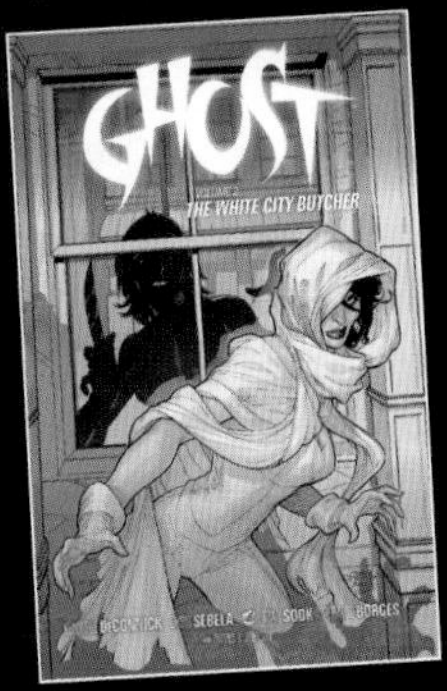
GHOST
THE WHITE CITY BUTCHER

GHOST

Kelly Sue DeConnick, Chris Sebela, Alex Ross, Ryan Sook, and others

Paranormal investigators accidentally summon a ghostly woman. The search for her identity uncovers a deadly alliance between political corruption and demonic science! In the middle stands a woman trapped between two worlds!

VOLUME 1: IN THE SMOKE AND DIN
978-1-61655-121-6 | $14.99

VOLUME 2: THE WHITE CITY BUTCHER
978-1-61655-420-0 | $14.99

THE OCCULTIST

Mike Richardson, Tim Seeley, and Victor Drujiniu

When a team of hit mages hired by a powerful sorcerer after him, it's trial by fire for the new Occultist, as he learns to handle his powerful magical tome, or suffer at the hands of deadly enemies. From the mind of Dark Horse founder Mike Richardson (*The Secret*, *Cut*, *The Mask*)!

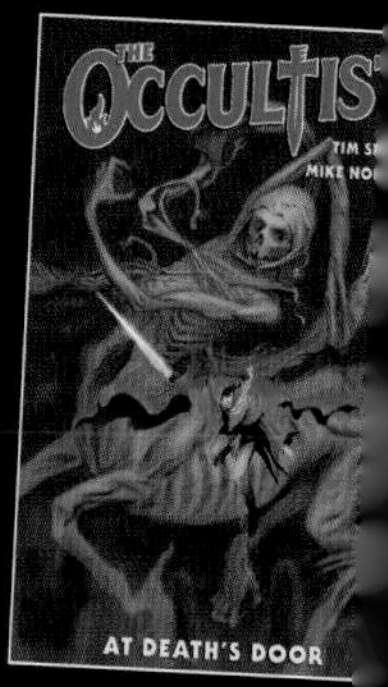
THE OCCULTIST
AT DEATH'S DOOR

VOLUME 1
978-1-59582-745-6 | $16.99

VOLUME 2: AT DEATH'S DOOR
978-1-61655-463-7 | $16.99

PROJECT BLACK SKY

CAPTAIN MIDNIGHT

Joshua Williamson, Fernando Dagnino, Eduardo Francisco, Victor Ibáñez, Pere Pérez, and Roger Robinson

In the forties, he was an American hero, a daredevil fighter pilot, a technological genius . . . a superhero. Since he rifled out of the Bermuda Triangle and into the present day, Captain Midnight has been labeled a threat to homeland security. Can Captain Midnight survive in the modern world, with the US government on his heels and an old enemy out for revenge?

VOLUME 1: ON THE RUN
978-1-61655-229-9 | $14.99

VOLUME 2: BRAVE OLD WORLD
978-1-61655-230-5 | $14.99

VOLUME 3: FOR A BETTER TOMORROW
978-1-61655-231-2 | $14.99

VOLUME 4: CRASH AND BURN
978-1-61655-518-4 | $14.99

VOLUME 5: LOST TIME
978-1-61655-644-0 | $14.99

BRAIN BOY

Fred Van Lente, Freddie Williams II, and R. B. Silva

Ambushed while protecting an important statesman, Matt Price Jr., a.k.a. Brain Boy, finds himself wrapped up in political intrigue that could derail a key United Nations conference and sets the psychic spy on a collision course with a man whose mental powers rival his own!

VOLUME 1: PSY VS. PSY
978-1-61655-317-3 | $14.99

VOLUME 2: THE MEN FROM G.E.S.T.A.L.T.
978-1-61655-506-1 | $14.99

SKYMAN

Joshua Hale Fialkov and Manuel Garcia

The Skyman Program turns to US Air Force Sgt. Eric Reid: a wounded veteran on the ropes, looking for a new lease on life. Ultimates writer Joshua Hale Fialkov pens an all-new superhero series from the pages of Captain Midnight!

VOLUME 1: THE RIGHT STUFF
978-1-61655-439-2 | $14.99

BLACKOUT

Frank Barbiere, Colin Lorimer, and Micah Kaneshiro

tt Travers possesses a special suit bearing technology that allows Travers to e in and out of our world through a shadowy parallel dimension—but he doesn't y how the device works or where it came from. With his benefactor missing, owerful adversaries after his "Blackout" gear, Scott must master the suit's erious powers and find answers before the answers find him!

VOLUME 1: INTO THE DARK
978-1-61655-555-9 | $12.99

AVAILABLE AT YOUR LOCAL COMICS SHOP OR BOOKSTORE! • To find a comics shop in your area, call 1-888-266-4226.
For more information or to order direct visit DarkHorse.com or call 1-800-862-0052 Mon.–Fri. 9 AM to 5 PM Pacific Time. Prices and availability to change without notice.